DONALD CAIRD

Aonghus Dwane

Donald Caird

Church of Ireland Bishop
Gaelic Churchman
A Life

the columba press

First published in 2014 by
the columba press
55A Spruce Avenue,
Stillorgan Industrial Park,
Blackrock, Co. Dublin

Cover by Sin é Design
Origination by The Columba Press
Printed by ScandBook

ISBN 978 1 78218 178 1

Front Cover Image
Donald Caird in the Chapter Room of Christ Church Cathedral
prior to taking his final service as Archbishop, 7 April 1996. Also pictured,
Alison Finch (left), Eve McAulay (behind Donald) and Heidi Kinsella (right).
(Image courtesy of *The Irish Times*)

Back Cover Image
Donald Caird (in Aran sweater) with brothers Muiris and Seán Ó Guithín
and their sister Máire in 1986. Donald's daughter Helen
is pictured to the far right.
(Image courtesy of the Caird family)

Do mo mháthair,
Margaret Philomena Dwane (1933–2001)
agus mo dheartháir,
Colm Pádraig Seosamh Dwane (1963–2001).
I ndílchuimhne.

Contents

Foreword

Anyone who has known Donald Caird, in whatever capacity, cannot fail to have been impacted by him. Not a dominant or forceful personality in any conventional sense, the open friendliness, precision of mind (occasionally accompanied by a charming absent-mindedness), fascination with life and people, undemonstrative yet profound Christian integrity, and puckish quick-wittedness, combine to make an encounter with Donald Caird something to be relished at the time, and then recalled with great happiness.

This biography by Aonghus Dwane, which happily never descends into hagiography, carries us from the early days as a quiet and studious little boy in Dublin suburbia through to the 'safe lodging' in old age at the Brabazon Home in Sandymount. Proper time and space is allocated to Donald Caird's youth, student days, on through the years of his early ministry in Belfast, Portora Royal School, St David's College Lampeter, and hence back to Dublin, Rathmichael parish, and the utter contentment of married life with Nancy, a partnership that brings warmth into the lives of many of us, well beyond their family circle. After his short sojourn as Dean of Ossory, there followed the distinguished and hugely effective episcopal ministries in Limerick, Ardfert and Aghadoe, Meath and Kildare, and finally Dublin.

A foreword is not a book review, and it is for the reader to find his or her favourite encounters in this biography, but a few personal comments remain. The first is that Donald Caird's immense personal courage, utter integrity and lively commitment to the Christian cause has unquestionably affected the current landscape of the Church of Ireland for great good. To give but one example, Wilson's Hospital School in Westmeath might well not have survived (let alone flourished as it has done) without his single-minded determination. Although heavily involved in what we casually call the central Church, and frequently producing statements on behalf of the Church of Ireland that were truly magisterial in their depth, he was a dedicated diocesan bishop also. Secondly, he has never misused his great gifts and talents, or debased them by one iota. Through his ministry, Donald Caird certainly did not suffer fools gladly (if at all), but he never used his tremendous intellect or quick zany humour to demean another human being. Finally, we will always associate Donald Caird with the Irish language, and in a particular way. For someone who learnt his Irish as a young man rather than as a child, the language has seemingly permeated his whole being. In contrast even to other equally fluent Irish speakers, Irish is an integral part of him. Yes, he could speak *as Gaeilge* for public purposes, but the use of Irish is clearly as natural to him as is breathing.

In being profoundly grateful for Donald Caird and all that he means to us, we are also very thankful to Aonghus Dwane for undertaking this study.

✠ The Most Rev. Richard L. Clarke,
Archbishop of Armagh,
Primate of All Ireland

Acknowledgements

I am very grateful to Donald and his wife Nancy for their graciousness and assistance over a number of years in providing me with valuable information for this biography (including access to Donald's archival material) and sharing with me their fund of personal anecdotes and memories.

This book – in some ways a hybrid of biography and memoir – draws heavily on the reminiscences of a number of people who knew Donald Caird personally (some since childhood) and through his long and varied ministry. I can scarcely thank them adequately for their kindness and generosity in granting expansive and detailed interviews to me, but it is very deeply appreciated. This project could not have been undertaken without their contribution.

My thanks to Ann Caird, John Caird and Helen Caird for sharing with me their experiences growing up as the children of a bishop and reminiscences of their parents Donald and Nancy.

Ms Elizabeth Caird furnished me with valuable background information in relation to Donald's father George Caird, George's first wife Elizabeth (née McDonald), and Donald's half-siblings (the late Norman Caird, Phoebe Fenner and James Caird). Both she and Mr Ken Ryan gave me helpful information on his Broadbent and Strachan ancestors.

The following individuals granted me interviews for the book: Rt Rev. Robin Eames, former Archbishop of Armagh; Rt Rev. Walton Empey, former Archbishop of Dublin; Rt Rev. John Neill, former Archbishop of Dublin; Rt Rev. Samuel G. Poyntz, former Bishop of Connor; Rt Rev. Paul Colton, Bishop of Cork; the Ven Gordon Linney, former Archdeacon of Dublin; Rev. Canon Adrian Empey; Rev. Canon Ginnie Kennerley; Rev. Gillian Wharton; Msgr Padraig Ó Fiannachta; Dr T.K. Whitaker; Dr Kenneth Milne; Dáithí Ó Maolchoille uasal; Mr Vincent Denard; Mr David Neligan; Mrs Stella Bell (née Woods); Mrs Muriel McCarthy; Mr Cyril Patton; Dr William Vaughan; Mr Basil Waugh; Mrs Olive Waugh and Mrs Frances Pakenham Walsh.

The Rt Rev. John McDowell, Bishop of Clogher and former rector of St Mark's, Dundela, gave myself and Donald a most informative tour of the parish in 2009.

I would like to record my deep appreciation for the contribution of the late Valerie Jones, who was diocesan communications officer in Dublin and Glendalough during Donald's time as Archbishop, and who granted me a detailed interview in 2010. *Ar dheis Dé go raibh a hanam dílis.*

Dr Kenneth Milne, Church of Ireland historiographer, warmly encouraged this project since its inception, for which I am very grateful indeed. I wish to thank both him and Mr Diarmuid Scully, lecturer in history at University College Cork, for reading over a draft of the manuscript and for making helpful comments and suggestions.

I would also like to express my thanks to the following who assisted in various ways:

Dáithí Ó Maolchoille, Cumann Gaelach na hEaglaise; Dr Raymond Refaussé, Representative Church Body Library; the Very Rev. Dermot Dunne, Dean of Christ Church Cathedral; Rev. Garth Bunting; Dr Eoin MacCárthaigh, Roinn na Gaeilge, Trinity College; Clíona Ní Shúilleabháin and Trevor Peare of Trinity College Library; Anne FitzGerald, John Coman and Sinéad MacBride of the Secretary's Office, Trinity College (for facilitating flexible arrangements to enable me to work on the project); my colleagues in the Secretary's Office, Trinity College and the staff of Read's in Nassau Street.

The dedication and hard work of Fearghal O'Boyle, Patrick O'Donoghue, Shane McCoy and the team at Columba Press ensured the publication of this biography in a short timescale, for which I am very appreciative. Generous support from Cumann Gaelach na hEaglaise and the General Synod Royalties Fund secured the publication of this book.

My thanks to the Most Rev. Richard Clarke, Archbishop of Armagh, for writing the foreword to this biography.

Finally, a note of appreciation to my father, Timothy Dwane, and my sisters Íde Dwane and Caoimhe Brouwers, for their love and support.

Go raibh míle maith agaibh uile.

Author's note

In this biography, I have employed the terms 'Catholic' and 'Roman Catholic' variously to refer to the largest religious community in the state. The Church of Ireland, of course, regards itself as catholic (but reformed), as do the other main reformed traditions. I am very conscious from my own upbringing that Catholics do not – generally – refer to themselves as 'Roman Catholic' and my usual preference is to refer to groups of people by the title they themselves use. However, as there are some references in the text also to the Catholic tradition in Anglicanism, it seemed appropriate to use 'Roman Catholic' in certain places (though not in all). It is of course used by the Catholic Church itself in ecumenical contexts and appears in addresses given by Pope John Paul II during his visit to Ireland, and in the title of the Anglican–Roman Catholic International Commission (ARCIC). I hope that the context will make clear my meaning in all cases, and that no confusion or offence is caused, as certainly none is intended.

In the text, where I quote directly from Donald Caird's addresses, sermons or writings, I have inserted such punctuation as considered appropriate. Any quotations in the text, where not accompanied by footnotes, are either from my interviews with Donald or such other interviewee as the context makes clear.

Any errors are, of course, my own.

Introduction

It is a source of particular pleasure for me that this biography is being published by Columba Press. I have a special affection for the Irish–Scottish saint, known also as Colm Cille, the dove of the church. My late brother's name was Colm, it is the name of my nephew/godson and I have worked as a project officer for Colmcille, the Irish–Scottish Gaelic cultural agency.

Colm Cille was an Irish-speaking monk of the sixth century who founded a monastery at Iona, and is credited with bringing Christianity to Scotland, converting many Scottish nobles in the process. To mention him is not inappropriate in an introduction to a biography of Donald Caird. The saint predates the 'unhappy divisions' occasioned by the Reformation and is revered by the main Christian traditions on this island and in Britain, with many Catholic, Anglican and Presbyterians churches in Ireland and Scotland dedicated to him. He is a symbol embodying complexity and inclusiveness, a bridge between traditions and nations.

The Church of Ireland's interactions with the Irish language reach back to the seventeenth century. It was William Bedell, Bishop of Kilmore (1571–1642), who made the first Irish translation of the Old Testament, published posthumously in 1685 along with a translation by William Daniel, Archbishop of Tuam, of the New Testament. As Provost of Trinity College, Bedell had required that students training for the Ministry who came from Irish-speaking areas should attend lectures in the language in order to be able to minister to the people. William Daniel (who himself died in 1628) had translated the Book of Common Prayer into Irish (printed by John Francke in 1608) and translations were also made of a number of subsequent editions of the prayer book. But in the main, the church was seen as an agency of the English state in its mission to 'civilise' (in other words, Anglicise) the Irish people, who were overwhelmingly Irish-speaking, and further its conquest of Ireland. The language was progressively banished from public life. The Anglican Church, of course, despite its sponsoring by the state, succeeded in winning the allegiance of only a small minority of the people. There was a further effort in the early nineteenth century, particularly in the west of Ireland, to win converts for the reformed faith through the strategic deployment of Irish-speaking clergy and the use of worship materials in the language (including the maintaining for a period of a Protestant school on the Great Blasket Island). This project enjoyed a limited measure of success, although many initial converts returned to Catholicism.

The influence of the state's national school system which promoted primary education through English, and the Great Famine of the mid nineteenth century, with deaths and emigration, accelerated the decline of the language. But all was far from lost. The language had become an object of interest to antiquarians and conservationists from the mid eighteenth century onwards. Assisted by access to universities and research materials, many individuals, including church ministers from an Irish Protestant background, were to the fore in such studies, including George Petrie (1792–1866) and the Rev. Maxwell Close (1822–1903), a founder of the Society for the Preservation of the Irish Language.

Prominent in the Irish literary and cultural revival of the late nineteenth and early twentieth centuries (known as the 'Celtic Revival') were a number of individuals from a Church of Ireland background, including the poet William Butler Yeats (1865–1939), the folklorist and playwright Lady Gregory (1852–1932) and the writer John Millington Synge (1871–1909). Douglas Hyde, from Castlerea in Co. Roscommon and the son of a rector, became fascinated by the Irish language spoken by the local people living in the area around him. Between 1879 and 1884, he published more than a hundred pieces of Irish verse under the pen name An Craoibhinn Aoibhinn, and helped to found the Gaelic League (Conradh na Gaeilge) in 1893.

These cultural developments were happening in parallel with a growing movement in the political sphere for Irish Home Rule, led by Charles Stewart Parnell (1846–1891), a Protestant landowner from Co. Wicklow. Parnell was leader of the nationalist party at Westminster and also an agitator for land reform in Ireland – which hastened the decline of the landowning Protestant ascendancy and triggered a long process of transfer of land to a mainly Catholic tenantry. The cultural revival together with political and land reform (allied to an older Fenian and Republican heritage which had in its pantheon such Protestants as Wolfe Tone, Lord Edward FitzGerald and Robert Emmet), formed a synergy which would inspire a new generation of revolutionaries mainly from the Catholic middle classes such as Patrick Pearse, Thomas McDonagh and others who went on to lead a rebellion in Dublin in 1916. The executions of the leaders of the Easter Rising (which had little initial support, and was seen as treacherous in view of the War which was then taking place), changed public opinion and led to the Sinn Féin election victory in 1918 and a War of Independence. Truce and treaty negotiations led to the partitioning of the island in 1922, with the establishment of the Irish Free State (a dominion which would progressively gain full independence) and the state of Northern Ireland (within the United Kingdom). The province of Ulster had been planted in the early seventeenth century, and its Protestant community (in contrast to other provinces) had a Presbyterian majority, of mainly Scottish background. Although the cultural revival had enjoyed considerable success there in the late nineteenth and early twentieth century, political independence was viewed by many northern Protestants as hastening 'Rome rule' because of the Catholic majority on the island, and with the nationalist desire for self-rule, the two national aspirations were set on irreconcilable trajectories. Partition became inevitable, creating a substantial disaffected Catholic minority within the Northern state.

Donald Caird's ancestors on his father's maternal side, the Broadbents, active in the commercial life of nineteenth-century Dublin, had probably been mildly 'Home Ruler' in sympathy, though they did not parade their religious or political affiliations. After independence in 1922, the Church of Ireland community was coming to terms with a new state and ethos very different from its own moorings in an earlier Ireland of establishment (until 1870) and ascendancy (the land reform of the late nineteenth century greatly accelerating its decline). The loss of many of its youth through service in the First World War (as attested to in the rolls of honour to be seen in many a Church of Ireland church) and the departure of the British military and civilian apparatus in 1922 had a demoralising effect and triggered the decline of the Protestant working class. As the new state bedded down, a number of influences combined to further push the Church of Ireland tradition from a central role to the margins of national life. Although the first Senate of the Free State had a number of Protestant and ex-Unionist representatives, it came to be seen as a transitional measure, and in retrospect as the high water mark of Protestant civic engagement with the new state.

The influence of the Roman Catholic Church's *Ne Temere* decree (of 1908) requiring children of mixed marriages to be raised as Catholic (which had accounted for some Northern Unionist fears of Catholic majority rule), and the psychological aftershock of some localised incidents during the War of Independence (mainly but not exclusively associated with republican targeting of loyalist Protestants), along with emigration in the early years of the State (to a more congenial environment in the North, or in Britain) coincided with the ascendancy of a new ethos emphasising Gaelic and Catholic elements of the national culture. These forces, along with the gaining of full political and cultural power by the Catholic middle classes, triggered a 'long retreat' by most Protestants in the South into the structures and supports of its own communal life at parish and national church levels. Many organisations such as the Boys' Brigade, Girls' Friendly Society, Church of Ireland Men's Society and Mothers' Union provided a social anchor there. Representative elements in the church's structure from select vestry to diocesan councils and synods and General Synod, provided an outlet for wider social energies, and the church also had its missionary and aid agencies. It all allowed for a fairly full life within a comfortable ethos, bordered and to a great extent defined-in-contrast by the larger external community, overwhelmingly Catholic.

Donald Caird (whose surname has Scottish Gaelic origins) remained loyal to, and yet transcended, his background. Raised a middle-class Church of Ireland boy in comfortable Dublin suburbia in the early years of the Irish Free State, his early exposure, in the Gaeltachtaí of Dún Chaoin and the Blasket Islands, to an ancient culture and language clearly had an enormous formative influence on him. Staying in the romantic setting of an Irish-speaking island open to all the elements of sun, wind and rain off the coast of Co. Kerry with a local family in the 1940s, his eyes were opened to a simplicity of life and quiet spiritual tradition very different from his own, yet one which he came to view with deep respect and affection. It was in his student days at Wesley College in the 1940s that he made his first encounter with members of Cumann Gaelach na hEaglaise (the Irish Guild of the Church). A number of the people he met had been involved from its earliest days, prior to partition, when there had been significant evidence of interest in the language among the Protestant and Unionist population generally. The Irish Guild of the Church was founded in 1914 with the aim of preserving the spirit of the ancient Celtic Church and promoting the use of the Irish language, Irish art and music in the life and worship of the Church of Ireland.

Laws in the independent state governing social mores – such as those on divorce (with a ban inserted to the Constitution in 1937) and on contraception – reflected a Catholic ethos. Such a counter-reaction was perhaps inevitable after centuries of state-sponsored Protestant ascendancy. The 1937 constitution included articles on social policy consonant mainly with Roman Catholic teaching, and expressly recognised the special position of the Roman Catholic Church as the guardian of the faith possessed by the vast majority of citizens (the same constitutional provision, interestingly, also recognised the Church of Ireland, along with various other religious communities). But while the public sphere was Catholic in atmosphere, the new state was no theocracy, and there was in the main a generous treatment of its principal minority. There were many comforting elements of continuity: in 1938, even as Donald prepared to begin schooling at Wesley College, Douglas Hyde, founder of the Gaelic League, was inaugurated as Ireland's first president. Bearing the appearance of an Edwardian gentlemen, his accession to office was a demonstration of the wide respect held for him in the new state's political establishment. The particular needs of Protestant schools were recognised and supported. Southern Protestantism retained many of the institutions which had buttressed its life prior to independence – Trinity College (where Donald studied in the late 1940s) remained a largely Protestant environment and *The Irish Times* had a slow transition from being a Unionist organ to a mainstream national newspaper, which was only fully completed by the 1970s. Involvement in business and professional life continued largely unruffled.

But the Protestant community made adjustments. Its schools had perforce to implement the new curriculum requiring study of Irish. An annual citizenship service was instituted in Christ Church Cathedral, to which politicians and members of the judiciary were invited. When a republic was declared in 1948 (the king having retained a formal role since 1922), the church altered its liturgy and began to offer prayers for the President instead of the monarch, the Primate John Gregg recognising that 'in our prayers, above all, there must be reality'. There might still be private viewings in parish halls of the coronation of Queen Elizabeth II in 1953 (and such interest in Royals was, and is, by no means confined to Protestants), along with some private pining in places for former belongings, but express loyalties were now to the changed order, and a new generation grew up with the Republic.

In the 1950s, Donald's ministry as curate, teacher-chaplain and lecturer successively, was spent in Northern Ireland (1950 to 1957) and in Wales (1957 to 1958). The Northern experience offered him an insight into the other side of partition since 1922: a state dominated by the governing Unionist party, the still-privileged position of the Protestant middle classes there (as well as a substantial Protestant working-class, something which had become largely absent in the South since partition) and an undercurrent of long-term Roman Catholic grievance.

Back in the South, with the celebration of the Golden Jubilee of the Easter Rising in 1966 (the Church of Ireland playing its part, holding services in diocesan cathedrals), the Archbishop of Dublin, Dr George Otto Simms, praised the efforts of the State to foster tolerance since independence:

> We are grateful across the span of the last fifty years for the goodwill, tolerance and freedom expressed and upheld among and between those of differing outlooks and religious allegiances. The words of the Proclamation that guarantee 'religious and civil liberty, equal rights and opportunities to all citizens' have brought help and encouragement to minorities during this period. There is a rock like quality about such elements in the formation of a State.

In his friendship with President de Valera, and his widely noted interest in the Irish language, the early Christian Church and the Book of Kells, Archbishop Simms gave a lead to his people, and must have had a certain impact on the then rector of Rathmichael in South County Dublin, Donald Caird (it was while rector in that parish that Donald met a visiting American from Nevada – Nancy Sharpe, who would open up a whole new perspective on life). Archbishop Simms demonstrated the value of engagement, and won wide respect among members of the general community, where he became a well-known figure through radio broadcasts and participation in public discussion. He was also a committed ecumenist, as was his successor Henry McAdoo, another Irish speaker, whom Donald referred to as his mentor.

In 1970, on assuming episcopal office himself in Limerick, Donald took up a theme which would resonate throughout his episcopal ministry there, in Meath, and in Dublin, directly encouraging the church's youth to engage in the institutions of local government, the Irish Army and the Gardaí. He was at the same time an advocate for his community, speaking out on mixed marriages and schools, two issues of key importance for its survival and flourishing. But such interventions, sometimes involving criticism of the Catholic Church or of the state, were no mere carping from the sidelines. Donald got involved. He served on the board of Limerick's Thomond College, the RTÉ Broadcasting Review Committee, the board of Siamsa Tíre (the folk theatre), and Bord na Gaeilge in the 1970s. In Dublin, he was a member of the Lord Mayor's Commission on Unemployment (1993–94) and the Lord Mayor's Commission on Cycling (1994–95). Such civic involvements, combined with personal friendships maintained across the traditions in the religious sphere (with such people as Cardinal Tomás Ó Fiaich and Archbishops Kevin McNamara and Desmond Connell) as well as in the civic and Irish language spheres, allied to his open and warm personality, meant that Donald Caird was widely recognised beyond the confines of his own community. He attended events and had many common interests with which to engage those whom he met. When he spoke out on public affairs, because they knew him already and felt he was genuinely interested in them, people listened.

When the modern Troubles in Northern Ireland took hold from the early 1970s, he became a consistent voice for moderation, fair treatment and reconciliation. His time in the North had given him some insight into the two communities. It would have been easy, against a backdrop of shootings and bombings and an association made by some of nationalism with violence, to have put to one side his interest in the Irish language during those difficult years. But he was never tempted to yield to 'the politics of the last atrocity', remaining committed to it, and seeing in it a vehicle for increased mutual understanding and common ground. Douglas Hyde was his hero and he referred in a number of addresses to Hyde's disappointment when politics came into the Gaelic League in 1915. Prior to that, there had been wide enthusiasm for the language across the religious traditions. While an advocate of active citizenship by the members of the Protestant community in the South, Donald called for the development of a broad and inclusive concept of Irish national identity, where all traditions could find their place without sacrificing their heritage. Following the signing of the Anglo–Irish agreement in the mid-1980s, and as the peace process developed in the 1990s, differences of emphasis in the Church of Ireland, North and South, were reflected in the respective statements of Robin Eames as Archbishop of Armagh and Donald as Archbishop of Dublin (though they maintained a strong mutual regard).

Economic expansion in the 1960s, membership of the European economic community from 1973, and the increasing influence of media such as television, coincided with the coming to power of a new generation of politicians to bring about a greater liberalism in attitudes and public discussion in the Republic. Donald's time in office, particularly as Archbishop of Dublin in the mid-1980s to mid-1990s coincided with the great 'liberal agenda' debates on contraception, abortion and divorce; and his pronouncements stressed a distinction between church teaching and the civil law. Where there was no consensus on aspects of private morality, he believed the state should not enforce the ethos of a single religious tradition. He was at the same time frustrated with some media representations of the churches' stances, whereby Church of Ireland viewpoints coinciding with liberal arguments were frequently juxtaposed with reports of statements from members of the Roman Catholic hierarchy, appearing to pit the churches against each other. While seeing the matter in terms of civil law, he privately regretted the necessity of providing for divorce. He was a cautious traditionalist in many ways, and was wary of the ecumenical impact of moves to ordain women to the priesthood. But once the measure was approved by General Synod, as a loyal son of the church, he embraced the new dispensation.

In the difficult economic climate of the 1980s and early 1990s, local initiatives took place in the dioceses of Meath and Dublin to assist the unemployed – promoted by Donald in perhaps a reflection of a social concern inherited from his father George (and seen also in his half-brother Norman's career in the Department of Social Welfare). A number of events combined in the early 1990s, in the second half of his tenure in Dublin, to lift national spirits, which in turn triggered economic development and greater openness. In the political sphere, fresh developments such as the election of Mary Robinson as president, a successful Irish presidency of the European Council and the developing peace process were mirrored in the sporting world with the participation of the Irish soccer team in the 1990 World Cup, and in the cultural sphere with a string of Irish successes in the Eurovision song contest and the phenomenon of *Riverdance*. In the social sphere, laws on contraception were liberalised, homosexuality decriminalised and (towards the end of Donald's term), the ban on divorce was removed. Such liberalisations released cultural energy in wider society, and the Church of Ireland's distinctive contribution to debate found a ready listenership, with politicians such as Senator Mary Henry, Senator Catherine McGuinness, Senator David Norris and Ivan Yates TD making key contributions to match those of church figures such as Donald himself, Dean Victor Griffin, Archdeacon Gordon Linney, Bishop Samuel Poyntz and Walton Empey. The Protestant contribution to the health service, traditionally expressed through the Adelaide hospital, faced challenges with proposals to develop a new hospital complex in Tallaght, Co. Dublin.

It must be recalled that, in the period of Donald's episcopate, references to 'the minority' in the State were understood to refer to the Protestant community. In the time since then, many other minority groups and traditions, social and religious and ethnic, have come to find their place in Ireland. Donald Caird combined social and civic engagement with a robust defence of his own tradition. He led by example in his community and functioned as an exemplar of his tradition to those outside it.

As he approached retirement, he struck a wistful note when asked about his view of partition:

It was very sad that this country had to be partitioned. Not only would we be a much more integrated and cohesive society, but we would have been on much better terms with our UK neighbours had the intentions of Home Rule been effected. I can only look back on the rebellion of 1916, the war with Britain in 1921, and the Civil War which followed, as really great tragedies in Irish history. If these events had never occurred Ireland would have emerged as a great liberal and independent society. Also I believe our relationship with Britain would be far happier than it is at present.

But he did not lose himself in such might-have-beens. The Republic was there, and his view was that its Protestant citizens – while preserving their identity and voice – had a full part to play in building up all aspects of its common life.

CHAPTER ONE

Childhood, Education and Training for the Ministry
(1925–1950)

Family background

The Irish Free State was barely three years old and had recently emerged from a debilitating civil war when Donald Arthur Richard Caird was born on 11 December 1925, in a nursing home at 37 Lower Leeson Street, Dublin 2. He was the only child of the marriage of George Caird and Emily (née Dreaper).

George's father was a Scotsman, John Anderson Caird. The origin of the Scottish surname is the Gaelic word *ceard*,[1] which means 'a craftsman, a travelling tinker who repaired pots and kettles, and a worker in brass'. John (born 1854) hailed from Arbroath, the great woollen manufacturing industry and jute capital in the nineteenth century. He went south to work in the woollen industry in Manchester, and it was there that he met Dubliner Emmeline Broadbent (born 1857), who had come over to study music.[2] The Broadbent family had been active in business life in Dublin city in the late eighteenth and nineteenth century, with an iron foundry business and interests in woollen mills at Palmerstown (the latter may have been an interesting point of connection for Caird). They owned the King's House in Chapelizod, near Dublin.[3] Robert Broadbent (Emmeline's father, Donald's great grandfather) was married to Alice Margaret Strachan of the Strachan mining family.[4] John Caird married Emmeline in 1882, and came to Ireland to live with her parents in the King's House. Donald recalls his grandmother, Emmeline, telling him that she remembered, as a young girl, two pictures hanging in the hallway of the King's House. One depicted Gladstone and bore the caption 'Our Leader'. The other picture depicted Charles Stewart Parnell, and was captioned 'Our Hero'. This seemed to encapsulate the liberal and moderately nationalist outlook of the family.

John and Emmeline had three daughters and two sons. George was the second eldest child and was born in the King's House in 1886. Alone of the children, his baptism was recorded at Lucan Presbyterian Church. This may have reflected some fluidity between the Protestant denominations

1

within the family, but in the 1901 census all of the family are recorded as belonging to the 'Irish Church', meaning Church of Ireland. George was educated at the National School in Castleknock, and in the Merchant Taylors' school. He suffered an injury as a young man, while watching a game of quoits – a traditional game involving the throwing of metal, rope or rubber rings over a set distance, usually to land over or near a spike in the ground. One of the metal rings missed the target and hit George just below his right knee, severing a nerve running to his foot and resulting in him walking with a limp for the rest of his life.

George worked for some time in the civil service, subsequently studying accountancy, and going to work in the Chief Engineer's Department of the Great Southern Railway, where he was a clerk involved in costing projects. He married his first wife, Elizabeth (née McDonald) in 1909, at twenty-three years of age. In 1911, they were living at 13 Halliday Square, Aran Quay, the census of that year recording 'Methodist' as their religious denomination. They had three children, Norman, Phoebe and James. In 1918 they were residing at Garden View Villas, Chapelizod, when Elizabeth died at the age of thirty-four, having suffered from pulmonary tuberculosis for some eighteen months prior to her death (this was possibly complicated by influenza from the epidemic of 1918). George's mother Emmeline lived nearby at Hillview, Chapelizod.

George met his second wife, Emily Florence (née Dreaper), in 1922 and they were married at Holy Trinity Church, Rathmines, on 8 August 1923. Emily was the second eldest in a family of five daughters and two sons of the late James Campbell Hill Dreaper (who had been an accountant and chemist) and Isabella (née Jackson). The Dreapers came from Ahascragh in Co. Galway, where they had land and business. On Emily's mother's side, the Jacksons were from Co. Carlow and had some property interests in south Dublin city.

Many of the Dreaper children were recorded in the 1911 census as working, Emily and her sister Ellen as Iron Manager's assistants, a brother as a general law clerk, two other sisters as a draper's assistant and office assistant respectively, and a younger brother as an unemployed clerk. The youngest daughter Isabella (known as 'Tuss') was still at school. Twelve years later, before her marriage, Emily was living with her widowed mother Isabella at 5 Ashfield Road in Ranelagh.[5]

Childhood in Ranelagh
George and Emily Caird set up home at number 10 Cullenswood Terrace (later renumbered 88, Ranelagh), located on the prominent Georgian

terrace in the very centre of the south Dublin suburb of Ranelagh. The houses on the terrace were two-storey, over a basement with steps up to the front door, and the Cairds' house (now a medical practice) was at the southern end, bordering Chelmsford Lane. At this time, Ranelagh was a middle to upper-middle class area with many doctors and solicitors resident there. Religiously, it was a mixed community of Protestants and Roman Catholics. There was little motor traffic on the roads, and the most common method of personal transport was the bicycle. The clanging bells of the number 11 electric tram would be heard as it plied its way northward from Clonskeagh, along Chelmsford Avenue and down Leeson Street into the city, the conductor having from time to time to adjust the trolley connecting with the overhead electric wire. Some intrepid folk would hold on to the destination board which ran along the lower deck, as they cycled alongside!

A short distance away in the opposite direction, at the junction of Sandford Road and Marlborough Road, was Sandford Church of Ireland church – the Cairds' parish church. In this era, there would have been several services held each Sunday, including Sunday School, Morning Prayer, a special children's service in the afternoon and an evening service. Various youth organisations were active in the parish, including scout troops and Girl Guides. The parish was presided over by the formidable Canon William Nesbitt Harvey, a man of great intellect but a somewhat eccentric personality.

Donald's father George was a tall, slim-ish, good-looking man, but with a strict nature. He would sit in his armchair, smoking his pipe, and had a habit of making humorous asides or quips. He had an active social conscience, and was involved in some charitable work directed towards the unemployed.[6] Donald recalls his father 'smoking all the day', while his mother Emily would smoke a cigarette after dinner. She is recalled as a quiet character. She was a thin woman but noted for her beautiful long hair, which grew white as she got older.[7] Occupying what must have been a sometimes uncomfortable 'outsider' status with regard to George's three older children, she was particularly devoted to her own son, Donald.

There was a substantial age gap between the young Donald and his three half-siblings. The eldest, Norman (almost thirteen years older), went on from Leeson Park National School to the Mountjoy School in Mountjoy Square, walking there each day from Ranelagh. He left school early and began work at the age of fifteen. Norman began working with invoices and costing in various employments, and became an Employment Clerk with the Dublin Employment Exchange in 1934. He studied at night for a degree in commerce at University College Dublin, and worked his way up through the ranks in the civil service. In August 1939, Norman moved out of 88 Ranelagh on marrying Jane 'Pansy' Lamb, whom he met in the Glenwick Cycling Club.

Phoebe, eleven years older than Donald, boarded at the Bertrand and Rutland High School for girls in Eccles Street on the northside of Dublin. Subsequently, she lived in 88 Ranelagh for a period, and it was then that her young half-brother became more aware of her, although she would be out at work during the day. She was recalled by Olive Waugh who came to know her later as being 'very funny' and very clever. She was 'wonderful with her hands', making her own coats and hats. In 1940, she married Hal Fenner, a Roman Catholic, who was working in the motor repair industry.

In the early years of her marriage to George, Emily cared for his youngest son Jim, but at only twelve years of age (when Donald was three), he was sent to the Hibernian Marine School on Seafield Road in Clontarf (later amalgamated with other schools, including the Mountjoy and Betrand and Rutland schools to form part of today's Mount Temple Comprehensive). Jim would pay visits to the Caird home in Ranelagh from time to time, before going to train on a ship on the River Fal in England in 1933 for the merchant navy, being made a cadet at the age of sixteen.[8] Donald recalls Jim writing home on the occasion of his sixteenth birthday from Vladivostok, where his ship was icebound for three months. Of his three half-siblings, Donald was closest to Jim, and recalls him bringing a present of 'magic boxes' on a visit home from Japan in 1937, two years before the War. He was commissioned as a British naval officer in 1939. Jim married Ethel Luke, like his brother Norman having met his wife through the Glenwick Cycling Club. Donald recalls as a child perceiving a sense of 'loneliness' in Jim (despite his close relationship with Emily) and a 'desire for independence' in Phoebe, which may have been how his half-siblings' sense of loss of their own mother came across to him.

The Cairds had not long been living at 10 Cullenswood Terrace when Emily's younger sister Isabella and her husband John R. (Jack) Waugh, a doctor, came to live with them for a period, later moving to one of the neighbouring houses in the middle of the terrace. In 1938, Waugh purchased number 1, the house on the northern corner of Cullenswood Terrace bordering Chelmsford Road, and established a doctor's surgery there. The Waughs had two sons, Desmond and Basil. Basil, of slight build and timid disposition, was closest in age to his cousin Donald, with Desmond some five years older. The older boy tended to exert his more dominant personality over Basil and Donald, leading the latter to become adept at devising wiles and stratagems to counter or deflect such behaviour. Desmond Waugh would later follow his father into the medical profession. Another sister of Emily's, Frances ('Fanny') was also living on the same terrace, married to a doctor, Dick Nightingale. The Nightingales had three children, Oswald, Lavinia and Sylvia, also first cousins of Donald. Emily enjoyed a very close relationship with the other members of her family living nearby, and they would regularly call in to each other's houses.

At the age of three-and-a-half, Donald began attending the small preparatory Selskar School in Ranelagh, which was located near Elmwood Avenue. This consisted of a large single room with twenty to twenty-five pupils. Donald recalled Mrs Moorhead, his teacher, as a staunch Church of Ireland lady who would begin the school day with prayers. After about a year and a half there, instead of going to Sandford Parish National School, he was sent for his primary education to a private school run by Miss Bertha Guilgault at 93 Marlborough Road, not far from the family home. Miss Guilgault was of French Protestant stock, and a daughter of Professor Leonie Guilgault, Professor of French in the Royal University. Donald recalls her as being rather dowdily dressed, wearing her hair in a bun and sporting small wire-frame glasses. Another pupil there, Cyril Patton, recalls her as 'warm but strict', and not inclined to put up with nonsense. She was small, 'like a sparrow', recalled Stella Bell (née Woods), a neighbour (and later a fellow pupil of Donald's at Wesley College).

There were steps up to the front door of her establishment, in a red brick Georgian house. The classroom was inside on the left, open double-doors linking the front room with the room behind. By means of this device, Miss Guilgault could herself instruct the single class of between ten and twenty boys and girls in Scripture, English, Geography, History, French, Writing and Arithmetic. She had two sisters, who like herself did not marry, and who resided with their father at Hauteville in Leeson Park: one sister taught French at Wesley College and the other kept house. The Guilgaults were strict evangelical Protestants.

Donald's cousin Basil Waugh was also a pupil at Miss Guilgault's, and it was at the school that Donald first met his lifelong friend, Cyril Patton, about thirteen months younger than himself. The Patton family lived on Sandford Road, about halfway between Cullenswood Terrace and the school. Cyril's parents were Presbyterian, who attended Adelaide Road Presbyterian Church. As the rector of Sandford Parish was not inclined to accept non-parishioners into the national school, Cyril was sent to Miss Guilgault's for his primary education. He was brought to school by his mother on the first day, Miss Guilgault greeting them at the door of number 93, and asking them to wait a moment. She then brought out a young boy, introducing him to Cyril: 'This is Donald, and he will look after you.' The two boys were put sitting together and became firm friends.

Along with Basil, Donald and Cyril would play at each other's houses in Ranelagh (Cyril recalls that his or Donald's family home was a 'second home' to each boy). They would also go down to nearby Herbert Park in Ballsbridge to play 'cowboys and Indians, all the things boys do, we were quite normal'. The Waughs had a boxing ring set up in their house, and would have Donald over to box with Basil, to the disapproval of the protective Emily. The Patton and Caird parents knew each other to greet, but were not socially close. A 'quasi-religious meeting' for children was held on Friday evenings, run by the sister of Miss Guilgault's who taught French at Wesley. This meeting was held in number 16 St Stephen's Green (a building owned by the Presbyterian Association) and as attendance seemed to be expected of them, Donald and Cyril would go along, cycling there from Ranelagh as they got a little older.

As a child, Donald accompanied his parents to Britain on holidays each year, the family frequently staying in a private hotel in Gower Street in London, a city his father 'loved'. They took excursions out from London, journeying for example to Plymouth; and on one memorable occasion when Donald was just four years of age, taking the Flying Scotsman train from London to Scotland. He has a vivid memory of a 'fine looking young man' on the train in handcuffs, being accompanied by a policeman. Donald's father took pity on this prisoner and gave him his cigarette case filled with the cheroots he smoked. Donald recalls visiting Arbroath with his father in 1934 and a man showing them the house, named 'Lambeth' where George's father John Anderson Caird had been born. Back in Dublin, 88 Ranelagh was named 'Montrose', in an echo of these Scottish origins.

Wesley College years (1935–44)

Mainly at his mother's instigation, it was decided that Donald should attend Wesley College, the Methodist school located on the southern side of St Stephen's Green, Dublin, but with pupils mostly drawn from the Church of Ireland. Wesley had been founded in 1845 'for the purpose of affording a thorough literary, scientific and commercial education, with a sound, religious, and moral training, in strict accordance with the principles of Wesleyan Methodism'. The college motto, in Greek, was *panta dokimazete to kalon katecete* (prove all things, hold fast that which is good), a phrase from Scripture (1 Thessalonians 5:21). The school, an impressive three-storey pointed building with a large spire, was co-educational, with about three hundred and seventy pupils. Girls accounted for about half of the student population. This coeducation was strictly supervised, and during Donald's time as a pupil there, boys were still being addressed by their surnames only, while girls had their surnames prefixed by 'Miss'.

Presiding over the school community was the Principal T.J. Irwin, a Methodist clergyman. He was a tall, angular man with bushy eyebrows, who remembered every child's name.[9] Irwin's unimpressed response at Donald's first interview, on learning of his quixotic primary education, was 'I suppose you learned politeness and French!' Wesley had a three year preparatory system, Prep C to Prep A, followed by First Form in the secondary system, and Donald started in Prep C class in September 1935, aged nine.

The teachers were an eclectic bunch, ranging from Dr John Conway, the Maths teacher who might surprise you with a belt of a book on the head from behind if you were being inattentive; Mrs 'Sandy' Alexander, the strict History teacher and headmistress of the girls; 'Curly Willie' Wilson, the Latin teacher; to 'Ma' Burrows (so-nicknamed because she had two sons in the school).[10] Stella Bell (Donald's classmate), recalls the studious boy sitting up near the top of the class: 'He was very quiet. To my recollection, he kept to himself, he wasn't one of the wild boys! … he was shy.'

While there was a variety of religious allegiance represented among its pupils, Donald recalled Wesley having at the time

a distinctly Methodist atmosphere, and the form of service in the beautiful school chapel was characteristically Methodist, based mainly on the scriptures, Old Testament and New Testament and on the splendid collection of hymns to which the Methodist tradition is heir, written many of them by John and Charles Wesley and used throughout the world by Christians of all traditions. There was a certain upbeat and evangelical flavour about these services, which was neither mindlessly enthusiastic nor oppressively puritanical, and which appealed to teenagers and young people generally. The school chaplain at the time was later to become a distinguished Professor of Psychiatry in Dublin University, and he certainly had the knack of reaching young people in a relevant and effective way.[11]

The custom at the school was that the girls played hockey while the boys played rugby at the Wesley pitch in Donnybrook or in Bloomfield,

Leeson Park. Donald played for two years in the Junior Cup rugby team, and later, in 1943 and 1944, in the Senior Cup team.

> Trying to coax a thin spray of cold water from a very inefficient shower in the corner of a dilapidated hut on the College sports field at Donnybrook, grandiloquently referred to as the pavilion, in order to wash off the caked mud of an hour and a half's vigorous play on a very wet and muddy rugby pitch was certainly a moral challenge which I don't think even John Wesley had thought of as a character building exercise for his adherents,

observed Donald.[12] By tradition, Wesley played a Senior Cup match against Portora Royal School in Enniskillen every year, the respective teams alternating visits between North and South. It was on the Wesley Senior team's visit North in 1943 that Donald first made the acquaintance of one Sam Poyntz, a popular and solidly built Portora player. Donald was a wing forward and Poyntz a hooker in the front row. Poyntz was 'a great man for gathering support', with cries of 'oh, Poyntz, pass to me!' or 'Sam!' abounding.

In the summer, the girls at Wesley would play tennis, and the boys cricket, although this was not a sport in which Donald took much of an interest. He played both tennis and badminton: 'anything with a racquet, I had a quick eye'. At home in Ranelagh, the family had its own table tennis team called 'Thomond' (so-called because one of Donald's uncles came from Limerick), which played in all the major Leinster tournaments. Donald's maternal aunt, Tuss Waugh, was an accomplished table tennis player, taking part in several international tournaments in places such as France and Czechoslovakia.

During the years of the Second World War (known as 'the Emergency' in the neutral South), Wesley suffered from food rationing like everywhere else, and while, in best stoical tradition, hardly a match was cancelled, the customary spreads of tea and cakes laid on afterwards were somewhat circumscribed. Stella Bell recalls the benefits for Dublin day-pupils of befriending the boarders, some of whose families had shops down the country – in this way one might come by extra supplies of tea or butter to bring home, circumventing the rations. During these years, morning assembly would occasionally feature the reading out of names of old Wesleyans who had been killed on active service abroad with the Allied Forces, one of these being Douglas Doyle, the brother of a boy in the year ahead of Donald. The Principal, Dr Irwin, took a large number of Jewish children from refugee families into the school, learning at a relatively early stage, through family contacts in the Allied Forces, of the persecutions they were experiencing.

Donald recalled that:

Though we knew that we were living a reduced kind of life to what our pre-war predecessors enjoyed, there was a certain isolation and even tranquillity which made study even attractive in the absence of any other distractions. And, something that was widely observed throughout the Republic, there was very little illness – public health improved immensely. Most of Ireland's social problems were resolved by the war, there was a general levelling down; but areas of severe poverty remained. This temporary Shangri-La dissipated and vanished with the ending of the war.[13]

Reflecting later on his memories of Wesley, Donald said:

I think gratitude would be the only appropriate word to use, gratitude for the independence of mind and for the fulfilment of personality to its natural limits, gratitude for the competence with which I was taught a wide range of subjects ... gratitude that the spiritual values which were always evident, but never paraded, allowed us to distinguish between false emotion and solid values of personal integrity and service; between pious platitudes and honest statements of true concern.[14]

After Donald had started in Wesley, his friends, Cyril Patton and Basil Waugh, who had moved on to St Andrew's College, had initially kept up contact, making regular visits to the local Sandford cinema in Ranelagh on a Saturday night. As he progressed through secondary school, and having a somewhat shy and reserved nature, Donald became more serious, taking an increasing interest in academic pursuits and 'getting into the books in a big way' according to Cyril. He began to drop out of the frequent cinema visits, particularly as the Intermediate and Leaving Certificate examinations approached. Cyril recalls that Donald became more interested in the books, 'and me in the girls', while Cyril and Basil kept up the cinema visits, and began attending dances, or 'hops', their friend 'didn't do that sort of thing'.

First encounters with the Gaeltacht and Cumann Gaelach na hEaglaise
The Irish language was a compulsory subject in state examinations, in Wesley as in all other schools in the state. However, as it had not featured among the subjects he had learned at Miss Guilgault's private school, Donald took little interest in it:

There was abroad in those days a common view amongst schoolboys and girls of Dublin that the Irish language was something invented in some obscure department of the Civil Service for the specific affliction of the youth of Dublin – a sort of *Danegeld* imposed upon the dwellers of the Pale to punish them, if not for their treachery, at least for their lack of enthusiasm in relation to the maintenance of Ireland's cultural heritage.[15]

In Donald's early years at Wesley, the Irish teacher was Jim Slator, an overpowering figure whom he was not overly fond. He achieved the mark of two per cent in Irish at a term examination, a distinction which did not trouble him greatly. However Irish was a source of some anxiety for him as the Intermediate Certificate examinations approached. He was conscious that failure here would mean failure in the entire examination, despite his proficiency in other subjects. He applied himself to studying the grammar and memorised a vocabulary and half-a-dozen poems, learning Irish much in the same manner as he learnt Latin and Greek. It was for him a dead language, and while he performed creditably in the Intermediate examination, he had little ability to converse or even understand Irish when it was spoken to him. While his parents had nothing against the Irish language as part of the general curriculum, they had a practical attitude towards education, and felt the right choice needed to be made in relation to subjects being studied. From about third year onwards, Mr Paddy Clune, a Roman Catholic from the west of Ireland, was Donald's Irish teacher at Wesley. His classmate Stella Bell recalls Clune telling the pupils many stories to make the language interesting.

Donald says that his father George had a few phrases in Irish and knew Irish speakers – this may possibly have been through his work with the Great Southern Railway. It was around this time that he invited a friend to supper one evening, in order that he might assess Donald's competence in the language. This was Mícheál 'Eoghan' Ó Súilleabháin, author of *An Ghloine Dhroidheachta agus Scéalta Eile*, a book of short stories for children. Donald recalls being unable to understand much of what was said to him in Irish that evening. Ó Súilleabháin advised his father to dispatch his son to the Gaeltacht '*go dtí áit nach bhfuil focal Béarla le cloisint ann, agus ní fada go mbeidh roinnt mhaith comhrá i nGaeilge uaidh*' (to a place where not a word of English will be heard, and it won't be long until there is a good flow of conversation in Irish from him).

Following this advice, Donald was duly sent off to the Gaeltacht district of Dún Chaoin (Dunquin) on the Dingle Peninsula in west Kerry. He paid his first visit there in the summer of 1943, at the age of seventeen, just before his final year in Wesley. Accompanied by a friend from school, Eric Craven, he travelled down by train from Dublin to Tralee, the boys' bikes being carried in the guard's van. After overnighting in Tralee with friends of the Cravens, they set out for Dún Chaoin at the westernmost end of the Dingle peninsula, stopping for lemonade at the South Pole Inn in Annascaul. It was late when they reached the point before Slea Head where a stream crosses the narrow coastal road, and supposing it to be a river, they propped the bikes on their shoulders and waded across, amazed to find the water did not even reach their knees! The boys lodged in the house of the MacGearailt family. The *bean an tí* (woman of the house) was the daughter of the late writer and teacher Seán Ó Dálaigh, known as 'Common Noun'. She is recalled as a wonderful host and cook, serving up such treats as 'Queen of Puddings', a delicious bread-and-jam desert, baked in the oven. Meat or fish would be served at dinner, in the middle of the day. In conversations with Seosamh Ó Dálaigh, a collector of folklore and son of Common Noun, Donald learned of the breadth and depth of the Irish folklore tradition and its importance in the context of European culture.[16] One evening, the local Church of Ireland minister, Frank Roycroft, called in to the house, and invited him to attend the service in nearby Kilmalkeader Church the following Sunday. The boy duly went along to the little church near the Atlantic coast, and was astonished to hear morning prayer in Irish from the lips of the local Church of Ireland people, native speakers.

Donald also stayed for a period in the house of the storyteller 'Kruger' Kavanagh, a legendary personality, who had emigrated to the United States at the age of nineteen and occupied a variety of positions from nursing to public relations, before returning to open a guesthouse and pub in his native county. While staying at Kruger's, he was taken one evening to meet Peig Sayers, the renowned storyteller who had lived on the Blaskets, and was at that time living on the mainland in Baile Bhiocáire. Peig was seated by the fire, and questioned the young visitor – where was he from, was he enjoying his visit to this area, and so on. He recalls her as a kindly, friendly woman, who readily entered into conversation, and did not let it flag. She spoke unhurriedly and steadily, using simple language, understanding that Donald did not have fluent Irish. It was a simple chat about *cúrsaí an lae* (everyday matters). He visited her on a couple of occasions during visits in these years, Peig recognising him on his second visit and greeting him as 'Dónall'. Peig had been blonde and Donald says that in her younger days she had been known as 'Peig Bhuí'. Although in her seventies when he met her, she struck her young visitor as a good-looking and graceful woman. She had a face alive with amusement 'and you knew she was going to engage you in amusing conversation'.

Reflecting later, in an interview with Risteárd Ó Glaisne, Donald said that he derived enormous pleasure from his first visit to the Gaeltacht, and this increased with each subsequent visit he made.

> It is certain that I only gradually became familiar with their Irish … But I remember well how kind, gentle and patient the older people were with a youth who was doing his best to understand their speech … The old people of the Gaeltacht had time to reflect, and to ponder life. They did not need to get their philosophy second-hand from any source.[17]

It was a whole new world for the middle class Church of Ireland boy from the city, and Donald was enthralled. Kerry would continue to hold a special place in his affections for the rest of his life.

It was around this time also that he recalls being informed by a boy named Edgar (whom he knew from the Friday evening religious meeting in St Stephen's Green) that there were regular Irish language services taking place every second Sunday in St Patrick's Cathedral. He could find there a number of his own co-religionists fluent in Irish, which might be a source of inspiration to him. Donald and Edgar went along to their first Irish language service in the Lady Chapel of St Patrick's in October 1942, conducted by Canon Paul Quigley, an Irish speaker from the west of Ireland. Gathered there were members of Cumann Gaelach na hEaglaise, the Irish Guild of the Church (of Ireland), which had been founded in 1914. Also present was a group of pupils from Coláiste Moibhí, the all-Irish preparatory college for would-be primary teachers in Protestant schools. Donald made the acquaintance of its principal, Lil Nic Dhonnchadh.[18] Although his Irish was still poor, he was able to follow the rubrics of the service from his familiarity with the Book of Common Prayer.

The service made a profound impression on him: the prayers being recited from memory and hymns being sung enthusiastically by those present, the sermon being given in Irish, and people chatting in the language afterwards. 'I had never heard Irish spoken so beautifully, so fast, so colloquially.' Donald recalled one notable figure present:

> A small old lady, who wore pince-nez spectacles and who always arrived on an ancient bicycle wearing rather incongruously a long fur coat in the winter, which she managed miraculously to keep out of the spokes of the moving wheels, I learned to be the famous Dr Kathleen Lynn, the founder of St Ultan's Hospital … She looked so mild and spoke so gently that it was hard to believe that less than thirty years previously she had taken part in the rebellion of 1916 and had been a medical officer to the Irish Republican Army in the ensuing Civil War.[19]

Dr Lynn, who 'spoke Irish with an Oxford accent',[20] was anxious to develop the social side of life for those interested in Irish (particularly the younger members of the Church of Ireland), arranging mid-week *céilithe* and holding events in a basement of a house in Molesworth Street, known as the 'K' Club. It was at such social occasions that Donald came to know, in relaxed circumstances, other figures such as Harry Nichols, the Dublin city engineer who had been condemned to life imprisonment for his part in the 1916 rising, and the treasurer of the Cumann, Alfie Cotton, a Northerner and old IRA man:

> These people I would not normally have met and would certainly never have come to know intimately, where it not for Cumann Gaelach na hEaglaise. So, I date my genuine interest in Irish to this strangely mixed, if not maverick, company with whom I fell in almost by accident. I know that many of the leaders in the national cause in the past were members of the Church of Ireland, members of my own community – Wolfe Tone, Thomas Davis, Smith O'Brien, Charles Stewart Parnell – but they were figures of the past. Here, in this group, were living representatives of that same tradition, alive and well and speaking Irish.[21]

On 4 December 1942, Donald was proposed as a member of Cumann Gaelach na hEaglaise, by Albert Stokes (later, rector of Powerscourt). Another new member was Frank Blennerhassett (who would later become chaplain to Coláiste Moibhí). Donald was elected to its *Coiste* (committee) at the AGM held on 13 May 1943.

Trinity College years (1944–50)
Donald's initial inclination, influenced by his relatives in the medical profession and his own aptitude for scientific subjects, had been towards the study of medicine, and he went as far as sitting the entrance examination to study medicine at Trinity. However, childhood attendance at Sandford Parish Church and experience of its academically brilliant rector Canon William Nesbitt Harvey may have had an unconscious influence on his subsequent life choices. Harvey was not a man who shied away from controversy and was well able to take a stand *contra mundum*. Donald's family background was that of middle-of-the-road, undemonstrative Church of Ireland Protestantism, and early exposure to Miss Guilgault's evangelicalism, together with his own logical and inquiring mind, appears to have turned him against fundamentalism in religion. He recalls a turning point in his later schooldays, when he came across a popular book on philosophy in one of his uncle's houses and was deeply

impressed, 'this was real thinking – the most important [subject] you could do'.

In October 1944, at the age of eighteen, Donald entered Trinity College Dublin and embarked upon the study of philosophy. In the 1940s, Trinity College was a fairly intimate community of under two thousand students, the overwhelming majority belonging to one or other of the Protestant denominations, and the College itself retaining a Church of Ireland ethos.[22] In his first year at Trinity, along with philosophy, Donald studied Celtic languages, where Éamon Ó Tuathail, Eleanor Knott, Seán Beaumont and Gordon Quin were among his lecturers. He was also a member of the *Cumann Gaelach*, the student Irish language society. Timetabling clashes in subsequent years may account for his failing to take these studies further.

The School of Mental and Moral Science[23] in Trinity was very much orientated towards religion and the ministry at the time. The Head of School was the distinguished Professor of Moral Philosophy, the Rev. Arthur Aston Luce. Luce, a former chaplain of St Columba's College, had served in the First World War with the Royal Irish Rifles and was awarded the MC in 1917. He was Chancellor of St Patrick's Cathedral from 1936 to 1953. Luce was an authority on George Berkeley, the famous philosopher and sometime Bishop of Cloyne, on whom he published a number of works. He was a keen recreational angler, but had suffered personal tragedy: his wife and daughter both drowned accidentally in the Liffey at Celbridge, Co. Kildare, in May 1940.[24] A philosophy classmate of Donald's, Vincent Denard, recalls that Luce had a very strong personality, managing to hold the attention of his class without the necessity to be overly strict. He would encourage his students to ask questions, although many were not ready to do so, encouraging the more diligent Denard instead to ask the question so that they could continue taking notes or 'have a bit of a rest'.

Other staff in the School included the Archbishop King Professor of Theology, R. R. Hartford (assisted by George Otto Simms, Dean of Residence and Church of Ireland chaplain at Trinity, and Tom Salmon, a future dean of Christ Church Cathedral); J. E. L. Oulton (Regius Professor of Theology); R. M. Gwynn (Professor of Biblical Greek); G. V. Jourdan (Professor of Church History) and J. L. B. Barker (Professor of Pastoral Theology).[25]

His fellow students were a talented bunch; of the dozen or so students entering as junior Freshmen studying the Mental and Moral Science Moderatorship course, several would go on to occupy senior office in the Church, including Donald himself; Samuel G. Poyntz (his former rugby opponent from Portora and a future Bishop of Cork and later, Connor); Noel P. Willoughby (future Bishop of Cashel); Cecil J. Price (future Archdeacon of Glendalough); A.D.H. (Douglas) Northridge (future Archdeacon of Cyprus) and H.J. Stuart (future Chaplain-in-Chief of the Royal Air Force). Several of the students were pursuing Double Moderatorship courses, taking another subject in addition to philosophy: oriental languages in the case of Sam Poyntz; modern languages or English in other cases.

In a letter written to his friend Douglas Northridge on 20 March 1948, Donald was in something of a flap about 'schol':

> Dear Duggy, I'm writing this to you in case you have not seen the timetable and examiners for schol. [X] sent me a notice this morning indicating that Furlong was in fact setting two papers, Kant and pre-Kantian. My heart nearly stopped and I have not been able to do any more work this morning on the head of it. It struck me like a thunderbolt because [X] expressly said there would be no change from last year when I [asked] him on Thursday week last after lectures – please don't blame me from misleading you; up to this minute I've been working on the assumption that everything would be the same as last year; but this changes the whole complexion of the situation. We may as well make the best of it. Donald. PS I'm enclosing a copy of the time-table.

Despite this hiccup however, Donald succeeded in the onerous scholarship examination in philosophy, becoming one of the Scholars of the House in 1948 (which meant he could dine for free at Commons and no longer had to pay University fees).

Donald reflects on his study of philosophy:

> As Hume says: 'the word of metaphysics is a Republic: there are no people with more knowledge than anybody else', and you can wander for years in the blinding wastes of metaphysics and never get anywhere. I was good at science in the early days, and took a senior exhibition in chemistry when I went to Trinity College. I would love to have done everything, I would love to have done medicine also; my cousins, their fathers, all did medicine … Philosophy requires you to order your thinking in a strictly logical way. One of the useful studies of philosophy is that it helps you immediately and practically to discover what logical fallacy is taking you out of the mainstream, whether it's post-hoc, propter-hoc. I was good at logic.

Philosophy students in Trinity tended to gravitate towards the student Metaphysical Society, which would meet around three times each term. Students would present papers and give talks on philosophical matters.

On one occasion, the society hosted the renowned English philosopher and panellist on the popular wartime BBC radio series *The Brains Trust*, C. E. M. Joad. Donald recalls Victor Griffin (a few years older than Donald, who would later become Dean of St Patrick's Cathedral) as a very effective chairman of the society, and also a great speaker at meetings of the Phil. and Hist societies. He also remembers the Fianna Fáil leader Éamon de Valera addressing a meeting of one of these societies around the year 1948, shortly after a trip he had made to America, and informing the students of the phenomenon of 'drip-dry shirts' which he had encountered there.

Donald had a very distinguished academic career in Trinity, achieving first-class honours in his philosophy examination in each of his years studying the subject there, and garnering several prestigious academic prizes over the course of his time in College. He achieved Senior Exhibitioner (1946) in philosophy, Irish and chemistry; Kyle Prizeman in Irish Language and Literature and Prizeman in Semitic languages (Jacob Winegreen being the Professor). In philosophy, he achieved Prizeman in Mental and Moral Science, and was awarded the Lilian Mary Luce Prize for Berkelian Philosophy.

During his College days, Donald enjoyed the company of his immediate circle, made up principally of his fellow course students. A group of four or five, including Ruth Childers[26] and Douglas Northridge, would regularly go for coffee in the morning, frequenting coffee houses in the city centre such as Robert Roberts in nearby Suffolk Street, Bewley's Café or Switzer's basement cafe on Grafton Street. This practice of taking a morning coffee break would become a treasured part of Donald's life: 'I love a break in the morning and also in mid afternoon – always in my life I had that.' He valued the mental refreshment supplied by spending this time in relaxed company. While he does not recall any particular romantic attachment during his university days, he enjoyed social friendships with girls, and the occasional date involving a trip to the cinema in the company of two or three others. Samuel Poyntz recalls Donald, himself and their classmates as being 'all very much a band of brothers, we knew each other fairly well ...' A Christmas card to Douglas Northridge in 1948 displays his wry sense of humour: a gentleman, clutching lopsidedly a glass of wine, sees elephants flying in the air, the printed caption is 'my good wishes for Xmas are no illusion!' Donald has added an arrow pointing to the last word and the observation 'you cannot escape philosophical questions even at Christmas.'

He continued to reside at home in Ranelagh during his university years, despite the fact that his status as scholar entitled him to both free rooms and Commons from 1948 onwards. He was happier with this arrangement, valuing home life and the proximity of his relatives. He says of himself: 'I wasn't the Trinity type, I was always shy.' Beyond his immediate circle, he does not recall having a great deal of social life in Trinity, but a full life at home (including the family Thomond table tennis team) and in Sandford parish (where he also played table tennis at the youth club) compensated for this. He enjoyed his own company and relished returning home after eating Commons. 'I would sit with my parents and later go to my room to read.' Rather than play rugby in Trinity College, he maintained his interest in the game through the Old Wesley rugby team which included former Wesley students who had not gone on to university.

A contemporary of Donald's at Trinity, Frances Pakenham Walsh, who studied science, recalls some aspects of College life in the mid to late forties:

> We would go out ... Lincoln Place gate, I think it was Johnston Mooney's [café in Nassau Street] and that's where we [science students] congregated ... We were down on the far end [of the campus] ... Life in College for a woman was incredibly restrictive ... No women had rooms in College ... I lived in Trinity Hall [in Dartry, Dublin 6]. We thought it was perfect freedom having been at a boarding school! ... [female students] got three *exeats* [permission to remain out after 11 p.m.] a term ... and they had to know where you are going. As far as TCD was concerned, you could go to read in the Reading Room until nine or ten, but there was a 6 p.m. rule as a woman. You went to the porter's lodge, and you signed the time, then you walked across Front Square into the Reading Room, and ... signed again ... so there could be no dalliance en route! ... it was the same on the way out ...
>
> Student societies [meetings], if mixed, had to take place before 6pm. As a woman, the Hist and the Phil, all the interesting ones, [were] closed to us ... Any mixed societies, like [the Choral Society] took place in the afternoon, or [if there was a] concert, you got a special dispensation.

Immediately after the end of the Second World War in 1945, there was a big demand for university places as many people would have gone straight from school into the armed forces. A significant number of ex-servicemen from the Allied armed forces, from both part of Ireland and also from Britain and further afield, came as students to Trinity around this time and for a number of years subsequently. Pakenham Walsh recalls a tremendous influx of students in 1946/7 after the war, with demobbed people coming back to finish degrees or do degrees. They were Irish in the main, and added zest to college life – 'young men ... a bit older, you know, and some of them even had cars! ... That was an amazing breath of fresh air into Trinity.'[27]

In a newspaper interview in 1984, Donald was asked if he knew Gainor Crist, the model for the character 'The Ginger Man', in J.P. Donleavy's book of the same name. Crist had served in the US Navy in WWII and came to Trinity on the GI Bill which provided a range of benefits including College education for returning WWII veterans:

> Well yes, I didn't know him well. One day he attended a philosophy lecture I was at. Canon A.A. Luce, the professor, was reading out the attendance list, and after Caird he came to Crist. 'How do you pronounce your name?' asked Luce. 'Christ!', said Gainor. 'Well,' said Luce, 'for the purpose of the lectures, it will be pronounced Crist.'[28]

In the early years of his time in Trinity, in tandem with his study of Celtic languages, Donald maintained an interest in Cumann Gaelach na hEaglaise (the Irish Guild of the Church). At the AGM in May 1946, it was he who proposed a motion calling for the provision of a more complete translation of the Book of Common Prayer in Irish than that then available, as it would otherwise be impossible to comply with canon 45 of the Church canons. The existing translation of 1938 was described as being incomplete in respect of psalms, catechism, epistles and gospels; the spelling was incomprehensible in places; there were grammatical errors and use of Roman type.[29] A joint committee comprising representatives of the Cumann and Archbishop Barton was duly established and the process of preparing a new translation was begun.[30]

At the end of his first year in Trinity, in the summer of 1945, Donald paid his first visit to the Irish-speaking Blasket Islands, off the coast of Co. Kerry, in the company of two Trinity friends: Kestor Heaslip from Co. Cavan (who had some Irish, his mother being a schoolteacher) and Douglas Northridge (who had no Irish whatsoever). The little houses on the island were clustered in a village on the north-westerly side, facing the mainland across the Blasket Sound. Several houses kept visitors, and Donald and his friends stayed with the Ó Guithín family: two brothers, Seán and Muiris (who were in their thirties), their younger sister Máire and their mother, also called Máire. This Máire (the mother) was the daughter of Pádraig Ó Catháin, the 'Rí' or hereditary 'King' of the island. Donald would keep up his connection with the Guithín family up to his retirement, visiting Seán, Muiris and their sister Máire on several occasions long after they had left the island and settled on the mainland.

In common with many other houses on the island, the Guithíns' little stone cottage had two rooms and a loft sleeping area. The kitchen, dining and living area all constituted just one room. The little house would be swept out each day, and was kept very clean. Donald recalls that the roof was made of sailcloth and tar. The house was built into the hillside, and one particularly wet evening, a cow slid down the hillside, putting its two feet through the roof of the room in which the visitors were staying. Sheep would regularly fall over the cliffs on the island. Donald recalls the house being very comfortable, with a blazing fire in the hearth. An iron arm, called 'the cradle', would be swung in over the fire, and on this would be hung cooking utensils such as pots and a kettle.

The islanders were fond of playing card games in the evenings, particularly twenty-fives, and Donald (who had never played it previously) proved adept at the game, played at little tables in the houses. The players would play 'for pennies' and Donald recalls being rather embarrassed by the fact that by the end of his day, he had won more money than the Guithín family had charged for his stay there (thirty shillings per week). Donald and his two friends enjoyed swimming off the sandy *Trá Bhán* (white strand) on the island, where seals would frequently swim up alongside them. It was not a pastime the islanders themselves engaged in, having a traditional fear of the ocean and its vagaries. Days were spent walking on the cliffs and talking with islanders they would meet, or going out fishing in the *naomhóg* (a small canoe) with the islanders. Curiously, however, Donald recalls the islanders having a greater preference for eating eggs than fish. The island men were fond of smoking tobacco in a pipe, but it seems that the scholar Robin Flower (who made his first visit to the Blaskets in 1910 and was called *Bláithín* – little flower – by the islanders) had introduced the custom of smoking cigarettes, which was first taken up by the women, and later by the men.

Addressing the *Éigse na nGlintí* festival in Donegal in June 2000, Donald recalled the islanders, apart from the very elderly, setting out each Sunday to attend Mass in Dún Chaoin on the mainland, and the magnificent spectacle visible from the top of the cliff: several *naomhóga* sailing out, full of people, braving the frequently rough sea. He recalled it being said in Dún Chaoin that the island people could be recognised because of their habit of walking in single file, one after the other, their custom when walking along the very narrow cliffside paths on the island.

In another address, he recounted sitting on a cliff above the Strand, watching the islanders prepare to make this Sunday journey to the mainland, where they would also purchase provisions before their return. The women were dressed for Mass, in polished shoes, wearing their best scarves on their heads and walking down the path carefully, supporting each other lest they fall. The men were already down at the little harbour waiting for them, and the six or seven *naomhóga* ready in the water. Each person made the sign of the cross as he or she went into the boat. Out on the ocean, though the day was calm, there was movement in the water and the *naomhóga* rose and fell with the waves. Three or four men in each *naomhóg* sat on the benches rowing strongly and rhythmically, quickly putting put a good distance between the island and the boat. The women sat at the back of the boat, their arms around their children. The journey to Mass was long and difficult. Donald remained seated on the cliffside, watching until the *naomhóga* resembled small seabirds on the surface of the water, and then vanished from his sight. It was a long and dangerous journey, taking at least an hour and a half in each direction, for the purpose of the worship of God and thanksgiving for the difficult life they had. Donald felt he had learned a lesson from the loyalty and devotion of these good people, which would remain with him throughout his life.[31]

Donald formed an impression of the islanders as a very kind, considerate, and civil people.

> The magic of this beautiful island … worked upon my spirit and over the past more than forty years I have never escaped from its spell. The mysterious silence broken only by the lapping of the sea: the cry of the elegant seabirds circling the cliffs above the glistening, ever moving water: the quietness of the night emphasised by the long silent sweep of the arm of light across the dark dividing sea from the lighthouse on the neighbouring island of Tiarach, the dark craggy silhouettes of the other neighbouring islands of Inish Tuaisceart and Inish Mhicfhaoinleán, arising steeply from the dark silver-streaked sea on a moonlight night; swimming in the translucent water from a beach of firm white sand at the foot of the sheltering cliff, going out in the *naomhóg* to pick up lobster pots between the islands; sitting beside a turf fire after a day in the wind and sun and sometimes the rain, the room lit by a gentle oil lamp, talking in Irish to my hosts or playing twenty-fives with them at the table in the middle of the kitchen.
>
> Irish became for me the language of this gentle, life-lasting friendship with the people of this island; it opened for me the path into another world which lay so close at hand but which, without Irish was almost inaccessible. To have conceived a love for Irish in such romantic surroundings has left me with an indefinable thrill when I hear it spoken, often in very different surroundings. To learn another language is to gain another life, or at least to enter another world where the spirit may be refreshed and invigorated, and that is certainly true for the English-speaker who learns Irish.[32]

Back in Dublin, Donald's interest in Irish seemed quixotic to some of his Trinity fellows, Samuel Poyntz remarking: 'whereas some of us would be working in the summer … he would be down in Kerry with Pegeen

Sayers.' Poyntz recalls addressing Donald as 'Donald' but 'sometimes if playing up [his interest in Irish], I would have [said] "Dónall"'.

Donald had been obliged to suspend philosophy for a year in order to enter Trinity's School of Divinity in 1947 – the traditional route for ordination to the Church of Ireland ministry. The course in those days was, as George Otto Simm's biographer Lesley Whiteside describes it, 'academically rather than spiritually orientated', and it was not then a requirement that candidates for the ministry reside in community at the Church's Divinity Hostel in Mountjoy Square. Among Donald's lecturers were Raymond Jenkins (future Archdeacon of Dublin) and Cecil de Pauley (later Dean of St Patrick's Cathedral and Bishop of Cashel). He combined, in one year, two of the three-part Divinity Testimonium course,[33] completing the third part in 1948–9 along with his final year of philosophy. It was a heavy workload, but he was awarded his Divinity Testimonium in 1949, along with a First Class Moderatorship (BA) in Mental and Moral Science. The following year, 1949–50, saw him take four of the five parts necessary for the course leading to the degree of Bachelor of Divinity, but the completion of his course and thesis for the degree of BD would have to wait until after his ordination and placement as a curate.

Donald has never been expansive on the subject of his own religious vocation, but says his sense of God was 'reflected in creation'. In order to study philosophy in any depth, one cannot escape the question of religion, because of the enquiring nature of the discipline. In an interview in 1985, he said:

> I suppose I finally made up my mind halfway through Trinity. There were no religious in my family which, although churchgoing, was not particularly devout. My teachers were an influence here, J. E. L. Oulton, the Professor of Divinity, was one of the really great scholars of his day, and R. M. Gwynn, who was a Hebraist, was also a most distinguished scholar. It was a particularly good time for scholarship in TCD.[34]

Samuel Poyntz emphasises that the whole orientation of the staff teaching philosophy in Trinity at the time was towards religion. For him, philosophy was a 'great participation in preparation for [the study of] theology'.

It was at the Scholars' dinner in Trinity in 1948 that Donald fell into conversation with Douglas Graham, headmaster of Portora Royal school in Enniskillen. Graham, a brilliant classical scholar, had been Master at Eton and served in the British Royal Navy, as well as being a heavyweight boxing champion. He was anxious to secure Donald for his school, telling him he wanted 'first option' on him once he had completed his curacy. It was Northern Ireland, and St Mark's parish, Dundela, in suburban East Belfast, which would provide the setting for the first phase of Donald's ministry: 'the only place that there was a vacancy'.[35] In 1950, at twenty-four years of age, he was ordained deacon by Bishop Shaw-Kerr of Down and Dromore.

CHAPTER TWO

Curate and Teacher

(1950–1950)

St Mark's Parish, Dundela

In 1950, Donald started his curacy in the parish of St Mark's, Dundela, in strongly Protestant and Unionist East Belfast. This was new territory for the Dubliner. He had played rugby matches against Portora Royal school while a pupil at Wesley, and taken a short holiday in Portrush in 1947. He had also visited Newry, just over the border from the Republic, on one or two occasions.

The focal point of the parish was the imposing redbrick St Mark's Church, with its high tower dominating the surrounding area. Designed by William Butterfield, the renowned Victorian architect who had designed All Saints' Church, Margaret Street, in London, the church, described by Sir John Betjeman as 'Butterfield at his best', had been consecrated in 1878.[1] The church tower, in Donald's recollection, had a red light affixed to its top as it was in the flight path to the airport. The rector was Cuthbert I. Peacocke, who came from a line of bishops – his father had been Bishop of Derry and Raphoe, while his grandfather had been Archbishop of Dublin. Cuthbert Peacocke himself would later go on to become Dean of Belfast and Bishop of Derry and Raphoe. He had served in the British Army during the Second World War.

The young curate from Dublin lodged with Mr and Mrs Alex Brown at 53 Belmont Church Road, a comfortably middle-class residential area of redbrick Victorian houses in Dundela parish. He resided there on a full board basis, paying the Browns the sum of two pounds and five shillings per week. This would be his home for the next three years, and his room was on the second storey of the house. Another curate also lodged with the Browns. Alex Brown was a chartered accountant in sole practice, as well as being a committed parishioner of St Mark's. As a student, he had been involved in the distribution of arms brought into Larne by the Ulster Volunteers in 1913, and was noted for his organisational skills. The arms had been distributed as far as Co. Fermanagh, to people living in farm holdings. Brown had also served as a soldier in the Manchester Regiment in the British Army, and had been a scout with Lawrence of Arabia. Donald recalls Mrs Brown as a wonderful cook, and remembers how well-fed he was there, with the traditional Ulster fry of bacon, egg, sausages, black and white pudding served up each morning! During Donald's years in St Mark's, there were a few curates on its staff: senior curate G. R. Harden Johnston (curate 1946–56), Noble Hamilton (1947–51), Anthony Trotman (1951–2) and George Ridgway (1950–8).

As a junior curate, Donald worked a six-day week, with a day off on Monday. The working week would begin on a Tuesday morning. Following a hearty breakfast, he would cycle over to the rectory for a ten o'clock staff meeting, comprising the rector, the senior curate and the junior curates. This meeting would go on to lunchtime, and would cover updates on births, deaths and marriages in the parish, and visitation arrangements for the sick. Lunch might be followed by visits to hospitals and nursing homes, the senior curate occasionally dropping the others off at their various stops in his car. A coffee break at four in the afternoon at the imposing Robinson Cleavers department store, situated directly opposite Belfast City Hall on Donegall Square, was a cherished tradition.

After dinner at their respective residences, the evening might see the clergy helping out at the badminton club or with other associations in the parish, such as the cubs or scout troops, or perhaps attending at meetings of the Church of Ireland Men's Society. Many of these activities would take place at the magnificent Heyn Hall, a large parochial hall built in 1936 and donated to the parish by the Heyn family of the famous Heyn shipping line. The parish was divided up into different areas, each overseen by a member of the clergy, who would be responsible for visiting people in hospital from their own particular area of responsibility. Four visits a day might be undertaken, amounting to some twenty to twenty-five visitations in a week. The rector would note details of each visitation – parishioner's name and current circumstances – in a great leatherbound ledger, of which several volumes were kept. Visitation of schools was another important aspect of the work, organised on a diocesan basis, with a clergyman being introduced to teachers and pupils in primary school, and perhaps taking a class there. Secondary schools such as Campbell College, a Presbyterian foundation of several hundred boys, and the larger comprehensive schools would also form part of the visiting round.

Church services in the parish were held principally at St Mark's itself and at St Brendan's (located at Sydenham in the direction of the shipyard). Peacocke himself did not take early morning services, as he suffered from catarrh as a result of his war experiences. He was appointed

Archdeacon of Down in 1950, requiring his frequent absence from the parish on diocesan duties, and much of the organisational work fell on the senior curate, G. R. Harden Johnston. The curates would take services as required by the rector, perhaps two or three services per week each. At St Mark's, two services were held on a Sunday morning in Donald's recollection: at ten o'clock (the church being filled with people) and again at 11.15 (a slightly smaller number attending). The church had a distinguished choral tradition, and boasted a robed choir since 1939, but this was no evidence of high church tendencies, which in Belfast would have been regarded with tremendous suspicion as evidence of 'Romish' tendencies – the parish was firmly middle of the road Anglican. Donald had little knowledge of music, so Hugh Maskelly, a tenor in the choir, advised him to 'sit beside me at choir practice, and I'll teach you'.

The parish seems to have had its share of eccentric incidents: Donald recalls one occasion at Evening Prayer, when a regular attender, Mr Campbell, a senior civil servant in Stormont, was reading the lesson. For some inexplicable reason, one of the lady members of the choir suddenly threw a heavy book at this man, hitting him on the back of the head!

Another time, one of Donald's fellow curate lodgers was overcharged for some food at the grocery shop just around the corner from their lodgings on Belmont Church Road. Taking a pack of frozen peas and a pea shooter, this indignant cleric positioned himself at a window where he could just see into the shop, and shelled it with frozen peas 'all over the place'.

At this time, the parish of St Mark's took in the impressive Northern Ireland parliament building at Stormont, and a number of senior civil servants in the administration there, many of whom would have been English, were parishioners. Donald described the parishioners as 'on the whole a cultured group of people'. He recalled that Roman Catholic civil servants at Stormont tended to be mainly of Irish background. The largest concentration of Roman Catholics in the area of St Mark's was at Ballyhackmore, and Donald got to know the parish priest there very well.[2] He found little sign of religious bigotry in St Mark's parish, but 'while it didn't occupy their minds very much', he detected a certain latent apprehension of the nationalist minority (overwhelmingly Roman Catholic) gaining in strength and numbers, and ultimately forcing the North into unity with the Republic. He suspects a fear of 'Rome Rule' underlay much of this. Parts of the parish near the Harland and Wolff shipyards were solidly working-class people whom Donald admired for their decency: 'you only had to bring a hard case before them, and you got overwhelming generosity'.

Donald was ordained to the diaconate on a Sunday, and recalls on the very next day, Monday, being taken by the rector to Knocknagoney on the outskirts of the parish, to view a tiny cottage (which appears to have been a gate lodge). This was a broken-down edifice, with green slime on the walls. Peacocke said: 'I'm putting you in charge here, and I hope that before you leave, you'll have built a church.' The painting of the cottage was undertaken and pews were put in. In due course Bible study and other parish groups held meetings there. The place name Knocknagoney is an Anglicisation of the Irish place name *Cnoc na gCoiníní*, the hill of the rabbits. This was a new suburb created in the late Forties, as a result of the evacuation of working class communities from York Street in the city, which had been bombed during the war. A number of prefabricated aluminium dwellings had been transported into the area to accommodate the evacuated York Street community (these would later be removed, and houses constructed to create what is now the Garnerville estate). As a curate, Donald, who travelled in and out from Belmont Church Road on his bicycle, recalls regularly passing a long queue of eighty or more people standing at the bus stop in Knocknagoney, waiting to catch a bus back into York Street in the city, because the pubs were still located there. He entertained doubts about the advisability of building a parish church in the area, feeling that the Knocknagoney people might have been better integrated into the community of St Mark's church itself. However, the rector was doubtful that they would be easily integrated into what was a mainly middle-class congregation at the principal church.

As part of the church building effort for Knocknagoney, the parish had little cardboard money boxes made up, in the shape of bricks, which were distributed throughout the parish. Donald recalls making his rounds on a bicycle once per month to collect these boxes, and cycling back to his digs at Belmont Church Road with a large sack over his shoulders. He would empty out the boxes on his bed and count the takings. In due course, a small wooden church was built.[3]

The parish had its share of hard-nosed and astute businessmen, a number of whom served on its select vestry. One evening a meeting was called to discuss a recommendation from the rector to increase the salary of the hard-worked curates. The curates sat waiting in the scout 'den' in the Heyn Hall until it was their turn to be called in be 'questioned by this austere body all showing off their toughness and astuteness, one millionaire trying to impress another!' Donald was duly awarded his modest ten pound salary increase.

Cuthbert Peacocke's war experiences had left him with a strong sense of military discipline. He would ring his curate around mid-morning on his day off, and if he found him at home, would want to know why he wasn't out and about! Donald became friendly with a retired gentleman in the parish, Mr Sargaisson, who would take him walking in the hills on the outskirts of the parish on a Monday, sharing with the young curate his extensive knowledge of plants and nature. The pair would set off at about 10.30 in the morning, with a supply of sandwiches, and spend the day in the mountains, returning late in the evening for dinner with Sargaisson's wife and two children at their house.

It was while a curate in Belfast that Donald first made the acquaintance of the great Christian writer and apologist, C.S. Lewis, who was a native of St Mark's parish. Donald had read many of his works, including the *Screwtape Letters* while a student at Trinity. Lewis' mother had been lecturer in mathematics at Queen's University, and his father was a prominent solicitor in Belfast. His mother died when he was only five years of age, leaving her husband and two sons bereft. After briefly attending Campbell College, Lewis was sent to Wellington public school in England, and thereafter secured entry to Oxford. He served in the war, suffering an injury when one of his own side's shells fell short. This resulted in him having to spend eighteen months in hospital. He returned to take his degree in Classics and Philosophy in Oxford after the war, subsequently becoming a tutor in English language and literature. He was the leading figure in the atheist group at Oxford, but later came to question the philosophical basis of atheism and found it unsustainable.

Lewis was a cousin of the Misses Ewart, two sisters who lived at Glenmachan in Dundela parish in Donald's time there. He was a native of Strandtown in the parish, and had been baptised in St Mark's in 1899, by his grandfather the Rev. Thomas Hamilton, who was then rector of the parish. As curate-in-charge in the 1870s, Hamilton had overseen the building of the church. In 1935, Lewis and his brother Warren presented a stained-glass window to the church in memory of their parents, created by Michael Healy (1873–1941) of the famous *Túr Gloine* stained-glass studio of the Irish Celtic revival period. The window depicts St James, and the two gospel writers, St Mark and St Luke, on either side. Above the head of St James is depicted Saint Mark's Church. Another memorial window in the church is in honour of the Rev. Hamilton himself. Other gifts presented by Lewis family members to the church down through the years included a chalice and lectern.

Lewis would visit his relatives at Glenmachan each year, and walk in the Mourne mountains, sometimes staying in a cottage, and conversing over a beer with the local people he met. Being aware of Donald's interest in philosophy, the Misses Ewart invited him to a dinner at which their illustrious cousin would be present. Donald found Lewis to be a very pleasant and welcoming character, and warmed to him. Lewis drank beer at dinner, and relaxed at coffee afterwards, smoking a big pipe. Donald was to meet him on two or three further occasions, and he found Lewis to be refreshingly free from self-absorption, and keen to know the other person's position.[4]

Donald muses that divinity students tend to be among the best trained atheists, because they are obliged to study all angles of religion in the Philosophy of Religion course: 'their minds are raked'. A person grounded in philosophy is 'sitting an examination in faith every day'. This process of questioning the basis of religion can result in regular spiritual crises, and a constant struggle to hold onto faith, but also instils a rigorous discipline of thought: 'if you're not doubting [questioning], you're not thinking!'

In a reflection for broadcast by RTÉ in later years, Donald offers a moving cameo of an aspect of ministry in Belfast – the sense of duty and devotion of a young woman who became known to him in the parochial round:

> It was dark and drizzling, and the streetlamps were reflected in the wet pavements as I rode my bicycle to the church on the Hollywood Road in Belfast, for the early morning service on Christmas Day. She was cycling in the opposite direction in the nice dark blue uniform of a public health nurse. Her cheerful greeting lit up the morning. As we visited some of the same houses, I knew the great work she did, the comfort she brought, the assurances which she gave. She was no Florence Nightingale; she was witty and pretty and earthy, with a strong sense of the ridiculous and a capacity for droll self-deprecation which she delivered in a charming and distinct Dublin accent. She, her husband, and their two little girls lived in a flat over a shop in Strandtown. One of the happiest homes I had ever entered. Her husband, a fine looking man in his early thirties, was permanently confined to bed from a heart condition which befell him at the height of his career as a footballer. Before she went out on her rounds each morning, she had to set him up for the day; get the little girls ready for school, prepare their lunch and complete all the demands of the household. She was a carer at home as well as in the homes of her patients. But she never showed it. Their marriage was happy and fulfilled even though it was what was called then a 'mixed marriage' which could be difficult in Belfast in those days. Their humour, their sense of one another's worth, their thanksgiving for one another's love, and their courage and faith in meeting the problems life presented to them, made the story of Christmas Day a reality for them all the year round.[5]

Reflecting in later years on his Belfast experiences and the cultural adjustment required in moving from the recently declared Republic of Ireland to Northern Ireland in the 1950s, Donald wrote:

> Coming directly from the academic cocoon of Trinity College, Dublin, I found myself a curate in a large Belfast parish where I was the fourth ... curate and member of the parish staff. Coming from a reserved religious background where religion, though both sincere and influential, was also a polite concomitant of civilised living and was loath to parade itself publicly, I found myself in a city where the religious atmosphere could become superheated; where religion was often a major topic of discussion on the shop-floor, in the pubs, on the playing fields and very much on the streets; and where to profess the right religion in the wrong place could be at least embarrassing, even in 1950. In some parts of the parish the Scottish Irish accent was so strong that for several months I did not understand what people were saying to me, and we were all claiming to speak English.
>
> I started with a certain disadvantage, apart from that of coming from Dublin; I was known also to be Irish speaking, which was not really appreciated in some parts of the Protestant Unionist community. The language you spoke was one of the numerous tell-tale signs of where your heart was politically and religiously; and my speaking Irish was regarded as gratuitously confusing in relation to such important aspects of life. If I was unreliable in regard to politics, who could trust me in regard to religion!
>
> I remain ever grateful for the three and a half years I spent as curate in Belfast and my admiration for these hard-working, honest, forthright, courageous people is unbounded, and I can well understand how many American Presidents have traced their origin to these Ulster Scots–Irish. They were cautious and required some time to accept the stranger, but once accepted they remained staunch friends for life and after more than fifty years I count them amongst my best friends.
>
> My rector in Belfast had only recently returned to parochial life after a long period as a senior chaplain in the army. His curates soon learned that holiness is no excuse for lack of organisation, nor enthusiasm for lack of discipline. A rigorous training in the early period of one's curacy leaves an indelible mark on all subsequent stages of one's life in the ministry. Even now in retirement I can hear the imperious voice of my first rector saying to me 'Well now, what are you doing?' when I lapse into a reverie in a comfortable moment during the day. In Belfast I encountered for the first time in my life the phenomenon of Orangeism and which is now universally familiar through media reports coming out of Northern Ireland over the past twenty-five years. I learnt in Belfast that a harsh voice and firm countenance often conceals a warm and true heart and a great capacity for sacrificial giving, and also that other people may have

considerable difficulty in coming to terms with attitudes and assumptions of which oneself is hardly aware, but which are steeped in adverse significance for them and which need to be explained.[6]

Portora Royal School, Enniskillen

Fulfilling the promise he had made to Douglas Graham at the scholars' dinner in Trinity in 1948, Donald took up a post as assistant master and chaplain in Portora Royal School, Enniskillen. He started there on 6 January 1954, on the completion of his curacy in Belfast. Portora was one of a number of 'free' schools founded by Royal Charter of King James in 1608 as part of the Ulster Plantation settlement. The school enjoys a prominent situation on Portora hill just outside Enniskillen town, with a commanding view over Lough Erne, and its sloping driveway is entered through imposing black wrought iron gates on the main road from Enniskillen to Ballyshannon, Co. Donegal in the north-west. The school accepted only male pupils and had a student population of approximately three hundred and forty at this time. Distinguished old Portorans included playwrights Oscar Wilde and Samuel Beckett (as well as Samuel G. Poyntz, already mentioned, a future Bishop of Cork and Connor successively).

Donald taught English and Scripture in Portora, and also took some pupils from the South for classes in Irish.[7] A significant proportion of the students who boarded at the school were from the South, and Adrian Empey, a boarder there during Donald's final two years' teaching at the school, recalls farmers' sons from places as far afield as Wexford, Kildare and Tipperary being among their number. Empey recollects that even pupils from Northern Ireland tended to self-describe as Irish at that time, feeling that it was the subsequent Troubles, which began in the late 1960s which drove people into labels.

About half of the students in the school were boarders, the remainder made up of day-pupils from the broader hinterland of Enniskillen and Co. Fermanagh. The day-pupils benefited from the free education introduced in the post-war era under the Atlee government in the United Kingdom. The boarders came from diverse backgrounds. Some were the children of senior military personnel, others had parents living in British colonial outposts, still others were the sons of people in the professions: clergy, doctors, solicitors and businesspeople. Portora consisted of four Houses named after the provinces of Ireland: Ulster, Munster, Leinster and Connacht. Each House included boarders and day-pupils, and had two masters in charge. A highlight of school life were the House Plays, staged each March. These were organised by the boys themselves without supervision, and a well-known personality would be invited to the school to adjudicate.

Empey recalls the standard of living north of the border being noticeably higher than conditions prevailing in the depressed South in the 1950s, where emigration and economic stagnation went hand-in-hand. Portora usually entered a team in the Henley Regatta along with other public schools in Britain, but Empey disagrees with the suggestion that it was in the mould of the English public school: '[Henley] is upper establishment England on parade ... you knew you were a redneck when you entered, and maybe you were meant to know ...' The Portora rowers practiced on Enniskillen's Lough Erne where the school had its boating club, and Empey recalls its senior rowers competing against Trinity College – 'we wouldn't be as heavy or strong but we were fit! ... We trained every day, pretty much, winter or summer on that lake.' The school sports were rowing, cricket and rugby. Portora also had a Combined Cadet Force, trainees taking an annual trip to places such as Ballykinlar army base in Co. Down where they might learn how to handle open-range or heavier weaponry. Indeed, many past pupils of Portora went on to Sandhurst (Royal Military Academy) in England.

The entire school community dined together, the teachers sitting at high table. Empey recalls that, at breakfast, the boys would resemble fighter pilots 'scrambling for Spitfires when the Germans came in'. Morning Assembly, attended by pupils and teachers alike, with its notices and instructions, and details of upcoming matches, was as much 'a general meeting as a nod to God'.

As a teacher, Donald was 'terrible at keeping order'. Empey feels he was not cut out temperamentally for teaching adolescent boys, 'a whole lot of pimply teenage barbarians, really'.

> They used to rag him mercilessly ... You could push him to a point, and then there would be a flash [of anger] ... I recall on one famous occasion we barricaded Donald out of the classroom [and] we all ended up before the headmaster and got a taste of the cane for our trouble!

The 'mild and gentle' Donald's nickname among the pupils was a demonstration of boys' ironic humour: 'the Brute.'[8] However, he was held in great affection by them:

> They liked eccentricities ... even these barbarians, wrestling with pimples ... and all other things which seldom concerned learning ... we all knew he was very able ... and he occasionally talked to us about his life on the

Blasket Islands … He would do other things – I remember he wanted to learn some science [and I think] he used to go off [to the physics teacher] … you knew from that you had someone with a very enquiring mind, that he was a bookish man. We liked him as a personality and would have seen him as a character around the school … He was fairly 'unmuscular' [in physical appearance] and we didn't get 'muscular Christianity' from him either … I think he would have tried to expand on [Scripture], sowing on very stony ground.

In a term report card for Empey in 1957, Donald reports on his pupil's progress in English: 'He has worked well, his English style is very mature yet at times a little ponderous; he should do well in the juniors.' For Scripture, he puts: 'consistently good', to Empey's amusement: 'I don't know if it's good at disruption, or good at study,' he says, 'it is suitably ambiguous, and perhaps not untrue, in some mysterious way.'

David Neligan, a friend of Donald's in subsequent years, recalls hearing a story which demonstrates his ability to think on his feet. It seems the Portora school community, boarders and staff, were parading along to the Cathedral in Enniskillen, where they worshipped each Sunday, when Douglas Graham, the headmaster, suddenly looked around and asked 'well, who's going to deliver the sermon today?' It seems to have been generally assumed that Graham himself (who was a clergyman), or possibly the Dean, would perform this duty, but he said: 'Caird, you do the sermon.' Donald had to wrack his brains and come up with the goods!

Trinity College historian Bill Vaughan, who had been a day pupil at Portora, recalls an incident he witnessed:

I remember one night he pursued these poor divils from Enniskillen [town] who had been raiding the orchard in Portora. He comes down and shouts at them, and they take off [running] and normally that is all that would happen. But Donald pursued them on foot and ran after them until they collapsed! … [They were] a couple of lads … He came after them for nearly a mile and a half into the town. I saw them when they lay down on the ground exhausted and he came down, far from exhausted, and he denounced them and scolded them. People were coming out saying 'oh, your Reverence, I know these two lads, [they are] very respectable young lads,' trying to calm him down. I would say they never went into an orchard again … this was at about seven in the evening.

St David's College, Lampeter, Wales

After some three and a half years at Portora, Donald went to Wales in September 1957, to take up a post as Lecturer in Philosophy at St David's College (*Coleg Dewi Sant*), Lampeter. St David's was founded in 1822 as the first academic degree-awarding institution in Wales, and until its later absorption into the University of Wales, was the third oldest such institution in England and Wales, after Oxford and Cambridge. The College was founded by Thomas Burgess, Bishop of St David's, as a place in which ordinands for the (Anglican) Church in Wales, who for financial or geographical reasons could not attend Oxford or Cambridge, could receive a higher education. Reflecting in a newspaper interview later, Donald comments:

> Most of my pupils were Welsh-speaking but I never did learn Welsh myself. It was the best college in these islands for Celtic studies and Dai Marks ... was a Bard of Wales. There were three Bardic chairs and unlike other colleges, these were actual chairs very beautiful and ornate. Marks spoke fluent Irish too but his main language was Breton.[9]

Donald had rooms in the 'Canterbury' building on campus, a two-storey neo-Gothic structure, where his companion was the new lecturer in English, James Sambrook, who had arrived only a few weeks previously. The two would dine out together in one of the few eating places in Lampeter, or boil eggs in their shared electric kettle in Canterbury.

In an article published in 2003, James Sambrook recalls life in St David's at Christmas term 1957:

> When term began, Canterbury filled with about thirty would-be Ordinands and two other bachelor staff members, Stanley Boorman and Peter Morris. (Though I give Christian names here, this is unhistorical: we mostly used surnames only throughout my seven years in S.D.C.). Morris was lecturer in theology and Hebrew; Boorman was Professor of English and so was my boss in a two-man, or, rather, a man-and-boy Department.
>
> The other two man departments were Classics with Professor HA Harris and Frank Newte, History with Professor Daniel Dawson and Fred David, and Philosophy with Raymond Renowden (lecturer in charge) and Donald Caird; Welsh had one lecturer in Dai Marks, so had mathematics in Ruth Renowden (Raymond's wife); theology had the lavish provision of Bill Hunt, Professor Tom Wood *and* Peter Morris. Hunt, Wood, Caird and I were all new appointees; I was the only lay man of the four newcomers. Last, but most certainly not least, was the 'Prinny': Principal Lloyd-Thomas, whose toughness, courage and guile at this time ... was

countering the apathy of the University Grants committee and the machinations of the college's enemies, in order to secure our very survival.

Saint David's College was conceived in the reign of George III as an inexpensive country cousin of Oxbridge. Its tiny academic staff ... and small, all male, undergraduate body lived in one another's pockets as a sort of family: their shared home was a quasi-ecclesiastical building remote from the world ... There were 140 students. Most took a general BA (Lampeter) degree, but there were honours students in penny numbers: two or three in English each year, more in history, fewer in the other subjects ...

The College's old association with Oxbridge affected our teaching in so far as that those universities appointed the men who marked all the examinations ... a common need to outwit the examiners did much for teacher–pupil solidarity.

Lampeter students were expected to take their three meals in Hall every day, with the senior scholar intoning grace before dinner, Oxford style. Bachelor staff regularly ate in Hall at High Table under full-length portraits of our founder, Bishop Burgess, and other notables ... the portraits were of a higher quality than High Table food, which, in our poverty stricken state, was immeasurably inferior to any Oxford college I had eaten in.

Fortunately for the College we were able to keep an underpaid loyal domestic staff. We were waited upon, three meals a day, at table; our beds were made and our rooms cleaned. My 'bedder' was Miss Harries: leathery, wrinkled, of indeterminate age and the soul of kindness. She always put a stone hot water bottle ... in my bed ... before I was due to return to the College; she was distressed when, once, I came back early and slept in an unaired bed: she was sure I would get 'the rheumatic'.

Sambrook highlights an impish side to Donald's sense of humour, and details the rules governing student life at St David's:

Other long serving college servants included the brothers Stanley and Beale Mills, who tended gardens, waited at table and did many other jobs around the college ... Teddy Richards, known as 'Teddy Topos' because the college lavatories were his responsibility, was small, thin faced and dark complexioned; he scurried everywhere. I was assured by Donald Caird that Teddy Topos and his sister Minnie also ran a dancing school. Can this be true? Caird, as a compatriot of Swift and Goldsmith, was a master of the Irish cod, but nothing less than absolute truth must be required of a future Archbishop.

The entire academic staff, Oxbridge fashion, constituted the College Board ... Discipline was a frequent topic at board meetings because College rules were made to be broken. These rules, for instance, required students to be in their rooms by 11.00 p.m.; licensed premises were out of bounds (though alcoholic drink could be bought in the College buttery); the use of student cars during term was forbidden; students needed to have the permission of the censor before travelling more than five miles from Lampeter.[10]

A trip to Twickenham by Sambrook, Donald Caird and others to see a rugby match ended in a serious traffic accident outside Abergavenny:

That first term in 1957 is mostly a blur of lectures, tutorials and markbooks. The only event I distinctly recall is a day away to see the Oxford–Cambridge rugby match at Twickenham. Renowden drove Caird, Morris and me in his car, starting early in the morning, coming back late at night and colliding with a turning lorry on the outskirts of Abergavenny. Peter Morris was concussed and was kept in Abergavenny hospital overnight. The rest of us completed the journey by taxi. Next morning Renowden, Caird and I were carpeted by Prinny for not having told him we were going to the match! His crossness was, I think, a reflection of quasi-parental concern and alarm at having nearly lost a third of his teaching force in one traffic accident.

Meanwhile, back in Dublin, Donald's mother Emily, who had suffered a stroke in the mid 1950s, was being looked after by his father, George, in their Ranelagh home, with help from her sisters who lived nearby. Donald visited home during term breaks from Lampeter. He seems also to have maintained a connection with Cumann Gaelach na hEaglaise during the 1950s, Dáithí Ó Maolchoille recalling meeting him at St Finian's Church, Adelaide Road, after 1956, in a period where Donald was *ag múineadh sa Bhreatain Bheag* (teaching in Wales).

His talents were well recognised back home in Ireland, and when a vacancy arose in the parish of Rathmichael, he was contacted by the Archbishop, Dr George Otto Simms. Simms knew Donald as his time as Dean of Residence at Trinity College had coincided with Donald's student career there, and he indicated to him that the elderly age profile of most of the parishioners in Rathmichael meant that he would have plenty of time to continue lecturing in philosophy whilst attending to parish duties. The offer seemed an attractive one and his mother's illness was probably also a strong motivating factor; so after just one academic year in Wales, Donald set his face once again towards Ireland.

CHAPTER THREE

Rathmichael Days and Kilkenny
(1958–1970)

Early days in Rathmichael

In 1958, the incumbent at Rathmichael, the Rev. Augustine Sterling Bluett, was obliged to retire as his health had been failing for some time. He had studied medicine at Trinity College and served in the Royal Army Medical Corps in World War I, which left him with a severe form of deafness in which he had to endure continuous noises in the head. He had entered the ministry after the war, and been rector at Rathmichael since 1944. His love of gardening was evident in the charming rectory gardens which he left behind him.

Rathmichael, with its long history dating back to pre-Norman times, and historic associations with St Patrick's Cathedral,[1] still enjoyed a largely rural setting in South County Dublin in the late 1950s, and was regarded as a 'light duty' parish. Located south-west of Killiney and a few miles inland from the eastern seaboard, its beautiful little 'church among the trees', made of local granite, was situated at the junction of cross roads on the shoulder of Shankill – the picturesque setting augmented by a handsome Celtic cross in the church grounds in memory of a former rector. At this time, the 'Big House' was still a feature of the parish. An eclectic mix of parishioners included such figures as Lord and Lady Holmpatrick, Lady de Freyne, the Hannas (of the well-known bookstore), the Hewats and the Weir family (which owned the large jewellers' store on Grafton Street in the city). Many parishioners were professional people working in Dublin. Sprawling ribbon development from the capital had not yet quite reached as far as Rathmichael, and the old road to Bray was still in operation. The Ballycorus lead mines, associated with the Strachan family (distant relatives of Donald's on his father's side), lay within the parish boundaries.

On returning home from Wales in 1958, Donald resided initially with his parents at 88 Ranelagh. He undertook his Higher Diploma in Education in Trinity in the academic year 1958–59, combined with some teaching, and the taking of some services. As Kathleen Turner's *Rathmichael: a Parish*

History has it, he soon found himself bicycling ten miles to take services in Rathmichael each Sunday, the first of these being Holy Communion at 8.00 a.m. He was licensed as curate-in-charge for Rathmichael on 13 July 1959. He had purchased a second-hand Puch motor scooter (made by the famous manufacturing company in Graz, Austria) for the sum of £5 from his old Trinity friend Vincent Denard, who had previously toured around Spain on it. He soon pressed the 'rather dilapidated' scooter into service on the Ranelagh–Rathmichael run. Soon afterwards, he moved into the rectory in Rathmichael, a handsome cross-gabled redbrick house, on the southern side of the main road across from the parish church. One night, his scooter broke down on the hill at Balally. Unable to discover the cause of the breakdown as the streetlights had gone out, he rang a parishioner, Alan Grainger, for help. Grainger, in a later parish newsletter, recalled having to tow Donald back to the rectory in the pitch dark using a clothes line from his garden.

It was during Bluett's time as rector that Coláiste Moibhí, the Irish-medium preparatory college to the Church of Ireland College of Education, had come to the parish, with Bluett having chaplaincy duties there. Coláiste Moibhí was located at Shanganagh Castle. The original fifteenth century castle was situated at the northern end of the vale of Shanganagh, while the modern eighteenth-century castle (considerably altered in the nineteenth century) was situated on the left side of the old Dublin–Bray Road about a mile north of Bray town. A long avenue led from a fine castellated gateway on the main road up to the castle, which from its front had an uninterrupted view of the Wicklow Mountains. The Board of Works had carried out refurbishments in 1954, including the addition of a north wing containing four classrooms and a hall for the pupils of Coláiste Moibhí, and demolishing roof turrets which were considered dangerous. Valerie Jones, a pupil at the school from 1959 to 1961, recalls the old mansion with its beautiful ceiling and pictures hanging on the walls. The school community was presided over by principal Gladys Allen, 'a wonderful teacher, who could make the deadest stuff come alive'. The pupils assembled in the hall each evening, and for Religious Education on a Tuesday afternoon.

Jones recalls Donald coming out to the school on a visitation, his fair hair flying in the wind as he came up the long driveway on his motor scooter, wearing a duffle coat, and patting his hair down before coming in to see the pupils. He would give his classes in English; it appears, following his time in the North and in Wales, that his Irish had slipped back a little. The school had something of the 'hothouse' atmosphere of an all-girls establishment, with the male teachers and postman being the object of some fanciful teasing – Donald with his reserved and studious nature was not generally a subject of this. The school included day and boarding pupils, and Donald initiated a Sunday School for boarders who remained at the weekends. The girls would come over to the rectory on a Sunday, and Donald would take three or four of them out on a hill-walking expedition, returning for tea. His rather spartan bachelor furnishings in the rectory, apart from the kitchen or study, bemused some of the Coláiste Moibhí girls. In 1963, Frank Blennerhassett came to Coláiste Moibhí as teacher of Religious Education but Donald remained as chaplain to the school while rector at Rathmichael.[2]

He was instituted as rector of the parish on 24 March 1960. The church was packed for this service, with a choir being provided by the pupils of Coláiste Moibhí, and a reception held afterwards in the parish hall.

It was customary for the service of institution of a new rector that the candidate would suggest a preacher to the Archbishop, who would then invite this person to preach. Donald's choice was Canon William Nesbitt Wilson Harvey, rector of Sandford, Donald's childhood parish. Harvey, who had served in Sandford since 1921, happened to occupy the Prebendal stall for Rathmichael in St Patrick's Cathedral and was an extremely learned man. He had enjoyed a stellar academic career, achieving his BA degree in 1911, his Bachelor of Divinity degree in 1915, his B.Litt. in 1942, his doctorate in Divinity in 1947 and his M.Litt. in 1960. In fact, he was one of the relatively few senior figures in the Church of Ireland in possession of an earned doctorate in Divinity (as opposed to one conferred *jure dignitatis*) – another was then Bishop of Ossory, Henry McAdoo, and according to Valerie Jones the pair would josh with each other about this whenever they met. Harvey's repeated references in his address to the new rector as 'Donald Arthur Richard' caused some hilarity to the teenage girls of Coláiste Moibhí present. His appearances at the school for some time thereafter would be heralded by cries from pupils of 'here's Donald Arthur Richard!'

Rathmichael parish had declined in the latter years of Bluett's incumbency due to his age and health, and Donald found it in a rather moribund state. A parishioner, Frances Pakenham Walsh, recalls:

> He started to invigorate us ... slowly, there wasn't much left to invigorate ... He got going on various things ... He sort of got children involved in things ... He gathered up what youth there were and ... brought them tramping around the hills, that sort of thing, got a little youth club going ...

Rathmichael Table Tennis Club was inaugurated on 16 November 1959 with a party at the rectory, twenty-five people attending to play on three tables set up there. A year later, the club was in a position to enter two table tennis teams for the Church of Ireland League. In October 1960, a 'most interesting series of lectures' was announced, to last up to the following March. Various aspects of the Bible would be explored, for example *Archaeology and the Old Testament* and *The Dead Sea Scrolls*. This was followed by a further series a year later, including a lecture on *The Criminal in Christian Society*, an illustrated lecture by the churchwarden, Colonel Flewett, and a talk by a Moravian minister in Dublin, Mr Asbal, on *Tibet and Its People*.

As a single man in his early days in Rathmichael parish, Donald did not find the life a particularly lonely one:

> It is hard to get lonely in a parish – something is always happening. To get a quiet moment to yourself is quite difficult! People were very kind, they would ring up and say 'what are you having for supper tonight'. I would tell them [what it was] and then [they would say] 'oh that's awful, come over and have it with us.' This happened all the time.

On Sunday mornings after early service, Billy Gilbert the sexton would run over to the rectory, put the kettle on and have the bacon ready for Donald. The rector rarely had a day off as such, 'but [occasionally] I might wake up and there would be nothing to do, so I would go for a swim.' Cold water swimming, even in winter time, was a hobby of Donald's, mainly pursued at the bottom of Corbawn Lane, which led down from the main Shankill Road to the sea. Another regular swimmer at this spot was P. J. Hillery, a doctor who hailed from Co. Clare (and future President of Ireland). A favourite pursuit of Donald's, when he had the time, was coffee in town followed by a period browsing in the APCK (Association for the Promotion of Christian Knowledge) bookshop in Dawson Street (located next door to the Automobile Association, and across the road from the Mansion House). Donald recalls the shop's beautiful curved glass window (still to be seen), the carpets on the floor and the selection of books available, mainly APCK titles but also including some books on languages. It was 'one of the most impressive shops on the street'.

In addition to his parish responsibilities, Donald also pursued a number of teaching interests, in line with Archbishop Simm's earlier promise that he would be free to so do while at Rathmichael. After only a short time in the parish, he was contacted by the Warden of St Columba's College, Rathfarnham. A pupil in the school, Fergus Kelly (son of the renowned sculptor Oisín Kelly, a member of the Church of Ireland), wished to sit for a scholarship to Trinity College, and Donald was asked to give him extra tuition in Irish. He served as an assistant master at St

Columba's from 1960 until 1967, teaching classes in English in addition
to Irish. A colleague on the teaching staff (and lodger at the school) was
David Neligan, who describes Donald as a 'pretty shrewd' teacher: 'he
only taught the subjects he knew well.' Neligan offers the view that Irish
was not a popular subject at the school. A number of the pupils at St
Columba's were from Northern Ireland, and would not have taken the
subject at primary level there. A level of apathy towards the language
mirrored the view of the language in southern Protestant schools at the
time, Neligan opining that the teaching of Irish in such schools required
particularly inspired teachers. While Donald could display these
qualities, he was also a teacher with a 'light touch', and there was a
'certain amount of disorder' in his classes. In addition to this, Donald was
deputy lecturer in philosophy at Trinity College in the academic year 1962
to 1963. During this period, he would typically cycle from Rathmichael
(near sea level) nine to eleven miles uphill to St Columba's in
Rathfarnham (some five hundred feet above sea level) to take an early
morning class and later 'freewheel to Trinity College' in the city, where
he would give a lecture. On the return journey to Rathmichael in the
afternoon, he might stop off to visit a patient at Loughlinstown Hospital,
where, as rector of the parish, he had chaplaincy duties.

A later reflection captures a charming scene during his ministry in
these years:

> It was a small quiet private nursing home in Dublin suburb where many
> elderly people lived in friendly comfort and contentment in the twilight
> of their lives, when for some, the past was more vividly real than the
> present. An old lady who kept mainly to her own room had asked the
> matron to arrange for her to receive Holy Communion on Holy Innocents'
> Day. I had newly arrived in the parish and had not until then had an
> opportunity to visit that nursing home. Upon entering the room I was
> surprised to find it set out in a formal manner for the service – candles
> were lit on the small table, beautiful icons were placed on the cupboard
> beside her bed and a magnificent cross of Russian Orthodox design stood
> on another table. The old lady knew the Book of Common Prayer service
> by heart and joined in the prayers and responses. As I read the collect for
> Holy Innocents, tears ran down her face. At the end of the service matron
> brought in a cup of coffee and I had time to chat to the old lady. She spoke
> fluent French and Russian but she was obviously Irish. She explained that
> on Holy Innocents' Day she always remembered at the Eucharist the
> children to whom she had been governess and friend in St Petersburg
> before the First World War, the children of Czar Nicholas II who were
> murdered at Yekaterinburg in 1917. For her, they were the Holy Innocents.
> One meets interesting people in nursing homes.[3]

David Neligan and Dáithí Ó Maolchoille (a young accountant and learner of Irish, who was elected *cisteoir* (treasurer) of Cumann Gaelach na hEaglaise in 1963) recall regular meetings in the early 1960s of *An Ciorcal Gaelach*, a social circle for young Irish-speaking Protestants. It seems these gatherings were frequently held at members' houses in the winter months (including Rathmichael rectory on at least one occasion) and featured conversation, knitting for the women present, and occasionally some dancing accompanied by music on the piano or by recordings of well-known *céilí* bands. 'I can recall ... playing some dance music myself on the recorder,' says Neligan, 'it was a very powerful feeling to play this music ... and to see people leaping about in cadence on the floor ... an uplifting experience and I enjoyed it.' Oscar Willis, a teacher at Coláiste Moibhí, was another regular attender, as were a group of female national teachers. The writer Risteárd Ó Glaisne (a Methodist lay preacher and fluent Irish speaker, from Bandon in Co. Cork) was also a habitué of the *Ciorcal*.

An anecdote concerning Donald and a horse has acquired almost legendary status among his friends. It seems that the young rector had become irritated by the way some horses belonging to the Travelling community would appear regularly in the fields to the front of Rathmichael rectory. On one particular evening, on his arrival home, Donald found an unusually large group of horses in occupation. In a fit of exasperation, he opened the rectory gates and shooed them out. As he did so, he noticed that one of the equine trespassers had a particularly well-bred appearance, but thought no more about it. He closed the gates and went to bed. The next morning, he was aroused quite early by a telephone call from one of his parishioners, who said:

> Well, I'm terribly sorry, rector, to bother you, but when I was coming home – we'd had a very long day with the ... [hunt] and my horse was terribly tired and I was afraid that he would get lame. So as we came past your field, I'm afraid I allowed myself to put my horse in there for safe keeping, and of course I'll come immediately now and collect it.[4]

Alarm bells rang in Donald's mind and he hurried out on his bike, travelling up various bye-roads where he knew the Travellers were habitually to be found. He came across a group of horses, more or less intact as he had expelled them into the night, and there among their number was the 'noble, well-bred hunter'. The rector put a rope around this horse's neck, and managed to lead him back to the grounds of the rectory just in time in time for his unsuspecting gentlemanly parishioner to arrive, express heartfelt thanks and take the horse away – with perhaps some wonder at the fact that the horse was still sweating copiously, a day after the hunt.

Donald's mother Emily died in 1961 at the age of seventy-eight years, after suffering a further stroke. Her husband George had cared for her at home with Emily's neighbouring sisters calling in frequently. After her death, George lived alone in the house for a period, but lost interest in its upkeep, neglecting the garden which had been beautifully kept in former years. Finally, in 1964, he sold the house to some doctors, who established consulting rooms there. He went to live for a period of time with his elder son Norman (Donald's half brother), later transferring to a nursing home at Greystones. He died in 1966.

Engagement and marriage

A Rathmichael parishioner who played a pivotal role in Donald's life was the secretary of the parish's select vestry (the committee that has responsibility for the administration of the parish finances and care of the buildings), Mrs Kathleen Turner. Born in 1900, she was a woman of wide and varied interests: local history, art and sculpture, languages (she had taught French in Canada for a period), music, sailing, flying and gardening. It was she who would introduce Donald to his future wife: the American, Nancy Ballantyne Sharpe.

Nancy was the only daughter of Professor William Sharpe, a leading brain surgeon in the United States[5] and his wife Gwendolen (née Wolfe).[6] Gwendolen grew up in Maine, the third eldest of four children. She was an accomplished horsewoman, who had remarried. Her first marriage at the age of twenty-eight was to Edward Rochester, by whom she had two children, Dudley and Paul. In 1935, she married William Sharpe. Sharpe worked in New York and Nancy was largely raised by her mother in her home in the Sierra Mountains in Nevada, near the German settlement town of Minden. However she frequently stayed with another family, the Jepsens. While her father had come from a Presbyterian background, her mother was an Episcopalian (Anglican), and Nancy attended an episcopal secondary school, Rosemary Hall in Greenwich, Connecticut, singing in the choir there. Although baptised, she was not particularly religious in her youth, and was confirmed just before her marriage. A severe riding accident at the age of seventeen, while helping with the haying on a friend's ranch, resulted in a lot of physical pain during her senior year in school. In 1958, she graduated from Columbia University in New York with a Bachelor in Science degree in Physical Therapy. She subsequently worked in a physical rehabilitation unit at Boston

University Hospital, helping to treat amputees who had been injured in industrial accidents.

It was around the year 1960 (by virtue of contacts friends of her mother had with Mrs Kathleen Turner) that Nancy got the opportunity to visit Ireland. Turner extended an invitation to her to come and stay with her at her home in Shankill, Co. Dublin, in Rathmichael parish. Nancy duly came over, and availed of opportunities to pursue her horseriding interests. She kept her horse, Mulligan, in stables at the Phoenix Park racecourse, driving over there from Shankill in her little Volkswagen car. Around Christmas 1960, Nancy went to France to meet up with a friend of hers from America, Harriet Daniels. The pair set off on an epic car journey of eight months across Europe, taking in Austria, Belgium, Holland, Spain and Portugal, among other places. On their return to Ireland in late summer 1961, the pair concluded their trip with a visit to the Dublin Horse Show.

Severe weather in Ireland that winter, including snow and ice, prevented Nancy from continuing with hunting. Back in Kathleen Turner's house, she had time on her hands, and mused aloud that she might 'audit' a course (attend lectures only, without taking examinations) for the winter in Trinity College in education or psychology. Turner advised her to seek advice from the parish rector who knew Trinity well. Although Nancy had previously visited the church in Rathmichael and met Mr Caird, she had no more than a passing acquaintance with him. However, he came to visit, and discussed Trinity with her. 'That was really how we got to know one another, and then one thing led to another,' reflects Nancy. Donald was thirty-five, some eleven years older than her. David Neligan recalls hearing from his parents that around this time Donald developed a very severe earache as a result of his vigorous cold water swimming, and when hospitalised, was diagnosed with pneumonia. Nancy's concern and regular visits at this time, it seems, did not go unnoticed by Rathmichael parishioners: 'This was quite possibly when Cupid shot his dart.' The couple did not fall in love overnight, it was a more gradual process of getting to know each other and working out what each wanted for their lives, as Nancy attended her course and Donald continued with his work in the parish.

Frances Pakenham Walsh and her husband had a tennis court at their home at Crinken in Bray, and frequently hosted gatherings there on Sunday afternoons. Donald was a frequent guest, and one Sunday morning after service the customary invitation was extended.

'He said "could I bring Miss Sharpe?" and blushed up to the roots of his hair!' recalls Pakenham Walsh,

It was very informal … so they came and I can see them still sitting in this window seat [in the dining room where some of the guests were sitting or standing, having tea] utterly absorbed in each other. It was very early in their acquaintance too, and I thought to myself 'wouldn't that be marvellous?' and then (slapping herself on the wrist in mock rebuke) … 'don't be silly!' Then of course it developed.

Over the years, Donald had kept up contact with his friend from primary school days, Cyril Patton (now an accountant living in Carlow and married to Philippa). When visiting home from Portora or Wales, he would meet up with Cyril and Philippa, and after moving back to Dublin would occasionally call in to Cyril's mother's house, enquiring as to whether his friend might be coming up to the city any weekend soon. Patton recalls Donald having his scooter

and [on one occasion] was coming down to see us, and the scooter … probably second-hand … broke down! He eventually made it, somewhat late! … I think some part fell out and he couldn't find it and it was dark.

The Pattons moved back to Dublin in 1960. One day at his home in Mount Merrion, Cyril received a telephone call from Donald: were the couple at home? He would like to call in, and bring 'a lady friend' with him. Immediately, Philippa was on the alert: 'oh, this must be something important, he doesn't usually tout lady friends around!' They were astonished when Donald arrived in the company of a tall, elegant young lady, and Philippa and Nancy quickly struck up a firm friendship.

Up to this point, Nancy's intention had been to return to the United States. However, although she had enjoyed it, she was not keen on resuming the work she had been doing in Boston and felt herself at something of a crossroads in her life. Donald had only recently entered fully into parochial life following a period of teaching. Marriage was a serious matter for a clergyman, and not something to be contemplated lightly. As Nancy puts it:

Give and take a whole lot of things, the outstanding things were … he loved me and I loved him, I don't know how you know that but you just do … it wasn't love at first sight, but it wasn't after years either, and he had such a wonderful personality and sense of humour, such a vision of everything. I suppose to him, I brought a whole different aspect of life as well, and love. And so we decided that we would get married.

The couple got engaged, but kept the fact a secret until Donald would have a chance to inform his parish. Nancy moved out of Kathleen

Turner's house in the parish, taking an apartment in Donnybrook. In the autumn of 1962, she returned to the United States to see her mother, and after she had departed, Donald announced his engagement to his select vestry. The notice of their engagement was published in the New York Times on 11 November 1962: *Nancy B. Sharpe Is Future Bride of Clergyman: Columbia Alumna and Reverend Donald Caird of Ireland Are Engaged*. The notice also appeared in the Social and Personal column of *The Irish Times*. A prominent member of the parish took it upon himself to write to Nancy's mother in the United States, assuring her that she should be confident of the kind of young man that her daughter was marrying:

> ... my mother always appreciated that, because my mother was very sceptical, in fact everybody was very sceptical at home. You were marrying a priest, an Irish priest; of course the only priests in Ireland were Catholic.

The couple married in a snowy Vermont in the United States on 12 January 1963. The ceremony was held in St James' Episcopal church in Arlington, Vermont's Manchester Journal carrying a detailed report:

> The ceremony was performed at four o'clock by the Reverend Clement G. Blecher, rector of St James'. Decorations in the church included two vases of white chrysanthemums ... The bride was given in marriage by her brother, Dr William Sharpe. Her gown was of ivory coloured satin with long pointed sleeves, a princess waist and cathedral train ... She carried a cascade of large white orchids ... following the ceremony a reception was held at the Barrows House in Dorset.

A large group of guests, including the Jepsons from Nevada, family friends from San Francisco and other places gathered. John Campbell a former teacher who had received tuition from Donald in Irish when preparing for the examinations of the Department of External Affairs, was now Third Secretary in the Irish Embassy in Washington, and acted as Donald's best man. Harriet Daniels was Nancy's maid of honour. An especially honoured guest at the wedding was Kathleen Turner. Donald did not have any relatives present at the wedding; his mother had died and his father was in a nursing home in Greystones at this stage. The couple went on honeymoon to Montréal, where Donald met up with the newly enthroned Anglican Bishop there, Robert Kenneth Maguire, who was an old friend from Trinity College days. After Montréal, they drove around the coast of Maine (Nancy's brother William hosting them for two nights) before flying back to Ireland from Boston, to embark on their new life together.

Once installed at Rathmichael rectory, Nancy faced the task of making the house a home (clergy frequently have to furnish their houses themselves, previous incumbents having amassed their own collections over the years and taken it with them). Donald's collection consisted mainly of a few ping-pong or table tennis tables in the main reception rooms, a kitchen table and chairs, and a bed. Nancy had some of her own effects shipped over from America in containers. At first, the couple entertained mainly in the rectory kitchen which was warm and comfortable with its large Aga cooker: 'even George Simms, the Archbishop of Dublin, we had him in the kitchen. We had everything in the kitchen until we got a … dining room table and chairs'. Nancy attended auctions, and by this means gradually furnished the house. Being unfamiliar with Irish recipes, she made use of several American cookery books which she had brought over. These recipes were exotic in Ireland in the 1960s. She had also received a series of handwritten recipes from her sister-in-law Lois, compiled specially as a wedding gift: sweet-and-sour meatloaf and pasta recipes and suchlike. For desserts, Nancy would make apple crumble in the American way. 'People loved them. They were unusual … I steered clear of the Irish/English cooking.' For cooking, she used a little Tricity electric cooker, which she had installed because she did not know how to use the Aga and was unable to correlate the American temperatures and recipes with it (this innovation did not meet with the approval of the retained domestic help, an elderly lady whom Donald had inherited when he moved into the rectory). There were one or two culinary culture shocks in the early days:

> when I had my first entertaining, it was with our church warden [Colonel Flewett, who was] a bachelor … I thought, well, I'll do macaroni and cheese. I got out my recipe book, and I got the ingredients. In Rathmichael, there was a larder and in the larder there were canisters, tins, on which were written Sugar, Salt etc. So I used the flour, now the flour was strange to me. It said Flour so I used it. It was pink, so I thought: 'well, that's what Ireland has: pink flour'. We had pink macaroni and cheese. [The church warden] had two helpings of it. [In fact], it was custard powder. It could have been a lot worse!

Nancy soon installed her own choice of domestic help in the rectory. On Sundays, after Holy Communion in Rathmichael church, Donald would host a group of Coláiste Moibhí girls for breakfast in the kitchen. The girls would be expected to converse in Irish, which meant only Donald could engage with them. As they were also somewhat shy, Nancy and a church warden or two who might be present, would end up having a separate conversation in English across the room. Donald also had an active table tennis club based in the rectory. The couple were frequently invited out for dinner in the first year or so of their marriage, by parishioners anxious to get to know the rector's wife.

Married life at Rathmichael

On the plane journey home from America just after their wedding, Donald enthusiastically shared with Nancy two particular projects which he had in mind for the parish. One was his wish to start a dramatic society, and he said to Nancy: 'I want you to start a women's group.' The Rathmichael Amateur Dramatic Society was duly heralded with a notice in the parish notes for the diocesan magazine in March 1963:

> It is proposed to start a dramatic society in the parish which shall meet for the present in the rectory for play readings, and later shall present plays for public entertainment. I hope all persons interested in drama will support this society.

The first performance was held on 24 May 1963, and two further plays were presented the following November: *Send Her Victorious* and *The Shadow of the Glen*. Many prominent parish families such as the Ainsworths, Booths, Corrans, Graingers, Fellows–Prynnes, Tamplins and MacGillycuddys became involved. Frances Pakenham Walsh recalls:

> … that was a terrific thing for us all … and there was enough talent in the parish to scratch along. There weren't so many dramatic societies then, so anybody who got up and said their line, [the reaction was] 'aren't you marvellous!'

Donald himself took an active involvement as time permitted. Kathleen Turner's parish history records that 'at least one of his former parishioners had a vivid memory of him in one of Samuel Beckett's plays, sitting on the stage beside a hole into which he remained gazing in complete silence during the whole performance!' Nancy recalls that Donald had a wonderful acting talent, and in his heyday could take on any role: 'but of course he was absolutely maddening, because he could never remember his lines, so people [taking] their cues from what he was saying would be left …'. Donald also had a particular talent for mimicry, which his natural discretion would allow him to exercise only in private and trusted company.

About six months after Nancy's arrival, a meeting was announced for women in the parish, and chairs were set up in the rectory. Quite a number of people came along. Anxious to adopt a look-and-learn approach, Nancy had refused Donald's request that she chair the meeting. It proved a wise move, as there immediately arose a dispute between a group of women who wanted to start a branch of the Mothers' Union in the parish, and another group resistant to this. The latter included a prominent lady parishioner who had been divorced and remarried. Her basis of objection was the Mothers' Union's policy of not accepting separated or divorced members at the time. Ultimately, a new group called the Thursday Group was established.

Anxious to maintain his Irish language interests, Donald took Nancy to visit Inis Oírr, the smallest of the Aran Islands off the coast of Co. Galway, in the summer of 1964. In an account published in the journal *Focus* (edited by Risteárd Ó Glaisne) he described the journey out from Galway docks on the steamer Naomh Éanna:

> It was a dark cloudy day and the north easterly wind ruffled the seas. It was not difficult to distinguish the island people from the visitors, not just on account of their clothing and the strong bone [structure] of their faces coloured by the weather, but the manner in which they were gathered at the back of the steamer … sheltered from the wind … speaking in Irish.

On arrival near the island, a big iron door in the side of the steamer opened and large parcels were passed out from hand to hand into the awaiting currachs which would bring them ashore, barrels of black stout, bags of flour, a new bed, chairs … Islanders were waiting on the strand, including their host who took their bags and marched off ahead of them. Donald described the situation of the four villages on the island, all gathered so closely together that it was difficult to distinguish one from the other. The houses were neat and tidy, most now with slate roofs although houses with thatched roofs were still to be seen. Fishing and working the land were the main occupations for the men, while the women would knit and weave during the winter, and accommodate visitors in their own houses during the summer months. Donald had never tasted fish as delicious as that of the island. He and Nancy enjoyed the company of the other visitors, chatting to them until it was time to visit the pub, where the men of the island would gather almost every night, discussing events and surveying new visitors coming in. A pleasant evening would be spent chatting, playing darts and now and then singing a song. On returning to their lodgings, a cup of tea would be enjoyed by the fire in the kitchen with *na daoine is muinteartha agus is láí a casadh orm ariamh, muintir Inis Oi'ir* (the most friendly and pleasant people I ever met, the people of Inis Oírr).[7]

Back at Rathmichael, the rectory gardens were unkempt, as their maintenance had not been one of Donald's fortes in bachelorhood. A gardener, Joe Devlin (who was an 'Old IRA' veteran from the era of the War of Independence) set about creating some order and making a vegetable plot. A parishioner, Nora McConnell, gave Nancy the benefit of her wide knowledge and practical help and gardening soon became a treasured interest: 'They were great gardeners in Rathmichael.'

Since her marriage, Nancy had kept her horse Mulligan in the stable at the rectory. In February 1967, she and Donald became parents with the birth of their first daughter, Ann. During the pregnancy, they had a health scare when Nancy developed a malignant growth in her nose, necessitating medical treatment and reconstructive surgery. Much of the treatment had to be deferred until after her daughter's birth. Soon after this, Nancy became pregnant with the Cairds' first son John, born in April 1968. Right up to her first pregnancy, Nancy had continued to hunt with the Bray Harriers, striking up a number of friendships which would endure. She now found she could no longer hunt, if she were to lead rectory life and fulfil the responsibilities of motherhood: 'My priority is always to be where you need me to be.' The horse was sold.

Rathmichael parish blossomed under Donald's stewardship, and the church celebrated its centenary in 1964, with oil-fired central heating being installed and the pews refurnished. In 1965, Archbishop Simms came down to open the parish hall and an extension to the parish school, the latter having had grown rapidly under the guidance of its principal, Miss Hazel Jolley (now Mrs Crawford), since her arrival in 1962. The first edition of the parish newsletter appeared in October 1965. In 1967, the parish boundaries were extended to take in the townland of Cherrywood together with the portion of Loughlinstown lying to the west of the main road, areas which had previously formed part of Killiney parish. The object of this realignment was to bring the ancient boundaries of some neighbouring parishes more closely into line with modern roads and housing developments.[8] The parish notes in the diocesan magazine of February 1969 give a snapshot of the eclectic and vibrant life of the parish close to the end of Donald's tenure: a seventy-five per cent increase was recorded over the year in the number of pupils attending the day school, congratulations were extended to the Rathmichael Parish Dramatic Society on its performance of *The White Sheep of the Family*: 'a most accomplished performance of a brilliant and sophisticated comedy' and an illustrated talk at Rathmichael schoolhouse of a visit made by two parishioners to Jordan and Israel was advertised.

Moving to Kilkenny

Kathleen Turner's *Rathmichael, a Parish History* records that: 'The red and gold roses planted by Nancy Caird in the Rectory Garden were in full flower when in June 1969 the rector announced that he had been invited to become Dean of St Canice's Cathedral, Kilkenny.' While Donald's promotion was greeted with pleasure in the parish, it was accompanied by great regret that he was leaving them. His academic and philosophical interests had been noted by the similarly scholarly Henry McAdoo, the Bishop of Ossory, who invited him to take the office of Dean of Ossory. During that summer, however, he was struck by illness, developing a severe case of mumps in an outbreak which affected the east coast of the country at the time, and which resulted in the deaths of four men. Encephalitis developed as a complication of the mumps, resulting in a delay of some months in the move to the deanery in Kilkenny. Donald was cared for by Nancy at home in Rathmichael rectory during his illness: 'he was very ill for a whole year after that. He was weak the whole time he was Dean of Ossory.'

On their eventual move to Kilkenny, the family settled into the old deanery next door to St Canice's Cathedral. On 3 September 1969, the service of institution and installation of Donald as dean took place in the presence of the Minister for Defence, Mr James Gibbons TD; the Mayor; members of the Corporation; and ecumenical representatives from the Roman Catholic, Methodist and Presbyterian Churches. One hundred and fifty Rathmichael parishioners travelled down for the occasion and attended the reception in St Mary's Hall, Kilkenny. In his sermon at the institution, Bishop McAdoo spoke of the Troubles which were then beginning to ignite in Northern Ireland, beginning with attacks on civil rights demonstrators, and stressed the basic Christian principles of justice and freedom, 'which alone would secure a lasting settlement of the present distress'.[9]

A busy round of decanal duties and parochial responsibilities in the Kilkenny and Freshford group of parishes (where the dean was also rector) quickly ensued. Donald and the diocesan curate, Rev. David Woodworth, announced a series of addresses for Advent 1969, the diocesan magazine notes observing that:

Our church makes few demands on our time outside the services on Sunday, and it is our duty as members of the Anglican Communion to support the ancient custom of the church to hold special services in Advent when we prepare to celebrate the greatest event in church history, the revelation of God in the person of Christ.

In the New Year, the 'greatly loved and appreciated' David Woodworth and his wife Mary departed for Bandon, Co. Cork, the parish notes striking a wistful tone:

We look before and after / and pine at what is not; / and our sincerest laughter with / some pain is fraught.

An epilogue service was planned for 9:15 p.m. on Sunday evenings in the summer months of 1970 in order to 'allow those who have spent the day away in the country or at the seaside to complete their day with an act of thanksgiving for all the joys of their life'. A project was underway to amalgamate three Church of Ireland national schools in the diocese through the addition of new classrooms and other facilities to Kilkenny city's Model School. Donald himself was given added responsibilities, being appointed director of ordinands for Cashel and Ossory in summer 1970.

He recalled a national service held by the Masonic order in St Canice's Cathedral during his time there, recalling that the cathedral was filled with Masons in their aprons:

All gorgeous looking things, gold insignias etc. So few of them were Church of Ireland, there were Jews, Mohammedans ... that amazed me. They were charming people and made a nice financial contribution to the upkeep of the place.[10]

Speaking about his parochial experiences for an American audience in 1997, Donald recounted:

We moved to Kilkenny to St Canice's Cathedral, one of the most beautiful 13th century buildings in Ireland with a perfect round tower standing beside it. To live in the middle of the city, albeit, a medieval city required considerable adaptation, including the disappearance of the horse. Kilkenny is a magnificent city dominated by the Cathedral and the great Norman castle of the Duke of Ormond ... We enjoyed our short sojourn, less than two years, in this beautiful city where life still showed distinct traces of the Norman feudal system. On a parochial visit to one of the great houses I asked a retired admiral with a distinctly Norman name how long his family had been attending the cathedral; he replied 'since 1260 without a break', despite frequent rebellions, civil wars and reformations. Kilkenny was like that.[11]

The Cairds' stay in the medieval city was short, as still higher office beckoned for Donald. His nomination as bishop to the See of Limerick in the summer of 1970 was noted by Bishop McAdoo as giving 'great satisfaction to all who wish to see his many gifts used in the widest possible way ... he will be much missed in the field of the numerous civic commitments in which he was involved'.[12] A note from Donald and Nancy recorded their sadness at having to say goodbye to Kilkenny 'so soon after settling in this beautiful city'. No other parish could have so securely captured their affections in such a short time. Particular thanks were expressed to their 'good and great Bishop, Dr McAdoo, and his wife'.[13]

CHAPTER FOUR

Bishop of Limerick, Ardfert and Aghadoe
(1970–1976)

Consecration and Enthronement

The forty-two lay and clerical members of the Episcopal Electoral College met in Christ Church Cathedral, Dublin on 31 July 1970 to select a successor to Robert Wyse Jackson, Bishop of Limerick, Ardfert and Aghadoe, who had recently retired for health reasons. After day-long deliberations, Donald Caird was duly elected. The diocese mainly covered the counties of Limerick and Kerry, *The Church of Ireland Gazette* noting that it was a sparsely populated area (in so far as the Church of Ireland was concerned), with a Church population in the region of 2,300.[1]

The bishop had his *cathedra*, or seat, at the medieval St Mary's Cathedral in Limerick city (the other cathedral in the diocese, St Brendan's at Ardfert, was in ruins, having been destroyed by fire in 1641).[2] Its principal urban centres were Limerick city itself, and the towns of Tralee and Killarney. Also located in remote districts within the diocesan boundaries were two traditional Irish-speaking *Gaeltachtaí*: in Corca Dhuibhne on the westernmost end of Kerry's Dingle Peninsula and in the central and western part of Uíbh Rathach, the neighbouring Iveragh peninsula. In its geographical, social and linguistic breadth, this diocese would provide ample scope for the new bishop's cultural and pastoral interests. The Bishop's House on Limerick's North Circular Road had as its immediate neighbour, the palace of the Roman Catholic bishop, Henry Murphy.

Letters and telegrams of congratulation on the appointment came in from such varied sources as the leading ecumenist Fr Michael Hurley SJ (signing himself 'the Jesuit in whom there is no guile'); Raymond Renowden, Donald's old head of department at St David's, Lampeter; the select vestry of St Mark's church, Dundela, Belfast; Donald's half brother Jim; Cóilí Conneeley with whom he had stayed on Inis Oírr and his former rector at Sandford, William Nesbitt Harvey. John Campbell, writing from the Irish Embassy in Paris, composed a ditty:

> An episcopal flyer named Caird / once remarked, thinking not overheard / 'While the Ossory scene / Is all right for a Dean / I'd to Limerick prefer being preferred.' 'Would mechanic or priest or gas fitter / As career', mused our Donald, 'be brighter?' / Then was heard, with composure / While toying with a crozier / Mutter 'motor or meter or mitre?'

Donald was consecrated bishop by Dr Alan Buchanan (as Archbishop of Dublin and Primate of Ireland) in Christ Church Cathedral, Dublin, on the feast of St Michael and All Angels, Tuesday, 29 September 1970. The preacher was the Rev. Noel Willoughby, a former classmate of Donald's in Trinity. Noting that the consecration of a bishop should always be held on a Sunday or Holy Day, his theme was St Michael and the Angels, in their struggle and witness to God. The Christians of the early church took as their inspiration and hope the Lamb, a symbolic vision of Jesus. He was the Christ – Crucified – Risen – Victorious. Willoughby cautioned against excessive readiness to embrace new trends in theological thought:

> Reaction, no less than in-action, has its dangers ... new things are apt to impress us enormously so that automatically we think what's new is true ... While all this debate stimulates thought and delights the theologians, it has nonetheless confused and perplexed many people of every denomination, not all of whom can be dismissed as theological squares and unthinking diehards (I am sure that the parish clergy here have experienced this concern from their own pastoral ministrations, and they also know that when they visit a bed of sickness what brings hope and comfort is not the latest theory but the fact of God's love and forgiveness in Christ). And it is ... to this basic doctrine, that Michaelmas day points – steering us through the fads and fashions of religion.[3]

To be a bishop is to be a community, as well as a religious, leader, and also a public figure of some consequence, and among the dignitaries of church and state present in Christ Church to greet the new bishop were Colonel Seán Brennan, representing President de Valera; Minister for Justice Des O'Malley, representing the Taoiseach and government; and Dom Paul McDonnell, representing the Abbot of Glenstal.

A fortnight later, on 13 October, Donald sought admission to the cathedral of St Mary in Limerick for his enthronement by knocking in the traditional style on the great west door three times with his Pastoral Staff. Upon being admitted by the representative of the dean, he declared 'open me the gates of righteousness, that I may go into them, and give thanks unto the Lord'.

Addressing the assembled clergy and laity (including civic dignitaries), Donald admitted that, when he was asked whether he would permit his name to go forward for consideration for the bishopric, his first instinct was to refuse as he had served so short a time in Ossory. However he was counselled by the Bishop of Ossory, Dr McAdoo, in these words: 'You have not sought to go, it is not your choice, it is the wisdom of the church under the Holy Spirit; if you were chosen, you must go.'

Paying tribute to his predecessor, Donald noted that he must look beyond the cathedral and the city to the scattered communities of town and village where the thinly distributed Church of Ireland population lived. The smallness of the Protestant community should not, however, be a cause of despair or apathy in relation to the affairs of the nation: 'The voice of conscience, though small and still, will be effectively heard and respected when it was impartially expressed in issues that concern the whole community.'

Taking up a theme that would find repeated expression in his public utterances in subsequent years, Donald urged that the church's young people would be 'encouraged to take a full part in the civic life of country and city in all the agencies of local government'. The scattered nature of the community posed challenges in respect of providing for education, both primary and secondary, and difficulties for young members of the church in finding marriage partners of their own tradition. Referring to the symbolism of the shepherd inherent in the office of bishop and signalled in the pastoral staff, he said that, although it might seem to smack of paternalism in this age, it was a picture that came to us with the authority of the New Testament and the unbroken traditions of the church – it was not meant to suggest a blind, unthinking, sheep-like reaction on the part of the flock:

> The work of the Shepherd is to lead, to guard and to feed the flock, so that each member may come to maturity in the spiritual aspect of their lives and achieve that self-fulfilment which St Paul indicated when he prayed that the Christian might reach the full measure of the stature of Christ.[4]

A reception was held after the service in the Parkway Motel, the Mayor of Limerick telling the Bishop he was coming to the city at time of expansion. Replying to the various speakers, Donald made witty reference to the linkage of his name in Scottish Gaelic with itinerants, pointing out that since his ordination twenty years previously, Limerick was his seventh diocese. However, having come there, he would now try to amend his 'Romany ways'.[5]

The Bishop's House and Family life

After an initial period residing in Limerick's Ardhu Hotel while the Bishop's House on North Circular Road was being renovated and readied for their use, Donald, Nancy, their two young children Ann and John, and a nanny (Joan Dargan, who had come with them from Kilkenny) moved into their new home. Built *c*.1845, its unusual appearance had been described by the previous bishop, Robert Wyse Jackson as 'Victorian acrobatic'. It featured two wings at forty-five degree angles at either side of the central bay section, which had a Tudor-style porch topped by decorative turrets (Nancy later decided to have these removed as they had the effect of blocking light into the upstairs landing window). Among the house's other features were a large dining room, drawing room and nine bedrooms, three of which were situated in the dormer attic.

The ground landlord of this property was the legendary Limerick figure Feathery Bourke. According to Donald, Bourke had grown a large business from the sale of feathers, which he collected from various sources such as chicken slaughterers, selling them on to feather packers. Donald recalls him as 'one of the most charming and handsome men in Limerick'. Following the death of his wife after only eighteen months of marriage, it seems Bourke had become reclusive and of somewhat dishevelled appearance, selling various properties he owned and going to live in a modest dwelling in Limerick city. Each year during the Cairds' time in Limerick, they would receive a note from Bourke stating that he would like to 'come and walk my property' on a specified day. The Cairds would give him tea in the drawing room, and Bourke would reminisce about his background and adventures. 'He was charming … very well educated and extraordinarily polite.' He would say to the Cairds 'oh yes, you're keeping my property beautifully, thank you', following up his visit with a polite note of thanks.

The Bishop's House was hidden from the main road, and over-shadowed by a venerable copper beech tree of great vintage, 'with a big trunk and the perfect balloon shape that is the copper beech', dominating the garden. Nancy recalls that herons from the nearby River Shannon would come to nest in the tree, their loud squawking making a din at night. The Cairds had inherited a gardener from Donald's predecessor, and under Nancy's direction, the task of restoring the gardens was begun. She recalls turning to her gardener for advice at one point, when pellets from an air gun, being fired from the opposite side of the road, began landing in the garden of the house, even hitting the windows of Donald's study. The gardener, who seemed to have very effective contacts, reassured her that he would put a stop to it, and there was indeed no recurrence.

Nancy ensured that the Bishop's House was put to use as a centre of hospitality and entertainment for the wider community, and family friends visited from time to time. A newspaper profile published some months after their arrival in the city noted her interest in charitable work and in availing of opportunities for meeting a wide selection of people beyond the confines of the Church of Ireland community. She made the observation that 'being American is something of an advantage: At home we are not conscious of any religious split. Over there, the people I knew were the people I knew, and never confined to any religious sect.'[6]

In the early 1970s, Nancy had been approached by parishioners in Limerick and asked to take on the task of reviving the local Mothers' Union (MU). The organisation generally had been riven by controversy because of its refusal to admit or retain members who had been divorced, even in cases where the divorce had not been sought by the wife. The ensuing rancour had left it in a demoralised state. Nancy agreed to take on the task on condition that she would be given such help as she needed by others. One of the principal benefits she felt she could bring was to offer the Bishop's House as a venue for meetings.

Because the organisation's diocesan president lived in Killarney, Nancy took on duties at both city parish and wider diocesan level. She was appointed head of the MU Literature Department, and would speak about publications brought out by the MU internationally: books and leaflets on topics such as parenting and marriages. Inexperienced as a speaker, she found this a help: 'you have something specific to talk about'. She travelled to different areas in Limerick and Kerry, facilitating gatherings of women. Growing in confidence, she served later as diocesan president of the MU. At a wider civic level, she became a member of the National Council for the Blind, providing opportunities to make personal contact with a variety of people in the general community. She viewed the provision of hospitality as one of the most important contributions she could make: 'we lived in these great houses, [my view was] let people use them'. The couple entertained for various church and civic groups, inviting people from the city and counties Limerick and Kerry there for dinner – a new Aga cooker was installed in the kitchens and an extensive set of cutlery built up, which would last them for many years.

David Neligan recalled, while visiting Donald and Nancy in these years (possibly while they were still at Rathmichael), observing their daughter Ann, a 'robust little girl' of about two or three, out playing in the garden and falling in the mud. He remarked that the children had the 'energy and strength that [Donald] had'. Ann and John, Donald and

Nancy's children, were soon attending St Michael's national school on Pery Square (where Walton Empey's sons were also pupils). Ann recalls St Michael's as a fairly intimate school community of one hundred to one hundred and fifty pupils, with about fifteen pupils in each class, boys slightly outnumbering girls. The Cairds' second daughter, Helen, was born in January 1972. A typical day for Nancy in the year 1973–74 would see her drive Ann and John to school, having breakfast in the car as they waited in line for an allocation of petrol during the oil crisis of that year. This might be followed by some duties at home and shopping. In the afternoon, she did taxi service, ferrying the older children in the car to various after-school activities while baby Helen was strapped into the back. Ann joined the Girls' Friendly Society and John the cub scouts (soon going camping with them to places like Cratloe in nearby Co. Clare). Nancy might attend meetings (in line with the various responsibilities she had taken on) in the afternoon, while Joan, the housekeeper, minded Helen. In the evening, the family would gather to have dinner in the kitchen, prepared by Nancy. It was a hectic life, but 'back then, we had unbounded energy and we enjoyed it'.

John recalls life as a young boy in the Bishop's House around the year 1974:

> It was a beautiful house, with its own grounds – a childhood playground. It had bigger gardens then than now. Bishop Newman lived next door. It was a lovely, leafy beautiful place, with lovely stables. It was a rather sheltered upbringing. I joined the choir at St Mary's Cathedral in 1974 – I was about six. [There was] a family called Gardner – Mrs Gardner and her husband, the verger, and their daughter Constance. They lived ... at the back near the vestry. [Mrs Gardner would] brush everyone's hair and polish our shoes, she'd only blue polish and everyone got [this] regardless of [the colour of their] shoes!

Donald had an Irish Terrier, and John would frequently accompany his father on walks with the dog down the North Circular Road and out along Barrington's Pier, Donald swinging his blackthorn stick (made by Canon Dan Heavener, an American of Irish heritage who had come to Co. Limerick, and whose hobby was the fashioning of such accessories). Donald would frequently step out sporting an Aran sweater and Aran cap. Walking and cycling were the Cairds' favourite pastime as a family. Towards the end of their time in Limerick, they acquired a Swiss au pair, Beatrice, to mind the children (who would move on with them later when they transferred to Leixlip).

The dioceses

The first year of his Episcopate saw Donald enter upon a wide range of public duties, from attendance at 'a reception for the three astronauts lately rescued from space', a school prize-giving and the opening of an art exhibition to sitting 'through a display of ladies fashions in the very front seat'. He took part in joint blessings of an engineering works, a hosiery factory and a bank, addressed the Gaelic League, the Credit Union of Ireland, the Vocational Teachers' Association, the Lions International Congress, 'and to crown the year, I had my photograph taken with the Rose of Tralee'. As bishop, he could avail of the services of a secretary, Valerie Stevenson, to handle his growing workload.

With responsibility for a large, sprawling diocese covering counties Limerick and Kerry, and a scattered, mainly rural Church of Ireland population, long car journeys became an essential feature of Donald's working life. Diocesan council meetings had to be held in each of the constituent dioceses: Limerick on the one hand, and Ardfert and Aghadoe (Kerry) on the other. In the rural parts, particularly in Kerry, the church community were farming people in the main.[7] This meant that meetings would have to be held in the evening, after working hours on the farms. In remoter parts of Kerry, it would be necessary to stop and stay somewhere overnight en route.

Addressing the synod for the Ardfert and Aghadoe (Kerry) portion of the united dioceses at the end of his first year, he humorously referred to the task of making contact with its people and parishes as 'trial by journey', noting the challenges this posed for clergy in travelling long distances in the course of their work and the difficulties faced by national (primary) schools in terms of pupil numbers. There were, for example, one-teacher schools in four disparate areas: Tralee, Ballymacelligott, Castlemaine and Killarney. He highlighted a need to coordinate the parish system,

> formed in the days of horse transport, when the journey of fifteen or twenty miles was something to be carefully considered and not lightly undertaken; but now we live in the days of the fast and comfortable motor car, where the journey of fifteen or twenty miles should not take half an hour, and the clergy can move comfortably from congregation to congregation.

A group ministry scheme for the parishes of Tralee, Camp, Ballymacelligott and Listowel was proposed, whereby clergy could share duties and 'each man will be able to exercise his specific talents for the benefit of the whole group' and benefit from mutual support.

Addressing the diocesan synod in October 1972, Donald humorously noted that 'the first year of one's episcopacy in a new diocese is often described as the "honeymoon period" when it is said that "one can do no wrong". The second year is regarded as a period of disillusionment, when "one can do no right" and the following year is a period of indifference when "it does not matter what one does".' However, his experience of his second year, when he had a chance to visit the various parishes in 'a cool hour' (more relaxed circumstances than the big occasion of a bishop's first visit) led him to find,

> contrary to the cynical predictions ... not disillusionment, but a most encouraging record of quiet devotion and service in the church, a concern for and a firm commitment to the Christian way of life as presented in the Anglican tradition of the Church of Ireland.

In Limerick city, Donald's predecessor Robert Wyse Jackson had overseen the formation of a single parish out of five former parishes: St Mary, St Michael, St John, Holy Trinity and St Munchin, resulting in the strengthening and cohesion of Church life there, centred on the cathedral and St Michael's in Pery Square. The parish and cathedral had the right to appoint a rector for the city parish, but the appointment of a dean was the prerogative of the bishop – the dean chosen was normally in fact the rector. Dean Maurice Talbot had been obliged to retire after suffering a stroke within a short time of Donald taking up office, meaning a replacement had to be found to manage the work of the diocese along with himself and the archdeacon. Dublin-born Walton Empey, a man of great personal charm and warmth, was at this time rector of Stradbally, Co. Laois, whence he had come on returning from Canada in 1966. The son of a clergyman, Empey had been a pupil at Portora Royal School in Enniskillen (his younger brother Adrian, as we have seen, was also a pupil there in Donald's time as chaplain). After a curacy in Glenageary, he had spent six years in Canada. He was married to Louie, and the couple had three young boys (a baby daughter would be born shortly after their arrival in Limerick).

Empey recalls picking up the telephone in Stradbally and Donald was on the line. He would like to interview Empey as a prospective dean of Limerick: 'I went and was interviewed by the nominators about almost everything except what I actually believed in ... My wife had become secretary of Stradbally Steam Society, and [the nominators] seemed more interested in that than what I believed in!' He more or less forgot about it, until he received a follow-up call from Donald about a month later –

would he accept the position as dean? Empey recalls that Donald stated his income would be a certain sum, which appeared generous to Empey. However on each subsequent phone call, the sum seemed to reduce, until, as he recalls with amusement, he was finally moved to ask: 'Bishop, am I going to have to pay to come here?' Apparently, in his predecessor's time, payments in respect of a number of hospital chaplaincies had gone directly to the dean, but were henceforth to be regarded as diocesan income. However, he accepted the position, which represented a promotion in the structures of the Church.

In Limerick, Empey recalls himself and Donald as young bishops 'sharing their inexperience' and learning from each other. Donald had a 'glass half full' outlook, which could sometimes tip over into an almost reckless optimism. In the early 1970s, there was a great deal of expansion in the Limerick region generally as part of the industrial development surrounding Shannon airport, which was Ireland's only transatlantic hub. Some of the companies in the industrial estates were bringing in workers from places such as Germany. The Shannon Free Airport Development Company (SFADCO) had founded a new town, Shannon, in the area. In 1972, with support from SFADCO, a National Institute of Higher Education was established in Limerick (Dr Edward Walsh was appointed its first director, and was noted for his ambitious vision for economic development) and a National Technological Park was located nearby.

Donald felt that the dioceses should be preparing for a large influx of people as a result of these developments. Addressing his diocesan synod in October 1971, he hailed the plans for a university which 'could have as many as eight thousand students on its books'. The presence of a large body of students and university staff would transform life in Limerick, and present a 'great and invigorating challenge'. Noting the number of large industries being developed on the outskirts of the city, which would bring into the community people from churches on the continent of Europe, he said that we 'should make contact with the home churches of these people so that we will know how best to serve their spiritual needs when they come to our community. I hope to set up a committee to pursue this problem during this coming year ...' Empey however felt that there would be 'slim pickings', at best, for the Church of Ireland, and indeed the much anticipated influx to the parish did not materialise – although there were some newcomers such as German industrialist Dr Tiede Herrema, his wife and their two boys, who enrolled in the national school.

Donald recalls that St Mary's Cathedral was kept open during the day on a regular basis during his time in Limerick. The walls of the medieval keep by the river, about ten feet thick, were part of the ancient fortress of Dónal Mór Ó Briain, King of Munster. The cathedral graveyard had been a common burial place for both Catholic and Protestant prior to the Irish Church Act of 1869 (which disestablished the Church of Ireland) and it housed the vault of the Barrington family, connected with the famous Limerick hospital. It appears that fishermen had an ancient right of burial in the cathedral grounds. In 1976, as part of the King's Island festival celebrating the folklore of the fishermen of the Abbey and Shannon, Donald spoke knowledgeably about the tradition of the fishermen and praised the links the festival established between them and the people of the parish.

Limerick prison was situated within the diocese and, up to the early 1970s enjoyed a relatively relaxed regime. Donald recalls strolling past the jail one day and being hailed by a chap painting a railing, who said to him 'oh, you're the bishop – do you know me?' 'I can't say that I know you, who are you?' Donald replied. The man said: 'My brother and I were put in prison here because we used dynamite to stun the fish in the River Laun.' (As Bishop of Limerick, Donald had ancient fishing rights in the same river, in Co. Kerry.) The man then called over to his friends 'hey, hey, the bishop's here!' It seems that when the case had come before the courts, the Judge had taken a poor view of the offence, but as the brothers came from 'a good family', they were given certain privileges when taken into prison. One of the duties assigned to them was this task of painting the railings.

Donald could be a rather excitable driver. On one occasion, the bishop and his dean were in his car, and Donald drove the wrong way up a one-way street in Limerick city. A taxi came down in the other direction, and the driver rolled down his window and shouted across 'it's a one-way street!' Donald, who had something of a short fuse on occasion,[8] retorted robustly, but immediately afterwards realised that in fact the taxi driver was in the right.

> Now this is Donald, he took the number of the taxi and when he got back [to the Bishop's House] he immediately telephoned the taxi company and asked who the driver was [and to be put in touch with him]. [The driver] telephoned (expecting an earful, I suppose) but Donald wanted to apologise.

He invited the driver up to the Bishop's House, where the pair sat down, had 'a few beers' and proceeded to enjoy a convivial chat about Limerick, Donald learning a great deal about the city from his guest.

Donald's propensity for 'nodding off' and 'power napping' was legendary among his family and friends. Walton Empey recalls one occasion when he and Donald drove to a meeting in Dublin, each driving for half of the journey on the way there. As they prepared for the return journey late the same evening, Donald set out the driving duties to his dean: 'Now, Walton, you'll drive to Naas, I'll drive to Mountrath, you'll drive to Nenagh …' They got into the car and Donald soon nodded off. He dozed as they passed Naas, Newbridge, Kildare and Mountrath, and it was when they had reached a point about twelve miles outside of Limerick city that Donald roused himself with a snort and a cough and exclaimed, 'Oh, are we in Naas?'

In contrast to the farming and Gaelic aspects of parts of Kerry, Donald's diocese, on the Limerick side, included Adare and the surrounding rolling countryside, home to some wealthy residents, and the riding of horses to hounds. On one occasion, an elderly gentleman of English background living in Adare passed away, and at his burial the local hunt decided that the entire pack and as many members as possible would grace the ceremony. Donald conducted the service. As the burial was taking place, the huntsman began playing his horn, and the tune played was *Gone to Ground*.[9] A pack of hounds came racing through in pre-arranged theatrical fashion.

With characteristic self-deprecating humour, Donald recounts an occasion in October 1973 when the American network NBC's television programme *Today* was being broadcast from Ireland, featuring an interview with him and the Roman Catholic Bishop of Killaloe, Michael Harty. The interview was to be filmed at a promontory on Slea Head on the Dingle Peninsula near Ventry, with the two bishops instructed to travel there to meet the anchorwoman Barbara Walters at about 11am on a Friday. The segment took the form of a conversation between the two bishops, looking to camera, and the Blasket Islands visible out to sea behind them. Their 'conversation' was triggered by questions posed off-camera by the anchorwoman, which would be subsequently edited out. On the appointed day, however, torrential rain and wind lashed the Peninsula from the sea. The Catholic Bishop was wearing spectacles, and the driving rain made it impossible for him to see anything. *Bhí an gaoth ag séideadh eadrainn* ('the wind was blowing between us'), recalled Donald, as they struggled to maintain their 'conversation' with Ms Walters, who was all the while safely ensconced in a hut, firing out the questions to them. The islands were described in the television introduction as being Gaelic speaking, and accordingly the bishops were instructed to answer one or two questions in Irish to create a romantic impression for the American viewers. 'We did this [interview] for half an hour and we were soaked through, and then finally she said: "This is going out [on television in the USA] at 6 or 7 a.m. on Monday morning".'

Following the interview, the two bishops went to have coffee in a covered area nearby with Ms Walters and her young daughter who was accompanying her. The little girl was running in the rain on the hillside, and her mother jumped up to grab her, resulting in both slipping in a cow pat and ending up covered in cow dung. This presented a sorry picture as the respected US anchorwoman was wearing 'tigerskin tight breeches and thin narrow boots' at the time.

The interview was recorded on a Friday and by coincidence Donald and Nancy were due to fly out to San Francisco the very next day with their two children to visit Nancy's mother Gwendolen and fulfil an engagement in New York. They were woken up by Gwendolen in San Francisco on Monday morning to watch the broadcast:

> I never looked so bedraggled in my life, soaking wet and my hair was wet and my eyes were closed because the rain was very sharp. The Roman Catholic Bishop could not see anything through his spectacles, and we were shouting out [our replies] apparently to nothing, because [the interviewer] was out of view. At about 12 [o'clock] a friend of Nancy's who had seen the programme, telephoned from New England and exclaimed 'oh Nancy, I was watching [the programme], and I always assumed you had married an idiot, but ...!'

In the course of their American trip, Donald and Nancy travelled to New York to attend the sixty-seventh annual dinner of the American Irish Historical society in the Waldorf Hotel in New York – a gala occasion attended by leading figures in the Irish American community including Cardinal Terence Cooke. Among the guests were Peter J. Brennan, US Secretary of Labour, and the Irish actress Siobhán McKenna. Donald gave the benediction in Irish.[10]

Early on in their time in Limerick, Donald and Nancy adopted a practice of taking a break in the summer on the Dingle Peninsula, staying in the little parish of Killiney, near Castlegregory. They would stay in the modest sexton's cottage next to the small church there. Helen as a baby was bathed in the kitchen handbasin. Three weeks were spent there each August, Donald taking summer relief services at Killiney church (where attendances at services would be augmented by summer visitors from the United States, Britain and continental Europe), and occasionally driving over the Conor Pass to Kilmalkeader, where he would hold services in Irish for the tiny Church of Ireland community living in that area.

Some time after the birth of Helen, Donald's predecessor Robert Wyse Jackson recommended to the Cairds that they purchase a permanent holiday home (which might also serve as a retirement home) and recommended the district of Camp, where he himself had a place. The advantage of Camp was that it was on the Dingle Peninsula, but close enough to both Tralee and the road which went over the mountains to Castlemaine. As well as the Dingle peninsula, this location allowed easy access to the southerly Iveragh Peninsula. Donald and Nancy placed the search in the hands of a local auctioneer and in the meantime continued to holiday in the area and stay at Killiney. An old house in Camp named Kilgobbin Lodge was identified as suitable. It had been owned briefly by a surgeon from Northern Ireland, John Robb. (Robb was a liberal Protestant from Northern Ireland who in the early 1980s founded the New Ireland Group, which set out a vision of Ireland distinct from traditional Unionist and Gaelic/Catholic perspectives. In 1982 he was appointed to the Senate in the Republic.)

Although Kilgobbin Lodge was in a ramshackle condition (initially consisting of a two-storey house and a shed to the rear reached from the upper storey), the Cairds found it charming with just the right amount of land suitable for their needs, and so they purchased it. Ann recalls the early days: 'It was like camping inside a structure ... For us and friends coming to stay, [it was] a seven bed dormitory. The place was falling down and ... slime running down the walls to the open drains.' Under Donald's and Nancy's supervision, a local builder, Eugene Deane, set about gradually renovating and extending the house and converting the shed into an extension. While Kilgobbin Lodge remained a 'work in progress' for the next twenty years, it was quickly made habitable enough, and the first summer the family stayed there was in 1976, Donald's final year in the diocese. This would become for the future the place where they spent all of their holidays: summer, mid-term breaks, New Year and Easter. Each summer, Nancy would go there with the children a week or two in advance of Donald. Donald would join them for August, relaxing and unwinding from the pressures of work. Nancy and he entertained friends there, and friends of the children would come to stay. They took trips around the Dingle Peninsula, encountering people such as Dáithí Ó Maolchoille from Cumann Gaelach na hEaglaise and his wife on holidays in Ballyferriter with their sons. It was through the purchase of the house in Kerry, and the haven it provided in later years, that a key link was forged in a chain which had begun with Donald's boyhood experience in the Kerry Gaeltacht.

Pastoral concerns

As bishop, Donald was 'Father in God' to his clergy in the dioceses. Paying tribute to the clergy in his presidential address to the Limerick Synod in 1975, he noted that:

> The privilege of priests is to be daily concerned with the 'things of God,' to have as their daily task the conduct of worship, the administration of the sacraments, the teaching of religious knowledge, the counselling of men and women seeking the way of God in the various crises of their lives, the visiting of the sick, the representation of the church in many and various functions in the community, the administration of schools, and all the organisations of the parish.

This posed a strain on clergy, who needed the support and encouragement of the laity. He quoted Cardinal Suenens of Belgium who had recently summed up the position of those in ministry: 'they carry the torch of the gospel, but others see better than they do by its light.' Those who exercise ministry, Donald said,

> need to be reminded of their humanity, they need relaxation, encouragement, a change of scene, a change of work, new insights into the ways of living and thinking of those whose lives are far removed from their own, so that refreshed they may return with greater vigour and renewed vision to the task to which they have been commissioned.[11]

Noting the recent decision of the General Synod to accept the auxiliary ministry (now known as the non-stipendiary ministry, whereby persons might be ordained while continuing secular vocations), his belief was that

> our church shall be ... enriched and strengthened by the devoted service ... of men who will bring a wide and varied experience through their secular occupations to bear on the essential work of presenting the gospel of Christ to the world and of encouraging people who may be alienated from the church, to discover the relevance of the Christian gospel and the life of the church in fellowship and worship, for themselves and their society.

A youthful sense of enthusiasm found expression in his interest in, and enjoyment of, the company of young people. In 1972, he became chairman of the Church of Ireland Youth Council. Robin Eames (who became a bishop in 1975 and was elected Archbishop of Armagh in 1986) said he associated Donald in this era with him heading off on camping expeditions with young people. To those who would express some concern for his welfare while roughing it, Donald would cheerily respond 'I'm as young as they are!' 'Are you sure you will be all right under canvas?' 'Good gracious yes, I'll be fine under canvas – as long as it doesn't leak!' Wales was visited once or twice on such camping expeditions. A particular source of satisfaction towards the end of his period in the diocese was the offering of a grant by the Minister for Education, through the Church of Ireland Youth Council, for the conversion of Muckross church into a resident youth centre. This would allow groups of young people to come to engage in outdoor activities in the beautiful surroundings of Killarney.[12] A no less important illustration of his practical concern for the position of young people – foreshadowed in his enthronement address – was the devising of plans to establish an introductions service to enable young Church of Ireland men and women to meet possible marriage partners. The outlines for the Contact service were worked out by the bishop and the Rev. Ted Woods in the drawing room of the Bishop's House in Limerick.[13]

Education

As much as with marriage, the maintenance of the Church of Ireland's community and sense of identity was bound up with education and schools. Villiers School on Limerick's North Circular Road was the only school under Protestant management between Sligo to the north, Cork to the south and Kilkenny to the east (serving not only the Church of Ireland, but also the other Protestant denominations). Donald declared that 'the life of the Protestant community in Limerick, and the whole South West region is intimately, indeed vitally, concerned with the future of Villiers school.' The extensive catchment area made it necessary that a large proportion of pupils should be boarders. Its future, in the light of Department of Education requirements concerned with schools' viability, would be a challenge for the Protestant community, which could 'derive inspiration from the imagination, courage and tenacity of the Limerick University Project Committee, the crowning achievement of whose work was celebrated … with the official opening of the National Institute for Higher Education at Plassey'.

Within a year, an Advisory Committee under the joint chairmanship of the Church of Ireland bishops of Limerick and Killaloe had devised detailed plans for the renovation and expansion of Villiers' boarding premises, the reorganisation of its grounds and the extension of its teaching accommodation, with a view to meeting Departmental requirements.

In late 1975, Donald reported to his synod a detailed feasibility study of the number of potential pupils for Villiers school had been sent to the Minister for Education:

Villiers continues to grow, having something in the region of one hundred and ninety pupils this term which means that the school has doubled its size in ten years, so that in four years it should reach the sacred number of three hundred which would justify expenditure by the Department of Education. The Villiers board, Headmaster and staff are to be congratulated on the way in which they have kept the school going under very difficult circumstances.[14]

However, in the area of primary education, the Minister for Education had recently 'surprised the country' with a proposal to end the system of the single clerical manager in primary schools 'which had existed for more than a century'. Management committees were now to be formed for every primary school, and the payment of a capitation grant of £6 per child – replacing the previous grant system for primary schools – would be dependent upon this. While every parochial primary school under Church of Ireland management had duly set up a management committee, there were anxieties over whether this form of grant would be adequate to meet the needs of the smaller two or three teacher national schools common to that Church: 'I would suggest a minimum grant of £500 per annum ... should be offered and a form of capitation grant should operate above this for the larger schools.'

Civic and ecumenical affairs
Because of his leadership and representational role, a bishop has a busy round of church and social engagements to fulfil, both within and outside his own diocese. For Donald, as Bishop of Limerick, these included conducting a Quiet Day for the Dublin Guild of Lay Readers at the Divinity Hostel; attending a lunch hosted by Nancy Lady Dunraven in Adare Manor, Limerick; attending a community presentation in Waterville for retiring Church of Ireland rector Canon J. L. Enright and giving the address at the official opening of the Bach music festival in Killarney's Muckross House.[15] He also maintained his connections with Northern Ireland. An illustration of his schedule is seen on one weekend in 1974. On Friday, 1 November, he preached at All Saints' Church, Waterside in Derry. Sunday, 3 November, saw him participate in two services: a youth service (where as chairman of the Church of Ireland Youth Council) he gave the address; and another service where he also

preached. On other occasions, he was the guest of honour at a prize day at Portora, and preached at Knocknagoney in his old parish in Belfast in the presence of a paramilitary-style band of men wearing earrings, sunglasses and football jerseys.

A controversy erupted briefly in the media in Limerick in 1973, concerning the sale by the Limerick Protestant Young Men's Association (LPYMA) of disused sports grounds to Limerick Corporation. The Corporation made an offer which was not found acceptable by the LPYMA, which then applied for planning permission to use the site for housing development. When the Corporation refused to designate it for this purpose, the Association appealed to the Minister for Local Government, James Tully (a TD for Limerick). Representations were made through the Minister for the Gaeltacht, Tom O'Donnell TD. Minister Tully approved planning permission for the site, which had the effect of appreciating its former value and resulted in the Corporation paying £40,000 for the site. Allegations were made that the price had been inflated by almost ten times its former value as a result of the planning permission, *The Sunday Independent* dubbing the affair a 'mini Watergate scandal'.

The Limerick Leader ran a story headed 'Bishop: I contacted Alderman Coughlan' claiming that Donald as Bishop of Limerick had acknowledged contacting Alderman Stephen Coughlan TD with a view to the LPYMA getting a 'reasonable return' for their ground. The article claimed that the bishop, in reply to questions submitted by journalist Billy Kelly, had said that he had made representations to Minister Tully, Minister O'Donnell, Alderman Coughlan and other members and officials of Limerick Corporation on the matter, adding that he 'did not want to be drawn into any political controversy in this matter'.[16]

A few days later, the paper published a letter from Donald, stating that he did not discuss the issue with Stephen Coughlan at any time prior to the Minister granting the application [for planning permission for housing].[17] Coughlan himself had denied leading any deputation or doing anything other than passing on representations 'in the normal routine manner'.[18] The affair appeared to fizzle out almost as quickly as it had begun, the Limerick City Manager stating that the price had been quoted at £45,000 eighteen months previously, and that he considered the purchase figure of £40,000 to be reasonable.[19] The journalist, accepting Donald's clarification, said the misunderstanding would not have arisen had the bishop been more specific in his replies to questions in the first place. It was possibly a disconcerting experience for Donald, and may have instilled in him a certain wariness of the media.

Donald's Catholic counterpart as Bishop of Limerick initially was his next-door neighbour, Dr Henry Murphy, succeeded in July 1974 by the conservative Dr Jeremiah Newman (whose personality was austere compared to Murphy's). In Kerry, he made the acquaintance of the colourful Bishop Eamon Casey. Donald and Casey commenced their respective stewardships of Kerry within a fortnight of each other, and would ultimately leave within a fortnight of each other, after tenures of six years. He enjoyed friendly relations with Casey,[20] but perceived in him a certain restlessness and difficulty in relaxing. On one occasion, he was a guest at lunch in Casey's house and met Annie Murphy, whom Casey introduced as his 'American cousin'. He found the Catholic bishop to be 'very generous, he gave a lovely dinner every year for the Church of Ireland clergy and we came to his house'. Casey would in turn be invited to the diocesan dinner held by the Church of Ireland. On one occasion, it seems Casey requested the use of an office in the Church of Ireland Hall in Tralee, as he lacked an office in the town himself. Donald readily agreed, but was left bemused when Casey publicly inaugurated the use of the office with a Catholic blessing ceremony in the presence of the press. Donald made the acquaintance of Cardinal William Conway during interchurch discussions on mixed marriage (as the working group on which they both served met on a number of occasions in the North). He found it interesting to observe how even the more evangelical Protestant representatives in the North seemed to relate socially on a far closer basis to Conway then he (Donald) did as a 'liberal Protestant' from the South. 'They all knew him as Bill and roared laughing at Belfast jokes I couldn't even understand.'

An occasion of civic and ecumenical celebration for the people of Kerry was the visit on 12 July 1974 of the President of Ireland, Mr Erskine Childers, to attend the rededication of St James's Church in Dingle following a programme of renovation, repair and redecoration. According to Donald, there had been problems with the spire of the church, and the architect advised it be taken down. Services in Irish were occasionally held there. The sexton employed at St James was a former Roman Catholic priest and the church had a 'vast' graveyard, where both Catholics and Protestants were buried. On one occasion, instigated by 'some fanatic', some children had broken the windows of the church, and Donald as bishop was called down. A local resident vowed 'we'll put all these windows back' and this was in fact done within a week.

Erskine Childers was the second member of the Church of Ireland to hold the office of President (the first was the very first holder of the office, Douglas Hyde, a member of Cumann Gaelach na hEaglaise). A civic dinner given in the President's honour by the people of Dingle was attended by representatives of church and state including Bishop Casey. Praising the work of the local minister, the Rev. Trevor Sullivan, Donald signalled the intention that in future the church would be used for cultural purposes, lectures and exhibitions, but this would be no innovation – the medieval churches had been the centre of cultural activities, and their restriction to liturgical purposes came later. Taking up the theme, President Childers, speaking the same evening, stated that the church, as reconstructed, symbolised for him his most important objective as President – to encourage community consciousness in which all of the people and the Christian churches would participate.[21] St James's continues to be an important cultural venue in Dingle and musical sessions in the church have been broadcast on RTÉ, the national television service.

The nation was shocked and saddened just four months after the church's rededication, when the President suffered a massive heart attack while delivering a speech at the Royal College of Physicians in Dublin on 16 November 1974. He died soon afterwards in hospital.[22] The state funeral took place in St Patrick's Cathedral, Dublin, and a memorial service was held subsequently in St Mary's Cathedral, Limerick, at which Donald gave the address. Replying to Donald's message of sympathy, the President's widow Rita noted that 'the tragedy is so much more than his family's: I grieve for the sense of loss which so many of the people of Ireland seem to feel, and I share your hope that the direction to Irish life which he gave will not be lost.'[23] It is believed that Childers may have tried to play a behind-the-scenes role in trying to ease the Northern Ireland conflict. In 2011, his daughter Nessa recalled a secret meeting which she had witnessed between her father and former Northern Ireland Prime Minister Terence O'Neill at Áras an Uachtaráin.[24]

The Irish language
His time as Bishop of Limerick, Ardfert and Aghadoe afforded Donald the opportunity to deepen his connections with Irish language and culture. In November 1970, shortly after his arrival in the dioceses, he gave an interview in Irish to the writer Mainchín Seoighe, which featured prominently on the editorial page of the *Irish Press* newspaper. The article ranged over his Scottish ancestry and the Gaelic origins of his surname, his upbringing in Dublin and time spent in Belfast, Enniskillen and Wales, as well as his early encounters with the language.

It recounted how, during his time in St Mark's in Belfast in the early 1950s, he had made the acquaintance of a small number of Irish speakers, *seanliobrálaithe* (old liberals) among Belfast's Protestant community, whose open-mindedness and live-and-let-live attitude had impressed him (an indication perhaps of a more relaxed attitude to matters of cultural identity which had existed in sectors of Northern Protestantism before the polarising consequences of the Troubles took hold from the 1970s onwards). Donald expressed the view that Irish unity was probably closer at that point (November 1970) than at any time since the foundation of the two states on the island.

Recalling holidays he and Nancy had taken in Inis Oírr, he expressed the wish to send his own children to the Gaeltacht at an early age, so that they could achieve a good *blas* ('taste') and knowledge of the language. However, he also hoped that they would learn French and German and spend some time in the countries where those languages are spoken. He recalled how, on a recent visit to Kerry, he had called to see Kruger Kavanagh with whom he had lodged on holidays in Dún Chaoin during his student days, and how Kruger, who had not seen him for more than twenty years, instantly recognised him. When asked what type of Ireland he would like to see in the future, Donald responded: 'It is my hope and my wish to see a united Ireland, North and South united in one country, a country in which each would have freedom to live their life according to their own beliefs and will, without threats from clergy of any denomination.'

The new bishop's engagement with cultural life in the dioceses was widely noted and appreciated. Shortly after his arrival, while still resident in the Ardhu Hotel, he hosted the Irish language writer Séamus Ó Cinnéide (Irish language columnist with *The Limerick Leader*) and the Bunratty Castle actor Jim Queally for coffee, and readily agreed to their request to make the disused church of St Munchin available for the Limerick Strawmen's *Spirit of Christmas* production. In Spring 1971, Donald spoke knowledge-ably on the literature and folklore of Scottish Gaelic at a celebration of Irish and Scottish Gaelic poetry featuring Somhairle Mac Gill Eathain, Ruairí MacThomáis and Domhnall MacAmhlaigh, among other guests and musicians. He delighted the Scottish guests and local Irish speakers with his talk.

When the renowned composer Seán Ó Riada was ill in hospital in 1971, Donald wrote to him, and shortly after his death hastened from an engagement in Dublin to attend a tribute in his honour in Limerick. While he had only made Ó Riada's acquaintance a short period prior to his death, he spoke appreciatively of the visit of his famous choir, *Cór Chúil*

Aodha, to the little church at Kilmalkeader on the Dingle peninsula, and Seán's promise to return any time that Donald requested.[25] Among Donald's other Irish cultural engagements,[26] he made the two hundred and seventy mile trip to Gaoth Dóbhair in the Donegal Gaeltacht to attend the *Éigse Uladh* festival, conducting *Ùrnaí na Maidne* (Morning Prayers) in the little Church of Ireland church at Bun Beag (where the preacher was the notable Irish scholar Canon Cosslett Quin), and he gave a lecture in Tralee's Benners Hotel to members of Conradh na Gaeilge, entitled 'My Odyssey among the Gaels'.[27]

Donald's son John recalls as a young boy in the early 1970s making visits with his father to the Ó Guithín brothers Seán and Muiris, with whom he had stayed when visiting the Blasket Islands as a student, but who now lived on the mainland in Dún Chaoin since the evacuation of the islands in the 1950s:

> Every holiday, summer and Christmas, we would visit them in their cottage. It was like stepping into a different world, two old men, bachelors, they had no English. One had a few words, as I would have German, but neither were fluent in English … It was hard to make out what they were saying. They had an open fire and a kettle over the fire … The little collie lying under the table, a bottle of whiskey on the table, the alarm clock – that was the furniture! The two brothers would sit at the table, [there were only] a couple of wooden chairs, an earth floor. There was a wooden bench, no couch and the dogs sat under the bench and the Sacred Heart [picture] was illuminated. They had no electricity, no running water. They were very content. [Us] kids would sit there and they would bring glasses of MiWadi, whiskey for the adults. They took us out one fine summer's day in a currach to the Blaskets, early 1970s. I was about seven. The currach was a fairly bouncy craft, it sits very high in the water, [it was] a wooden skeleton with skin [stretched] over it, tarred. It was a dangerous stretch of water between Slea Head and the Blaskets, with strong tidal currents. They were experts. The brothers rowed. A couple of miles. We walked up along an old track.

Donald made the acquaintance of the Dingle-based Roman Catholic priest and Irish language enthusiast Fr Pádraig Ó Fiannachta at a lecture and ecumenical service in Maynooth. Donald also addressed the conference of *Cumann na Sagart*, the Catholic association of Irish-speaking priests, on a few occasions. Ó Fiannachta recalls a relaxed dinner in Maynooth after some such address, early in their acquaintance, at which those present felt very comfortable in Donald's company. *Bhí an bua sin aige* (he had that trait about him). He perceived in Donald a man who had a great understanding of both his own and the Roman Catholic tradition, because of his grounding in both philosophy and theology. On another occasion, Ó Fiannachta recalled going to pay a visit to Bishop Jeremiah Newman in the company of Séamas Ó Cinnéide from *The Limerick Leader*. Newman was preoccupied with other business and able to give them only a little time, so they went next door to call on the Church of Ireland bishop. Donald, who was outside the Bishop's House painting, knew immediately who Ó Cinnéide was, dropped what he was doing, warmly welcomed the pair and invited them inside, where they had '*comhrá andeas*' (a very nice conversation).

There was a Church of Ireland tradition on the Dingle Peninsula. In the early nineteenth century, some proselytising missions of the established church did work in the district. The noted musician and collector of Irish music, Canon James Goodman (1828–96) had been raised in the Ventry area, the Goodmans' property bordering Pádraig Ó Fiannachta's family holding.[28] Kilmalkeader church, as we saw in the first chapter, was located there. In the early 1970s, the rector of Kilcolman, Rev. Chris Warren, who had a keen interest in Irish harp music, would travel there regularly in the summertime, sleeping overnight in a sleeping bag in the vestry. He would read the 8 a.m. service the next morning before a sparse congregation consisting of one or two local families and visitors to the district. It was he who established the keynote *Salmaireacht* service, held each August at Kilmalkeader 'to which Irish speakers from all over the country came, to take part in the service and to hear the famous [Cúil Aodha] choir founded by Seán Ó Riada'.[29]

In 1975, Donald was appointed a member of the state body for the promotion of the Irish language *Bord na Gaeilge*, by the Minister for the Gaeltacht and TD for Limerick, Tom O'Donnell. The chairman was Dr T. K. Whitaker, the talented permanent secretary in the Department of Finance who had played a strong role as economic adviser to Seán Lemass's government in the 1960s (which had set Ireland on the path to economic expansion and an open economy, leading eventually to membership of the European Economic Community). Bord na Gaeilge was not a statutory body at this time, but was constituted to advise the Minister on Irish language matters. Risteard MacGabhann, who served on the first board with Donald, recalls that the bishop was a dedicated participant in its deliberations. A newspaper account of an interview with Donald in 1985 records that, in these early years of the Bord, *naíonraí*, pre-schooling in Irish, was one of the principal issues on its agenda.[30] The Bord was later established on a statutory basis, and operates today on an all-island basis as *Foras na Gaeilge*, having been constituted a cross-border body under the Good Friday Agreement of 1998.

Northern Ireland Troubles

A period of prolonged conflict in Northern Ireland was triggered by loyalist reactions to civil rights demonstrators in the late 1960s. The collapse of the local Unionist administration which had governed since 1922, the institution of direct rule from London and the sending in of the British Army (initially welcomed by some nationalists as protectors against loyalist militias) led to a reaction and the growth of the Provisional Irish Republican Army in the early 1970s. The IRA launched a campaign of bombings and shootings of what it identified as British civil and military targets. As well as British army personnel, these included men and women of the Royal Ulster Constabulary and the Ulster Defence Regiment, the vast majority of whom were drawn from the region's Protestant community, of which Donald had personal experience from his time in Dundela.

Giving the address at a thanksgiving service for a new bridge linking Valentia island on the Iveragh Peninsula with the mainland in 1971, Donald said that what was needed in the country was bridges rather than bombs: 'For too long the people of the North and the people of the South have lived apart, in silent isolation, without serious endeavour to understand the life and thought of the other, and in this isolation fear and suspicion has grown, culminating in the current tragedy.' He expressed the belief that political differences could not be settled by force, as, in accordance with the biblical precept, violence could only beget violence. What was needed was a patient moving forward through an effort of common understanding and appreciation of the other's viewpoint 'with the deliberate intention of building up a fund of common human interest. We must build bridges from ourselves across to our neighbours, running in both directions so that a true community may grow'.[31]

He later recalled in an interview with the author that in the period 1973–74 'when the IRA was very active in Kerry', it 'ruined everything', people were afraid to 'put money into things' there.

The use of the denominational terms 'Catholic' and 'Protestant' on television and radio and in the press in reporting on acts of violence was deplored by Donald in his address to the Ardfert and Aghadoe synod in October 1974. Such usage 'is to imply religious motive to people of violence who were so obviously devoid of even the most rudimentary understanding of what Christianity is'.

Personal contacts in the church community (which spanned the border) could do much: he underlined the responsibility of Christians in the South to encourage through contact, concern and prayers, their fellow Christians in Northern Ireland to withstand violence and choose an equitable form of government, which would respect the legitimate aspirations of all, while noting that southern society was far from perfect. He warned both sides in the North that 'if you go on fighting one another, tooth and nail, all you can expect is mutual destruction.' His words at an ecumenical service for peace and reconciliation in November 1974 have a prophetic ring:

> If there is any lesson to be learned from history, it is that there is an end even to the worst of wars and civil conflicts. There must come a time of reconciliation and peace when the actions of extreme and violent men would seem like an ugly dream. To those who enter into violent conflict, history cautions (*non immemor in pace vivere*), do not forget that at some time you will have to live in peace and face the consequences of your action and live with those with whom you now fight.

An illustration of the climate prevailing in the South in the early to mid 1970s is given by Walton Empey. He had been driving back from a visit to Limerick prison (where, as dean, he had chaplaincy duties) when he encountered a crowd gathered near George's Hotel to listen to a man who was speaking. Rolling down the car window, he recognised the speaker from newspaper photographs as an IRA activist, wanted at the time by police in Northern Ireland. Agitated by this, Empey 'tore up' a sermon he had prepared for a service at the cathedral some hours later, delivering instead a discourse on the theory of the 'just war' and the dangers of violence. This was at a time when it was not customary for members of the religious minority in the Republic to speak out on such matters, for various reasons, including a sense of fear, but the sermon was reported in the newspapers. According to Empey, a Redemptorist priest in Limerick publicly criticised his sermon, labelling him a 'hypocrite who was speaking from a stolen pulpit'. However, Empey recalls Donald being strongly supportive of him. Another indication of the atmosphere prevailing at the time is provided by Empey's recollection that, on Remembrance Sunday each November, some Roman Catholic ex-servicemen (of the British armed forces during the wars) would attend the Eucharist in St Mary's Cathedral, Limerick, wearing their war service medals concealed under their raincoats.

Like Donald, Walton Empey (as dean, and later as bishop himself) strongly encouraged Church of Ireland people to play a more prominent part in public life in the Republic. He felt that Protestants in the South were being tarred with the same brush as their co-religionists in the North, where Ian Paisley's style of firebrand politics and the abuses and discrimination of the Stormont regime dominated press coverage of the province in the early 1970s, and attracted much international criticism. Empey was very conscious of his own Irishness, having served in the FCA, the local defence reserve in the Republic's army, but had a sense that some elements in the South saw Church of Ireland leaders like himself as what he termed 'half-assed Brits'. He felt a duty as a leader to give public voice to the Irish identity and loyalty to the State of members of the Church of Ireland.[32] He believes that Donald gave public and practical expression to this identity by his deep interest and involvement in Irish language matters.

Following the escalation of the Northern Ireland Troubles in the 1970s, Limerick prison changed from the relaxed environment described earlier to a maximum security régime, housing many Republican paramilitaries. The women's section housed the noted Republican activist and English heiress Rose Dugdale. On 26 April 1974, she had taken part in a raid at Russborough House, Co. Wicklow, the home of Sir Alfred Beit. The gang had pistol-whipped Sir Alfred and his wife before tying and gagging them. They then stole nineteen Old Masters valued at eight million pounds (including paintings by Gainsborough, Rubens, Vermeer and Goya). Dugdale was at the time pregnant with the child of another Republican activist Eddie Gallagher, and gave birth to his son Ruairí in prison in December 1974. The dean, as rector of Limerick city parish, was Church of Ireland chaplain to the prison and Donald recalls an anecdote concerning an encounter there between Walton Empey and Dugdale. 'And what [denomination] do you represent?' was the question fired at Empey by the prisoner. 'I'm an Anglican,' replied the chaplain. 'Well that's too bad, because I'm a Baptist!' Dugdale retorted (in fact, the family were believed to be Anglican).

The father of Dugdale's child, Eddie Gallagher was one of a four-member IRA gang which kidnapped the Dutch industrialist and Managing Director of Limerick's Ferenka factory, Dr Tiede Herrema, on his way to work on 3 October 1975. Herrema, his wife and their two younger sons Idza and Harm had moved to Ireland in September 1973 and were part of the worshipping community at St Mary's Cathedral, their sons attending Villiers School. The family was friendly with the Cairds. Herrema had been active in the Dutch resistance to the Nazis during the Second World War. His status as manager of a large multinational corporation was hoped to bring international pressure to bear on the government to yield to the kidnappers' demands: the release of three republican prisoners, including Dugdale.[33] The kidnapping attracted huge international media attention. In its immediate aftermath, Donald's

Catholic counterpart in Limerick, Bishop Newman, made contact asking what could the bishops do? Donald suggested a joint public statement pointing out the dangerous consequences for public life in Ireland of such actions, and the pair spent a night at the Catholic bishop's residence drafting a statement expressing 'dismay and revulsion'.[34]

Some time afterwards, Donald answered the telephone to Archbishop Alan Buchanan of Dublin. Buchanan said that he wanted Donald to pick him up at the See House in Dublin and come with him to the Dutch embassy to see what they could do to help matters. Buchanan had served as a chaplain with the parachute regiment during the Second World War, and was part of a group which landed at Arnhem in the occupied Netherlands. Buchanan survived and was taken prisoner by the Germans. As chaplain, he could have secured his own freedom but opted to remain with the other captured soldiers. As a retired Army officer, he had returned for several years to Arnhem to take part in the annual commemorative march into town. Unknown to him, Herrema's wife had served as a town councillor in Arnhem, and had also participated in that march. Donald drove to Dublin, collected Buchanan and headed for the Dutch embassy. On arrival, the ambassador greeted them, and informed them that Mrs Herrema had just returned from a visit home to Holland, where she had gone with her sons to seek political intervention. Donald recounts that it was there that Buchanan put a very direct proposal to the Garda Superintendent present: he wanted to offer himself as a captive in place of Herrema, believing that this gesture was owed to this great man of Holland who had taken part so bravely in the resistance, and had been an important contributor to business in Ireland. The Superintendent strongly advised Buchanan not to go public with this offer, informing the group that the case was in fact close to resolution at that point. Mrs Herrema then came in, and recognised Buchanan as the retired officer who had marched with her in Arnhem years before. It was a good moment in an extremely tense situation. Eighteen days after his kidnap, Herrema was finally traced to an end-of-terrace house in Monasterevin, where he was being held by Eddie Gallagher and another gang member, Marion Coyle. A siege there lasted a further seventeen days, ending unexpectedly and peacefully on the night of 7 November with the surrender of Gallagher and Coyle. The latter was subsequently housed in the women's facility at Limerick prison, where Dugdale was herself held. In his address to the Limerick diocesan synod, Donald noted that the crime had 'evoked the strongest national reaction in protest and in expression of sympathy for the wife and family of a very brave man'.

From 1971 until 1974, Donald served as a member of the Broadcasting Review Committee, appointed by the Minister for Posts and Telegraphs, Gerry Collins. Its brief was to 'review the progress of the television and sound broadcasting services since the enactment of the Broadcasting Authority Act 1960 … and to make any recommendations considered appropriate …' Among other members were Justice George Murnaghan (chairman); Donal O'Herlihy, Roman Catholic Bishop of Ferns; Bryan McMahon, the novelist and teacher (with whom Donald frequently travelled from Kerry to Dublin to attend the meetings); Donal Nevin, General Secretary of the Irish Congress of Trade Unions and T.K. Whitaker, Governor of the Central Bank. By the time the committee issued its final report in May 1974, a new Minister, Conor Cruise O'Brien, was in office.

Covering a wide range of broadcasting issues, the Broadcasting Review Committee's most controversial findings were its criticisms of RTÉ's coverage of Northern Ireland affairs. The report stated that though

> much of the reporting and commentary, particularly in the past two years or so, has been well balanced, the committee cannot regard RTÉ's treatment of Northern Ireland affairs in the period since 1968 as having conformed to an adequate standard of objectivity and impartiality.[35]

The earlier period referred to (1968–72) in fact coincided with the nationalist civil rights demonstrations and their forceful suppression by the Royal Ulster Constabulary, but also with the emergence of a campaign of bombings and killings by the Provisional IRA. The review committee's report came at a time of tension in relation to RTÉ's coverage of Northern Ireland. An order under section 31 of the 1960 Broadcasting Act had been made in 1971 by Minister Collins, instructing the organisation not to broadcast matter calculated to promote the objectives of any organisation engaged in or advocating violence as a means to attaining objectives. Its authority had been sacked in 1972 for not exerting sufficient discipline on broadcasters in this regard, after reporter Kevin O'Kelly interviewed the chief of staff of the IRA, Sean MacStiofáin, and included a report of the interview in a news programme. The committee's findings were criticised by the lead writer in *The Irish Times* in 1974 in an editorial headlined 'The Old Foolishness'. Surprise was expressed that 'such strictures should be made in a considered report of this kind without being backed up with some evidence or example'. Noting that objectivity is a criterion to be approached with some caution for those who work in newspapers or television, it queried the objectivity of those who sat on the committee on some issues, observing in relation to Donald and Bishop O'Herlihy: 'how objective are the two bishops on such questions as contraception and shared schools …?'[36] The editor of *The Irish Times* was Douglas Gageby. He had been an intelligence officer in the Irish Army, later moving to journalism, and was widely credited as editor with effecting the paper's transition from a largely Unionist organ to a mainstream Irish paper of record.

In 1976, Minister Conor Cruise O'Brien issued a new order under section 31, banning spokespersons for named organisations (including Sinn Féin, which was closely aligned to the IRA). This directive would remain in place throughout the period of the Northern Ireland Troubles, not being rescinded until 1994. Although seen as necessary for public order and security reasons, the ban was criticised for helping to foster a perceived climate in the RTÉ newsroom whereby issues and grievances in the nationalist community were not given comprehensive or balanced coverage in the 1980s.

Contributions to the Church nationally

The General Synod in 1971 appointed Donald a member of the Select Committee on the Revision of the Canons of the Church of Ireland, and he took over the chairing of this committee from 1973 – no small responsibility entrusted to a junior bishop. The previous chairman, Bishop Hanson of Clogher, had left to take up a professorship of theology in Manchester. The task of the committee was editing, revising and updating the canons – a substantive legal corpus which set out the rules for the liturgy of the church, including the conducting of services, ecclesiastical apparel, duties of clergy and the use of churches. The committee sought to recast the canons in an affirmative way, which would permit clergy and laity to do certain things, rather than set out a series of prohibitions as heretofore.

Presenting the committee's report to General Synod in 1973, Donald underlined the intention of the revision: 'to emphasise the positive and pastoral nature and intention of the canons and to remove the stringently juridical aspect which made the canons previously read like a set of Levitical prohibitions'. Recalling the last occasion when the canons had come dramatically before the Synod – the repealing of the famous canon 36 forbidding a cross on the communion table in 1964 – Donald observed that 'the long shadows cast by the bitter controversion of the mid nineteenth century in the Anglican Church were seen receding and allowing our generation to make its own decision in the light that we at present enjoy.'[37]

There was some animated debate at the 1973 Synod, one Northern speaker suggesting that 'just because some minority was breaking the rules was no reason for changing them'. The essence of the differences lay between those who held a 'low church' view in strict conformity with the tradition of the reformed church, and those who wished to see a recovery of elements of catholic practice. Captain A. Acheson of Dromore said he agreed with the affording of liberty of conscience to those of the catholic tradition but warned 'lest their liberty become another man's bondage'. Dean Tom Salmon of Christ Church Cathedral referred to the Church of Ireland as the 'ancient Catholic and apostolic Church' and said members were committed to hold in tension principles which are both Catholic and Protestant:

> Truth is something larger and more beautiful than can be conceived by any of our poor minds, much less comprehended by them. To seek to crystallise for all time the canons of 1870 as the norms of the church is to deny the very principles [on which] those who framed them based them.

The secretary to the committee was Canon Leslie Enright from Limerick, who did the detailed textual work to reflect its will. The committee brought its work back to General Synod in 1974 with a new text completely revising chapter IX of the constitution of the Church of Ireland. One outstanding point concerned the possibility of a stole being worn by a clergyman, and Donald, introducing the bill, said discussion on this point had been 'out of all proportion' to its significance. The house of bishops had affirmed that no particular doctrinal significance was attached to either a scarf or a stole.[38] The synod unanimously agreed to repeal the original chapter and replace it with the new text.

In 1973, Donald was appointed as the representative of the house of bishops on the council of the School of Divinity at Trinity College Dublin, again succeeding Bishop Hanson. The School of Divinity was responsible for the academic qualification of candidates for the ministry. At this time, under College statutes, anyone holding a professorship in the school was required to be an Anglican. As the school operated under the governance of the board of Trinity College, and the University was responsible for its academic validation, Trinity was anxious to have this denominational requirement relaxed. The wording of the statutes were recast in such a way as to allow for a more liberal interpretation, which permitted the school to secure the services of academics from other traditions where they had higher qualifications than members of the Church of Ireland. It was this change which allowed it in due course to appoint the theologian Seán Freyne as Professor of Theology. Donald in fact was to be the final nominee of the house of bishops appointed to the Divinity School council, which ceased to operate after his tenure.[39]

A move to Meath

In September 1976, news came that Donald had been elected bishop of the newly-united dioceses of Meath and Kildare. A civic reception was hosted by Killarney Urban District Council to mark his departure, a watercolour painting of Ross Castle by artist Sean O'Connor being presented to him. Paying tribute to Donald, Msgr J.J. Murphy, Catholic dean of Kerry, said that he had won the esteem, regard and affection of Kerry people, and this was not an easy thing to do as Kerry people do not always wear their hearts on their sleeves. That he had so succeeded was a great tribute to him. Expressing thanks, Donald noted that technically he was going from Kerry, but his heart would remain in the county and in fact he would be returning quite frequently as he was building his only home at Camp.[40]

In 1975 it had been decided to join the dioceses of Limerick, Ardfert and Aghadoe with Killaloe, and on the appointment of Donald's successor as Bishop of Limerick, the diocese duly expanded, resulting in a unit that now stretched from Kenmare in Co. Kerry to a point ten miles short of Galway city.[41] This was part of wide ranging proposals put forward by the Episcopal Reorganisation Committee, featuring the reduction in the number of Church of Ireland bishops from fourteen to twelve, and also uniting Kildare with Meath.

CHAPTER FIVE

Bishop of Meath and Kildare
(1976–1985)

Enthronement

Coinciding with Donald's arrival in 1976, the diocese of Kildare, previously annexed to Dublin and Glendalough, was being unified with Meath for the first time. Donald's translation meant he would be the first bishop of vast and sprawling united dioceses of some 2,800 square miles,[1] extending from Mountmellick, Co. Laois northwards to Kingscourt, Co. Cavan, and from Athlone, Co. Westmeath eastwards to Julianstown, Co. Meath. As well as a few larger towns such as such as Athlone, the territory was dotted with small towns and innumerable historic sites such as Tara (which had associations with St Patrick) and Clonmacnoise, the early Christian monastic centre by the Shannon (associated with St Ciarán).

The Bishop of Meath and Kildare is traditionally one of the senior bishops in the Church of Ireland, sharing the title of 'Most Reverend' only with the primatial bishops of Armagh and Dublin. Meath had been part of the northern province of Armagh in the church, but was now coming under the metropolitan jurisdiction of Dublin's Archbishop.

It was while taking part in the blessing of a new mental hospital in Killarney, jointly with Bishop Eamon Casey, that Donald was called to the telephone, whereupon the Archbishop of Dublin informed him that he had been the unanimous choice of the house of bishops. While Donald was aware that he was under consideration, his election nonetheless came as a surprise to him:

> I had asked the Archbishop for time to consider his proposal, but in fact I already knew that a primitive sense of duty would not allow me to refuse to implement the clear, indeed I believe, unanimous intention of the General Synod expressed in the bill … the moral, if there is one to be inferred from the story, is that reports of commissions appointed by the General Synod need to be studied urgently and in detail, because much sooner than expected they may impinge radically on one's own life.[2]

In his enthronement address at St Patrick's Cathedral, Trim, on the banks of the River Boyne, Donald noted that, relative to the dioceses' territorial expanse,

> the Church of Ireland community was small and in places widely scattered, but this must not breed a spirit of dejection or lead to a policy of withdrawal; it should rather lead to a determination to play the fullest part in the Christian community of which it was a significant part and where participation was not only expected but welcomed … Irish society, Christian for 1,500 years, has not yet reached the point of cynicism were numbers alone can determine the morality of an issue. We must take a full part in the community … Our young people should be encouraged to take a full part in the civic life of this diocese through all the agencies of local government.[3]

His call for full participation by members of the Church of Ireland, especially its young people, in every aspect of life of community life was repeated when taking his seat in the other cathedral of the united dioceses, St Brigid's in Kildare. In his sermon there, delivered in the presence of representatives of the national army (the military camp at the Curragh being situated within the diocese) and An Garda Síochána (and conscious no doubt of his role as chairman of the Church of Ireland Youth Council and vice chairman of the National Youth Council), he declared 'to live by the principles of our faith is not to alienate ourselves from the [wider] community.' Acknowledging the sense of loss attending the transfer of Kildare out of the episcopal see of Dublin and Glendalough, he said that

> the ability to promote change and to accept change is a sign of a living body and the ability to do this with grace and caring is the sign of a living church. My hope is that the union … will not be merely legal and formal but vital and effective, reflected in renewed fellowship and mutual commitment and felt in every family and by every individual in the diocese.

Five priorities for Meath and Kildare, described in 1984, sum up the key themes of his episcopacy there: (1) maintaining and developing its educational projects, including adult education; (2) bringing the Christian faith into the centre of people's lives, with an emphasis on its relevance to complex modern problems; (3) youth programmes for the church's youth, urban and rural; (4) dealing effectively with the problems of interchurch marriage and (5) generating sufficient confidence in our people to take a full part in the life of the nation, to contribute to community discussion and debate on political, social and ethical topics the insights and points of view of our members, so that the majority may be kept in mind that there are minority interests and points of view to be taken into account.[4]

Appointed directly to follow his sermon at the enthronement was the patriotic hymn composed after Church of Ireland disestablishment in 1871, *Lift thy banner, Church of Erin*:

Ages pass, yet with Saint Patrick / Firm we hold the faith of God, / With his 'Breastplate' armed, we follow / Where the Saints and Martyrs trod. Brave Columba's fearless labors, / Brigid's lifelong work of love, / Teach us to endure the hardness, / Till we reach the rest above.

Ivy House and Family Affairs

An important early issue was the identification of a suitable See House for the bishop and his family, as Donald's immediate predecessor had chosen to live in a vacant rectory in Meath. All three Caird children were attending St Michael's national school in Limerick, and Nancy and they remained there for several months while the task of locating and preparing the new house was under way. Donald took a room at the Divinity Hostel in Braemor Park, Rathgar in nearby Dublin. This was to become his domestic base for eight months, 'running the dioceses from boxes by his bed'. He had no full-time secretary, but could avail himself of the Representative Church Body typing pool. He managed to travel to Limerick on only a handful of occasions during this time. It was on one of these journeys that he had a car crash near Kildare. Just outside the town, a car suddenly came down the main road. This was driven by a man coming from a wedding in Kildare, who it seems had fallen asleep at the wheel, resulting in his car driving into Donald's and pushing it against the gates of the National Stud. The entire front of Donald's car was crashed in, and he suffered bruising to his legs and feet. The man's friends came and took him away. The proprietor of a nearby garage arrived at the scene and offered Donald another car in which to complete his journey. Ann recalls the family being very upset by this incident, combined as it was with the stress of being unable to move to Leixlip.

Eventually, Ivy House, a handsome Georgian house dating from 1730 and fronting on to the main street of Leixlip in Co. Kildare, was identified and in June 1977 the Cairds moved in. The children would attend St Andrew's national school in Lucan, a particular wrench for Ann and John, who were in higher classes and had already made their friends in Limerick. Ann says, 'I remember we were devastated moving. [We were leaving] all our friends … school, parties … a beautiful house, gardens. My world … fell apart when we moved. Joining school in sixth class was a difficult time, the others all knew each other.' The change of schooling proved an easier adjustment for the younger daughter, Helen.

In Limerick, the family had enjoyed being part of a closely knit Church of Ireland community within the city, where the children were together in school, in the choir, in cubs or scouts or Girls' Friendly Society, or taking classes in the Municipal School of Music. Moving to a small village represented quite a change, even if it was one located not too far from Dublin.

By road, Ivy house is approached from Dublin by passing over the Salmon Leap Bridge at the entrance to Leixlip, and taking an immediate left into the main street/Mall: 'if you didn't [take an immediate left], you go into [our] dining room!' as Nancy put it. Lorries frequently jackknifed due to the sharp turn, spilling their contents, including occasionally cattle, onto the bridge! Despite its prominent frontage on the main street, the house enjoyed a pleasant courtyard and secluded walled-in gardens to the rear with fruit trees, lawns, flower beds, shrubs and a vegetable patch, making it suitable for children and providing another gardening project for Nancy. The house took its name from a vast growth of ivy on the external front wall. One night there was a heavy snowstorm and a tremendous noise woke the family. They thought an aeroplane had crashed into the front garden. They went outside and saw that the ivy had fallen from the wall due to the weight of the snow, carrying some of the bricks with it: 'at four feet [thick], the ivy was nearly as solid as the wall', recalls Donald.

Because Leixlip was actually located in the diocese of Glendalough, Donald was in the situation of being 'a cuckoo in the nest', living in the diocese of a neighbouring bishop. Leixlip Castle had been the country residence of the Lord Lieutenant in olden times, and with its charming river and rural surroundings, provided a welcome break from the 'stench of Dublin', the court moving out there in the summer months. St Mary's, the Church of Ireland church, had a pleasant situation bordered by the river on one side and the Mall on the other. The little village had a small population at this time (which was before the arrival of the multinational Intel computer company) and the genial Church of Ireland bishop with the American wife and three children became a familiar sight. The Cairds came to love the village. Their daughter Helen recalls happy weekends playing in the garden of Ivy House, remarking twenty-five years later that she still dreams about it. Her brother John kept bees in the garden there.

Once installed in Ivy House, Donald was able to retain a part-time secretary, Mrs Chromer, who came in each day to attend to his correspondence and manage his diary. Nancy had a busy schedule, accompanying Donald to various diocesan events and carrying out some official duties of her own as the wife of the bishop, as well as ferrying the children to various activities, 'doing everything to enhance my father's position ...,' recalls Ann. She retained some domestic help for general housekeeping. On one occasion, the Cairds were expecting a large number of clergymen of the dioceses and their wives to dinner, when a power cut left them without power. Directly across the street lived the elderly Bewley couple (of the family which owned the famous Dublin coffee shops), who came to the rescue. Old Mr Bewley stood directing traffic in the centre of the main street as food was brought across the street to be cooked, and carried back to Ivy House.

Dogs were a consistent feature of the Cairds' family life over the years. Ann recalls that they had male dogs until they moved to Leixlip, when they got a female. 'She was hard work and would bite ... my mother got a male puppy to see would it soften her but she terrorised the poor creature! Eventually [we] gave him away to somebody else. We kept her. She would have to be put away when visitors arrived.' Ann and John soon started secondary school at Kings Hospital, Palmerstown, where they were able to settle and make new friends in the six hundred pupil school (John boarded there from his second year, Ann from her fifth year). On Sundays, while Donald customarily visited different parishes throughout the united dioceses, Nancy and the children attended church in nearby Maynooth or in the Dunboyne union of parishes, thereby getting to know people in these areas. This level of friendship and intimacy is made possible by the small, and familiar (and even at times familial) world of the Church of Ireland community in the Republic.

Ann reflected on being the young daughter of a bishop:

As a small child, I was not even remotely aware. It was a huge privilege – we lived in beautiful places. I now love old houses and gardens. Friends would come over and say 'wow, you live in a mansion.' We were fully aware we didn't own it but were minding it. I don't remember any negativity or being teased. [It was a case of] 'that's what she does.' [We went] to church a lot as kids ... when we moved to Leixlip, we would tend to, on Sunday, accompany my Mum with Dad to whatever parish – he was going all over the place, so we would go for a time. I remember it [as being] a bit tedious as a teen. There was a perception you were extra holy.

I was never particularly *bad*, I probably made the point in religion or scripture class of *not* doing well, I felt that it was overkill at that stage ... I would feel now [as an adult] I would have a very poor understanding of the Bible and where the books come from ... but I had a fairly normal upbringing. My parents were easygoing, they never rammed [religion] down my throat. Going to church was more solidarity [within] the family.

The Cairds continued to take summer holidays in Camp, Co. Kerry. With perhaps the glow of nostalgia, their daughter, Helen, recalls 'fantastic weather' there, her father doing 'a lot of reading'. Donald had a wide reading selection, including Irish language books, biographies (and a particular fascination with Winston Churchill according to Helen), books on heritage as well as material on philosophy. The Cairds might also take a boat trip out to the Blasket Islands, walking around the island, and climbing its hills. Helen relished 'the feeling of being out on the islands, the energy, the boat ride out. My parents used to take us out on a currach there – a very gentle boat ride, much nicer than the ferries, with no fumes'. When in Kerry around Christmas time, Donald would call in to see Seán and Muiris Ó Guithín and their sister Máire, Donald bringing a bottle of whiskey and conversing exclusively in Irish with his hosts.

Kenneth Milne recalls a long weekend spent down in Camp as a house guest of Donald. In the evenings, the bishop set out on a walk and called in on various neighbours there. He would

go in and sit down, and be totally at home in that milieu, and they all knew about him and they would ask about each other's families. He melted into the landscape there as one of themselves – that surprised me. I knew him in a more formal Dublin setting which he fitted into too.

However, the Kerry weather was not always reliable. On one occasion, on their way back to Dublin, the Cairds called to see Walton Empey, Donald's successor as Bishop of Limerick. 'You're looking fine, you're sunburnt' observed Empey. 'No,' replied Donald, 'this isn't sunburn, it's rust! It rained the whole time!'[5]

The dioceses

Kildare's separation from Dublin raised the question of how it would support itself financially. In a letter addressed to the people of his diocese in June 1977, Donald set out the challenge with directness:

The diocese of Kildare consists of ten unions of parishes, with ten incumbents, together with the chaplaincy at the Curragh camp. The total Church of Ireland population of Kildare diocese is 2,556 persons. 1,680 can be reckoned to be in the age group which bears the effective financial support of the parishes … from first of January 1978, the minimum [cost of each incumbent] will be at least £4,350, so that the overall cost of maintaining the clergy of the diocese of Kildare … will be not less than £43,500.

As no more than £4,500 would come from the Representative Church Body, he calculated that this would leave £39,000 to be raised locally – requiring a contribution of at least £50 from each adult to cover parishes' main expenses (excluding rectory and church maintenance and contributions to missionary and charitable work):

> But wealth is not evenly distributed, some families have small incomes and heavy outgoings, some of our people live on the old-age pension, some are unemployed, some live on sick benefit or on the blind pension. So to maintain the average, the burden necessarily falls on those who are better equipped to undertake it. The words of St Paul to the Galatians 'bear ye one another's burdens and so fulfil the law of Christ', find a peculiar significance in the context of our mutual responsibility to help in the maintenance of our church.

Addressing his diocesan synod in November 1978, Donald noted that since the reduction in the number of archbishoprics and bishoprics in the Church of Ireland by virtue of the Church Temporalities Act 1833, the Church's diocesan structure had remained remarkably stable. Since then, the Church had retained the same number of archbishops and bishops even though its population had declined by one third. Meath and Kildare together consisted of twenty-eight parochial units with twenty-eight incumbents ministering to congregations in more than one hundred churches each Sunday. There were nineteen primary schools (catering for some one thousand children) and one secondary school (catering for some three hundred). He estimated the Church population of the united dioceses at seven thousand.

Effective means of communication linking the various parishes were a vital element in fostering a sense of common purpose, and a new diocesan magazine encompassing Meath and Kildare was set for launch in January 1978. In his first 'bishop's letter' in the new publication, Donald reminded readers that:

historians and archivists treat diocesan magazines with seriousness and respect as a rich source of vital material for social, economic and other types of history but they are of much more than historical interest, they record the day-to-day, week to week events that constitute the life of the community parish by parish, the ongoing life that impinges more closely on us than perhaps any of the great world events which receive treatment in the national press ...[6]

Such diocesan magazines continue to provide an illuminating picture for the interested observer of day-to-day Church of Ireland life in parishes and dioceses up and down the country.

The Hill of Tara, ancient seat of the High Kings of Ireland, was one of the foremost sites of historical and archaeological interest in Meath and Kildare. According to tradition St Patrick lit a paschal fire on the Hill of Slane, which could be seen from Tara, in contravention of the law at the time. The picturesque Church of Ireland church of St Patrick is located on the hilltop, and an open-air service was held there each summer. The church features stained-glass windows by Catherine O'Brien of the stained glass workshop *An Túr Gloine* (O'Brien was a worshipper at St Bartholomew's, the Anglo–Catholic church at Ballsbridge in Dublin). 'When the sun comes in,' says Donald, 'it catches the light of the window and spreads it all over the church; beautiful dark blues and reds; it's magnificent.'

Another highlight for the Church of Ireland community in the midlands region was the open-air service held each July (since 1952) at the monastery of Clonmacnoise on the River Shannon. The monastic site (situated within the Church of Ireland parish of Athlone), was founded by St Ciarán in the year 545, and now consists of several ruined churches, high crosses and grave slabs. One roofed structure, Templeconnor, in the care of the Church of Ireland, holds about sixty people. The annual service would take place out of doors, with the large congregation numbering up to two thousand sitting around the grounds which slope gently down to the river. Clergy from various parts of the diocese would attend, a choir leading the singing. Many farming families would come along bringing flasks and a picnic lunch to enjoy after the service, making a day out of the occasion. One year, the President of Ireland had come to this service, arriving by boat on the majestic River Shannon, accompanied by a flotilla of pleasure boats.[7] An evocative photograph of the annual 'service that commemorates Clonmacnoise as a great medieval centre of holiness and worship' appeared in the National Geographic magazine in November 1978, depicting a windswept Donald striding forward amid the church ruins and round tower, in the classic scarlet chimere and black scarf of an Anglican bishop, clutching his prayer books in one hand and pastoral staff in the other.

Pastoral concerns

For any Church of Ireland bishop, as 'pastor pastorum' of his clergy in the dioceses, concern for them and a faithful recording of their deployments, institutions to parishes, retirements, deaths and other key developments formed a regular theme in synodical and other addresses, as well as in the monthly letter in the diocesan magazine. Dean John Paterson of Kildare (who came to the diocese in 1978)[8] took nine months' sabbatical leave in 1984 to visit India, Iran, Australia and the United States. The announcement of this was used as an opportunity for Donald in his diocesan synod address to express the view that every clergyman, at least once in the course of his ministry, should get such a period of sabbatical leave to see the church in operation in other parts of the world.

On his own role, he expressed the view that a bishop should be a colleague of his clergy rather than a schoolmaster, his function being to help and advise, rather than command and order – he was working with mature and spiritually-minded men (noting the possibility that women might be included later), and should ideally never need to invoke the authority which is given to him, spiritually and legally.

The creation of a laity informed in matters of theology and faith was the focus of a sermon given by Donald at the General Synod service in Dublin's St Patrick's Cathedral in 1978. There was a need for lay people to grow in the faith, and priority had to be placed on their training, education and encouragement. He decried developments in theology over the past quarter of a century whereby, he said, theologians had tried to strain out transcendental elements from the gospel in order to make it more acceptable to what was perceived to be the intellectual expectations of twentieth-century man. The more extreme forms of this movement, under the title of 'the death of God theology' had, he said, invaded news media and received great prominence, in the process losing the subtle and technical elements of theologians' arguments in order to present issues in a popularised fashion. This had a tendency to confuse the faithful. The Church's fundamental duty was to ensure that no generation of Christians would be left victims of a passing theological fashion. This duty could only be discharged if the Church had an effective system of communication and adult education. Referring to a book by the renowned Swiss psychiatrist and psychotherapist Carl Jung, *Modern Man in Search of a Soul*, Donald noted Jung's claim that nearly all those over the age of thirty-five who came to him for advice on the deepest problems of their lives were really searching for a religious answer, and that only this could restore to them the peace and confidence they sought and save them from the chasm of meaningless into which their lives threatened to fall. Jung had been aware of the irony that, in spite of the endeavours of some Christian scholars to remove transcendental and mystical elements from the gospel in order to make it more acceptable to contemporary man, evidence poured in from all sides that people were actually seeking the transcendental and mystical, 'albeit often in the most debased forms of spiritism, occultism and by the use of drugs'.[9]

The problem of unemployment in the Republic was a major concern in 1982 with more than half of the population in the Republic under twenty-five years of age, and more than two hundred thousand unemployed. Donald told his synod that:

> In the range of human experience, perhaps nothing is more deeply felt as the disappointed expectations of youth ... as Christians we have a commitment to help as far as we can those who suffer [unemployment] ... this experience knows no denominational boundaries and our concern must be for the whole of our society in this country, north and south ... wise heads, sympathetic hearts and determined and devoted wills are necessary to meet this challenge.

He established an advisory panel comprising two clergymen and two laypersons (including the director of the state training agency AnCO) to determine the extent of unemployment among young people in the diocese and to advise on ways in which it might be lessened. Interview sessions with unemployed youth were held at a number of venues, and while the problem was found to be less acute (in the Church of Ireland community) than had been expected, Donald reported the project's success in directing more than half of those interviewed into either employment or training schemes.[10]

Another area of pastoral concern on a national level was that of the remarriage in church of divorced people – a topic on which no easy agreement could be found. In November 1979, Donald had set out the crux of the problem:

> The church is faced with a great dilemma whether to condone easy divorce or to adhere to its ancient principle of refusing to remarry in church anyone who has been divorced and risk the danger of acting uncharitably and unjustly towards an innocent Christian and failing to fulfil the

supreme law of love. This is fundamentally a pastoral problem. How to deal in a loving way with those whose marriage has broken down, while yet respecting the words of Christ, the tradition of the church based on these words, and bearing witness of Christian standards to the world. There are many elements to be balanced here.[11]

It would be 1996, after Donald had retired, that 'the regulation of marriage discipline' in the Church to cover such cases would be finally approved at General Synod, requiring clergy to consult with their bishop in every case and seek his advice, and approving a service of preparation to be used by couples in all such cases.

Education

The Church maintained its vital interest in protecting its cherished system of education, key to the Southern minority's sense of identity. 'The secondary education system is denominationally-based and always has been,' Donald told journalist Deaglán de Bréadún in 1984. 'Of the twenty-six counties in the Republic, only eleven have Protestant secondary schools. If Protestants in the other fifteen counties wish to go to secondary school, then they must attend as boarders. This is, of course, very expensive.'[12]

When a system of free secondary education was introduced by education minister Donogh O'Malley in the 1960s, special provision had to be made for Protestant schools by way of a block grant, as most schools were under Roman Catholic management and the Protestant pupils were widely dispersed, meaning they had to travel some distance and board at schools of their own faith tradition (which were fee-paying). The Church of Ireland established a Secondary Education Committee (SEC) in 1965 comprising representatives of schools under Protestant management to organise distribution of the block grant in negotiations with the Department of Education. Donald recalled that Protestant parents with children of appropriate age applied to the committee (which included Presbyterian, Methodist and Quaker members) and their circumstances were assessed.

As chairman of the SEC for many years, having taken over in the 1970s from Bishop Gordon Perdue (who had overseen the rationalisation of the Protestant secondary sector through amalgamation of schools and other measures), Donald had a key role in the management of the block grant. 'We applied the block grant on a very strict basis – it was the income of the parents,' he recalled, in an interview with the author. Parents applied to the committee, making a case for the particular school they selected (for example, siblings of the prospective pupil might already be attending the preferred school). The committee made a decision on grants, and forwarded a list of approved pupils to the school, which passed on the benefit of the block sum it had received by way of a reduction in the fee charged to that pupil.

The committee reported each year to General Synod. 'We did as well as we could operating under the block grant,' Donald states, with some applicants inevitably feeling that they had not received a fair decision. Because of the size of the Church of Ireland community, people might become aware of the representative of the particular school area on the committee, and attempt to petition that person. However, 'the committee was coherent and could see from an informed position.' He instanced two cases where the committee were aware that there was wealth in business assets not declared.

Although there were vocational educational committees established in local areas, which set up secular day-schools, Donald says that 'some parents wanted a more academic orientation'. There had always been a strong Church of Ireland presence in the educational sector, 'and we were proud of educational standards, they constituted an area of concern for the Church of Ireland family'. He also felt that the proportion of Church of Ireland children going on to third level education was higher than the general norm. Four free comprehensive day schools were established under Protestant management; at Ashton in Cork, Mount Temple and Newpark in Dublin, and (in the late 1980s) East Glendalough comprehensive school. These were the only places a sufficient concentration of Protestant pupils could be found to make such day schools viable.

Wilson's Hospital (incorporating Preston School) was the boarding school under Church of Ireland management in the dioceses of Meath and Kildare, located in Multyfarnham, Co. Westmeath. Founded in 1724, the school was co-educational, a Georgian building standing on a site of more than two hundred and fifty acres, with extensive playing fields and recreational facilities. An advisory committee of experts in various fields was appointed in 1978 to review the school's operation and advise on future developments.[13] The first part of a renovation scheme took place in 1981, improving the boarding facilities for the pupils. This was the first stage in a plan to renovate the entire school and add a new teaching block so that the school could increase its capacity to two hundred and fifty or three hundred pupils within the following four or five years. While government assistance would be forthcoming for the building of a teaching block, the improvement to boarding facilities had to be done without state help.

A six-year-old Donald with his father George (left) and mother Emily (centre) on holiday in August 1932.

Donald (right) as a boy, with his friend Cyril Patton.

'Just before time Caird gained an unconverted try.' Donald (right, in the foreground) on the Wesley College rugby team, playing against St Columba's College on 12 February 1941. Wesley carried the day, 22–0. (Copyright courtesy *The Irish Times*)

Muiris, Máire and Seán Ó Guithín pictured outside their house on the Great Blasket Island in the 1940s.

Donald (second from right) with the Ó Guithín brothers and fellow Trinity student Kestor Heaslip on the Great Blasket Island, 1945.

Trinity College Dublin Scholars' Dinner, 1948. Donald Caird is in the back row, second from the right. (Copyright courtesy *The Irish Times*)

Donald walking in the hills as a young man.

Nancy Ballantyne Sharpe as a young woman.

Donald and Nancy's wedding
in Vermont, 12 January 1963.
Nancy's maid of honour,
Harriet Daniels, is pictured to
the left, and Donald's best man,
John Campbell, to the right.

Donald Caird striking the door of St Mary's Cathedral in
Limerick prior to his enthronement as Bishop on 13 October 1970.
(Copyright courtesy Independent newspapers)

A youthful Bishop of
Limerick on holiday in
Ireland with his young
family in 1973.

President Erskine Childers (centre, left) with Donald (centre, right) in Dingle, 12 July 1974, at the reopening of St James's Church after renovations. Pictured also are Bishop of Kerry, Eamon Casey (left) and Mrs Rita Childers (right). (Copyright courtesy *The Kerryman*)

Cardinal Tomás Ó Fiaich (partly visible on the far left) introduces Pope John Paul II to Donald Caird, Bishop of Meath and Kildare, at the Dominican convent, Cabra on 29 September 1979, during the papal visit to Ireland. The Pope and Bishop are smiling after exchanges following the Cardinal's introduction of Donald as a 'rara avis'. (Copyright courtesy Felici Photography, Rome)

Donald Caird as Bishop of Meath and Kildare being presented with a copy of *An Bíobla Naofa* by Msgr Padraig Ó Fiannachta (right).

Donald, wearing his Canterbury cap, reviewing the Irish Army as Bishop of Meath and Kildare.

A caricature of Donald published in *The Sunday Independent* in 1985. (Copyright courtesy Independent newspapers)

Donald as Archbishop of Meath and Kildare in May 1984. (Copyright courtesy *The Irish Times*)

Fellow swimmers from Rathmichael days meet again: President Patrick J. Hillery greets the newly enthroned Archbishop of Dublin in September 1985.

A development fund was established to meet the school's proportion of the overall cost of the renovations and maintenance, and Donald appealed for further support within the diocese, pointing out that the school gave a wonderful service to the Protestant community for the entire country, for a fee which well below that of other Protestant boarding schools. This situation was made possible because of a historic endowment for that purpose and because of the economic and efficient way in which the school was operated. The publication of *Meath and Kildare: An Historical Guide*, edited by Dean John Paterson and illustrated by the Rev. John Flinn, with notes supplied by clergy and pages assembled by parish teams, was hailed by Donald in his 1982 address as 'truly a diocesan effort', with profits from its sale going to the school's development fund.

In 1983, Donald was able to report that the new dormitory block was in place and school numbers were increasing ahead of estimations – now standing at 213 day and boarding pupils. Even such a success had its challenges: a strain was placed on accommodation resources for educational purposes, a problem which could not be addressed until the trustees had managed to clear the debt on the dormitory block. In his final report as bishop to the diocesan synod in 1984, Donald expressed satisfaction at the further growth in pupil numbers. If the physical development of the buildings could keep pace with the increase in pupils, they would already have a school of three hundred pupils, perhaps even four hundred. The first phase of the development plan had largely been completed, and the bulk of the cost of the first phase raised. The diocese would now address itself to phase two, and although government grants would cover the bulk of those costs, fundraising efforts would have to be maintained into the future, given that a school with beautiful but ancient buildings needed constant renewal and maintenance.

Donald's son John recounted to the author that, in this era, Wilson's Hospital School was

a dilapidated place, about to close. [My father was] heavily involved in the turnaround. He spent a lot of time there – there was a worry it would close – now it is thriving. I became aware of it more later. Recently there was a hall dedicated to him at Wilson's Hospital School. I think my father *knew* people with good business acumen, whether *he* had it [himself or not] … He never had any major business dealings himself, any property transactions or anything. To my knowledge. He had good friends who were accountants and stockbrokers etc. who could advise.

Even when he became Archbishop of Dublin, Donald remained a board member at Wilson's and was active in its continued development. Formerly, only bishops were governors of the school (who had their own dioceses to deal with) and Donald brought in educationalists like Kenneth Milne and business people such as solicitor Graham Richards, who would drive to Multyfarnham for governors' and committee meetings.

Donald's vision was that something could be done if a proper board was appointed. Donald took his colleague Walton Empey aback sometimes, in the sense of business savvy that he evinced in quoting developments on the stock market. Empey felt he had quite an understanding of finance and investments, and could 'hold his own with business people'.[14]

Ecumenism, the Papal Visit and Mixed Marriages

For the Catholic population, the pastoral visit of Pope John Paul II in late September 1979 (Ireland's first papal visit) was greeted with 'outpourings of joy and fervour', as *The Irish Times* put it, with huge crowds attending the various Masses associated with the visit and many more following the events on radio and television. There had been some hopes that the Pope during the visit would attend an ecumenical service in St Patrick's Cathedral, the national cathedral of the Church of Ireland, during the visit but his schedule did not permit this. However, the entire house of bishops of the Church of Ireland (along with representatives of other reformed churches) was invited to a reception hosted by the Papal Nuncio, Dr Gaetano Alibrandi, in the Dominican convent in Cabra late on Saturday evening, 29 September, to meet the pontiff. The Pope greeted them, saying 'Grace to you and peace from God our Father and the Lord Jesus Christ.'

Cardinal Tomás Ó Fiaich was by the Pope's side as he introduced him to each of the bishops. When he came to his friend and fellow Irish language enthusiast, Bishop Donald Caird, he said to the Pope 'this, your Holiness, is a *rara avis* – an Anglican Church of Ireland Bishop who is Irish speaking!' The Pope had spoken a little Irish a short time before this, in remarks at the reception, and he asked Donald, 'Did you like my Irish?' Donald recounts: 'I said "I thought it was excellent", and as [the Pope] was a very humorous and inviting type of man, I went on to say "if you continue to speak consistently, you could get a pension!"' The Pope was greatly amused and 'roared laughing'. A photograph of the occasion shows a highly amused Cardinal, Pope and Bishop of Meath and Kildare in the immediate aftermath of the exchange.

Addressing his diocesan synod a few weeks later, Donald recalled:

Such was the captivating charm of the man, and the overpowering sense of the occasion, that it was not easy to concentrate all the time on the contents of his speech [which stressed the Roman Catholic church's commitment to the pursuit of the unity of Christians] ... his audience responded to the Pope in the spirit of his address. Though tired to the point of exhaustion, he insisted on meeting everybody in the room and speaking with them with a gracious good humour. It was a memorable occasion.

In an RTÉ broadcast the same evening, Donald had spoken in Irish, welcoming the papal visit and expressing the hope that it would bring peace to the country and a deepening of the fellowship of the churches. He drew attention however to the difficult issue of mixed marriages, and explained the Church of Ireland position in relation to the Blessed Virgin Mary and the Roman Catholic dogmas of the Immaculate Conception and the Assumption:

> I did this in explanation of why we could not take part in the religious exercises at [the Marian shrine at] Knock with our Roman Catholic brethren ... not out of a spirit of controversy or from any desire to call into question either their integrity or the sincerity of their devotion, but because we could not do it with understanding (1 Cor. 14:15).

Interchurch marriage and the effect of the Roman Catholic Church's *Ne Temere* decree (whereby the parties had to make a solemn promise in writing to raise any children as Catholics) had long been a major concern for the Protestant community in the state, which had seen its numbers fall since independence. While much of the initial decline was accounted for by the withdrawal after 1921 of personnel in the Crown armed forces – police, army and navy – along with their dependents, the decline had continued, the Church of Ireland population standing at 145,030 in 1936, compared with 164,215 in 1928, and 249,535 in 1911. The decline was attributed by Primate John Gregg in 1939 to three factors: emigration, mixed marriages and late marrying. He urged the replenishment of the community's human stock through a fuller development of family life and the discouragement and prevention of mixed marriages.

The situation seemed almost to require social segregation of young people, as highlighted in remarks by Donald in a newspaper interview in Irish in 1970: 'for example I cannot say to a group of young Protestants "there is a *céilí* in the Hall tonight, you should all go there." Protestants in the North are looking at us in the South and on the manner in which [*Ne Temere*] impacts on us, and they say "look at them in the South; they will not even exist in another 100 years.'"[15] In addressing his diocesan synod in October 1972, Donald had observed that they were marking ten years since the Second Vatican Council, and the great promise and hope which had been held out both by the joint Anglican Roman Catholic Commission set up by Pope Paul VI and the Archbishop of Canterbury, and the greeting by the Pope of the Anglican Church 'as the ever beloved sister of the Roman Catholic Church'. He noted that the *Ne Temere* decree had been replaced in March 1966 by an 'instruction on mixed marriages'. The concession offered was that the non-Roman Catholic party would now be allowed to make the promise affecting the baptism and upbringing of the children verbally, rather than in writing. 'But to an honourable man/woman it makes little difference whether a promise is made verbally or in writing – in either case they will feel obliged to keep it.'

A new apostolic letter – *Motu Proprio* – issued by the Vatican in 1970 relaxed the requirements somewhat, in so far as the non-Roman Catholic party would no longer be required to make a promise but was to be informed of the Catholic partner's sincere promise to do all in his or her power to have the children baptised and brought up in the Catholic church. This remained unsatisfactory in Donald's view: 'to extract an oath from one partner affecting something that is their mutual concern, like the upbringing of the children, is tantamount to exacting it from both partners'. However he acknowledged the less harsh and rigid language of the new instruction compared to previous documents, suggesting it offered hope for further development.

Further developments flowed from the first formal Interchurch Meeting at Ballymascanlon, Co. Louth in September 1973. A joint initiative of the Irish Council of Churches (whose president was Archbishop Simms of Armagh) and the Roman Catholic hierarchy, the new forum would 'discuss questions of vital mutual concern to the Christian communities in Ireland'.[16] Initially, working parties were set up to discuss the issues of *Church, Scripture and Authority; Baptism, Eucharist and Marriage; Social and Community Problems;* and *Christianity and Secularism.*

Donald was appointed as one of the Church of Ireland representatives on the working party on mixed marriages. On attending an international consultation on the subject organised by the Irish School of Ecumenics in 1974, where the speakers included a number of scholars of international repute, he was disconcerted to find out that the requirements of *Motu Proprio* appeared to be capable of a more flexible interpretation by Roman Catholic authorities in other countries than in Ireland:

with a few notable exceptions, the regulations … are interpreted in the most rigid manner in Ireland still … the whole credibility of the Interchurch meeting will possibly depend upon the ability of the churches to reach a mutually acceptable agreement on the question.

The initial phase of the Ballymascanlon process concluded in April 1975 but the *Irish Times* headline of 24 April 1975 – 'Churches reach no settlement on controversial issue of mixed marriages' – did not make for encouraging reading. The report noted that

full recognition should be given to the basic principle that in a mixed marriage husband and wife alike have a Christian duty to contribute spiritually to the marriage, to their children's upbringing and to the general life of the home. Their obligations in conscience towards God and in relation to church membership are essentially of the same nature, whether explicitly declared or not. Each party must respect the inviolability of the conscientious convictions of the other and seek to resolve conflicts with the fullest regard for Christian truth and love.

Among its conclusions, the report stated that

churches have a duty to help mitigate [pressures on mixed marriages, which can be intensified by non-theological factors] by a more effective education of their clergy and laity in respect for the rights, both of those who belong to their own church, and of those whose traditions and convictions are different.

The report advised that

pastoral instruction and care should be undertaken by [clergy] in a spirit of mutual respect and trust. Where such a spirit exists it cannot but have a beneficial effect on the relationship of the married partners to each other.

The setting up of a standing committee to examine annually trends in mixed marriages in reporter John Cooney's words, left 'Protestant churchmen with a foothold in the door that the Catholic bishops feel they cannot authorise to be opened.' This presumably meant that while the formal position remained unchanged, a forum for continuing exploration of the issue existed. The clerk of the general assembly of the Presbyterian Church, the Rev. Jack Weir, described the standing committee as a mechanism 'not for dealing directly with individual cases but for reporting on practical issues raised from time to time and ways of clarifying or resolving them'. Archbishop Buchanan regretted that the mixed marriage report did not sufficiently reflect the deep sense of injustice felt by the people he served, while Donald suggested it was the best that could be arrived at in the present circumstances. Its recommendations, if carried out, could relieve the sense of injustice referred to by Archbishop Buchanan.[17]

Concerns for the sustainability of the Protestant community were again highlighted in Archbishop McAdoo of Dublin's warning in 1977 that integrated education was not a feasible project 'until there was a more Christian and equitable relationship between the churches on mixed marriages'.[18] In 1977, the Irish Association of Interchurch Families published a book *Two Churches, One Love* directed to people in mixed marriages, particularly engaged couples and their parents. In a foreword, Donald stated that for Christians other than Roman Catholics, the essential objection to interchurch marriages lay in the Catholic requirement that the party of that church was gravely bound to promise to do all in his or her power to have the children baptised and brought up in that faith. The declaration of religious freedom of the Second Vatican Council, which had recognised the right of the non-Roman Catholic partner to take a positive role in the religious upbringing and education of children, appeared to be pre-empted by this. The force of the Catholic Church's regulation depended on the interpretation placed on the words 'do all in his power', which was subject to different interpretations in different countries. Donald suggested a possible remedy might lie in an assurance being given by the priest conducting the marriage that he had duly put the partner of his faith in mind of his obligations concerning baptism and upbringing of children, rather than extracting a promise from the Roman Catholic partner.[19]

Not long after the Pope's visit to Ireland, Donald addressed the Association of Interchurch Families. The AICF provided a support network for interchurch couples, with couples being referred by clergy to it. Donald told the AICF that it would be very sad if the only response to the Pope's appeals over a whole range of areas would be a return to more conservative and traditional Roman Catholicism. Describing Pope John Paul II as 'a leader of such meteoric character that he can give tremendous power and energy to the institutions of which he is head', he predicted that ecumenism in the following decade would be slow and cautious. The Pope had met representatives of the reformed churches in Dublin and spoken in most gracious terms with an 'evangelical warmth' in his greeting, asking that no one would doubt the commitment of the Roman Catholic Church to Christian unity, but Donald noted that he had not touched upon specific problems of church unity, in particular mixed marriages (the Church of Ireland bishops when meeting with the Pope had submitted for his attention a statement of the Church's views and feelings on mixed marriages, in an illustration of the central importance for them of the question), and there was no indication of any radical change in the relationship of the churches or the addressing of this issue.[20]

It would be 1983 before a new Directory on Mixed Marriages was published by the Irish Roman Catholic bishops, updating a previous directory of 1976 by seeking to bring uniformity in the norms applied, where there had previously been variation from diocese to diocese. The position was now more in line with that observed in England and Wales. Although the directory's tone was acknowledged as being 'conciliatory and charitable' by Donald, he noted that there was little new in its content and that the promise required of the Roman Catholic partner remained central: he/she had to do 'everything possible, so far as in me lies, to have all the children of our marriage baptised and brought up in the Catholic Church'.

The situation, however, gradually improved over the years due to the practical work of the Association of Interchurch Families in supporting couples. By the 1990s, the problem of mixed marriages was increasingly being resolved by lay people themselves making up their own minds and couples taking the decision either to share their Christian faith in approaching the matter jointly, or sometimes, to the dismay of clergy, drifting away from both churches altogether.[21]

Interchurch relations was the main theme when Donald preached at the General Synod service in St Patrick's Cathedral in 1978. The central issues and points of difference in such relations might be the subject of discussions by hierarchies and commissions, he said, but ecumenism was a dangerous exercise when conducted without the participation of the members of the churches. The whole exercise was predicated upon an assumption of a growth of mutual understanding

> which implied careful and concerted study by the members of the churches involved ... of the great issues which divided Christendom and the greater issues in which Christians were united. This did not apply only to church leaders and theologians, but to the whole church, because ultimately the relationship of the Christian churches must depend on the consensus of their members.

He noted that Cardinal Basil Hume, the Archbishop of Westminster, had recently emphasised that in the Christian faith there was a hierarchy of truths towards which different communions of Christians might converge, leading to a form of unity not yet clearly foreseen by any of the churches involved.

Donald had been a founder member of the Christological group, a theological discussion group established in Dublin in 1967. Its membership consisted of professional theologians drawn from the Pontifical University at Maynooth, Trinity College, Queen's University Belfast and some others. The group met about four times a year, to receive a paper on a theological matter and have a discussion – 'we did not set out to reach conclusions.'

There were four members in the group from Maynooth, and Donald observed, in an interview with the author, that 'every one of them [ultimately] left the priesthood, and one the Roman Catholic church altogether'. This last was Mícheál Ledwith, whom Donald had found to be a 'brilliant fellow, the most brilliant of them all'. Both Donald and Kevin McNamara (Professor of Dogmatics in Maynooth, later appointed Bishop of Kerry) took a keen interest in process theology, largely built on the theories of the great English philosopher Whitehead 'who held that nature was an ongoing process rather than a thing, and Christianity fits into a universe that is not fixed'. Donald and McNamara interviewed Norman Pittenger, who had written on process theology and wrote up papers for discussion by the Christological group.

Northern Ireland Troubles
Some of the worst violence in the modern Northern Ireland Troubles occurred in the year of the Papal visit, with the killing of eighteen British soldiers at Warrenpoint, Co. Down in August, and the explosion of an IRA bomb on board a boat in Co. Sligo the same day, killing Queen Elizabeth's cousin Lord Louis Mountbatten and four other people.

During his visit to Ireland, Pope issued an impassioned appeal in Drogheda to 'the men of violence' in the IRA and northern paramilitary organisations to turn aside from their ongoing campaigns of violence:

> On my knees I beg you to turn away from the paths of violence and to return to the ways of peace … Let history record that at a difficult moment in the experience of the people of Ireland, the Bishop of Rome set foot in your land, that he was with you and prayed with you for peace and reconciliation, for the victory of justice and love over hatred and violence.

The IRA rejected his appeal, asking what had happened to the church's theory of the just war. Addressing his diocesan synod, Donald said:

> The tragedy for our country is that those to whom [the Pope] so graciously appealed have chosen to reject his appeal … The fear is that his appeal

rejected on one major issue, could possibly lead to rejection of other major issues to the great impoverishment of life in our country.

Such rejection would mean

> we would all as a nation have lost the opportunity of a lifetime to respond to the invitation to discover true reconciliation, to achieve that real mutual understanding which allows men to differ without quarrelling; an invitation offered by a man of patent greatness, holiness and deep concern for all mankind, the first bishop of Christendom.

Donald trenchantly criticised those who at a remove, facilitated violence. Those who planted the bomb and pulled the trigger might appear most heinous in the murderous chain of events. However, in terms of moral responsibility, those who supplied money, material and arms, however apparently far removed from the scene of action, however conventional or respectable, were equally guilty. Indeed, perhaps they bore greater guilt than the young men they encouraged to murder on their behalf.[22]

Six months later, on St Patrick's Day 1980, Donald became the first Anglican bishop to preach in Westminster Cathedral in London, at the invitation of Cardinal Hume. This coincided with an Irish-themed arts festival *A Sense of Ireland*.

The previous day, at an ecumenical service of prayer in the same cathedral, Cardinal Ó Fiaich had made a strong attack on violence during his sermon, delivered before a congregation of about two thousand people. He reiterated the Roman Catholic church's unequivocal condemnation of 'all such crimes' and its sympathy with families who had lost loved ones. The pleas of church leaders for peace had reached their climax in the Pope's plea at Drogheda. Addressing perceptions that Ireland lagged behind other countries in terms of ecumenism, he pointed to the monthly meetings of the church leaders, saying he knew of no other country in that part of the world where leaders of the main Christian denominations met each month to pray, plan and take counsel together. He emphasised the desire of many Irish men and women to see a United Ireland, which was 'no less worthy of support' than the desire of others to remain within the United Kingdom, and defended the right of 'Irish men, even Irish churchmen' to be critical of some aspects of British policy 'because they are conscious of their duty to point out that all men have human rights which must be respected and that even the State must at all times act in accordance with the law of God.' After this service, people departing were greeted with a silent demonstration from supporters of prisoners on the 'blanket' at the Maze prison in Belfast (who were protesting at the recent withdrawal of special category status).

Donald preached his St Patrick's Day sermon before a congregation including the Irish ambassador to London, Dr Eamon Kennedy; Seán Mac Réamoinn (the prominent broadcaster and ecumenist); and Lady Ewart-Biggs (the wife of the British ambassador to Ireland who had been assassinated in July 1976 along with his secretary). Tracing the life and character of St Patrick, he queried how the saint might advise us to proceed today. 'I think that he would advise against looking for miracles or happy accidents which might be mistaken for miracles.' Paying tribute to the often heroic endeavours of clergy, both Roman Catholic and Protestant, to keep a fragile peace and dissuade young people from joining or supporting violent organisations, he also acknowledged blame which the churches must accept, including

> their slowness to accept that differences in outlook and belief have proceeded from deep and genuinely held and rationally defensible theological pleading. The churches have too often fallen into line with traditionally linked political attitudes ... and have failed to find a common Christian stance in the face of violence and injustice.

In a commentary on the two Irish church leaders' sermons in the English Catholic newspaper *The Tablet* entitled 'Two Irish Voices', the Cardinal's remarks were contrasted unfavourably with those of Donald:

> To many there would appear to have been an ambivalent attitude in not explicitly naming the IRA as being mainly responsible for 'shootings and bombings, woundings and kidnappings' in the past decade in Northern Ireland ... The Cardinal's appeal to Catholics in Britain to put the case for their fellow Catholics in Ireland for Irish unification may have great historical justification ... but we cannot but feel that [it] was out of place in an ecumenical service ... laudatory references to the interchurch committee, popularly known as the Ballymascanlon talks, may sound like a beacon to a benighted Europe: actually it is a relatively modest, worthy and prayerful body whose meetings have not been as regular as was implied.

In sharp contrast, *The Tablet's* correspondent expressed regret that there was no room to print Bishop Caird's 'wholly admirable discourse' in full, quoting a passage illustrating his hopes for the future, which took the saint as his inspiration:

> Churches have in the past tended to keep one another at arms length from mutual suspicion of predatory intentions. These attitudes of the past,

deep-rooted in Ireland's history, have changed and are changing and our prayer must be that Christians in Ireland may find no reason to withdraw in fear from one another, but that Christians of all traditions may be free and equal to live and worship, to grow and expand their community in all parts of Ireland, knowing that their fellow Christians of other traditions present not a threat to them, but the opportunity of discovering Patrician comprehensiveness, the sense of oneness in Patrick which will take us along the road to a full expression of oneness in Christ.[23]

Protestant Citizenship

The theme of full engagement by the Church community in Irish public life was evident in many of Donald's statements in Meath and Kildare. For him, reasons for weaknesses in Protestant identification with the independent Irish state did not flow from external sources alone – it was also something to be addressed internally. He had made headlines in 1977 with a complaint that, in the General Election of that year, not one candidate was a member of the Church of Ireland. He placed the blame for this, and for the extremely low Protestant representation in the Army and Garda Síochána (both of which had won 'respect and admiration') squarely on the Church of Ireland community itself:

> In our schools, the Army and [Gardaí] should be presented to young people for what they are – an opportunity to serve the community well and to fulfil themselves in a satisfying and rewarding career. I know how well they are received in both services and where we do not respond the loss is ours.[24]

It was an exhortation he felt compelled to repeat at successive annual addresses to the diocesan synod and in other church fora.

An *Irish Times* editorial headed 'Revival' in October 1980 highlighted the small increase in the Church of Ireland population, and ranged over key topics such as Protestant emigration in the early years of the Free State, perceptions among Northern Protestants of the Republic, mixed marriages and Church of Ireland representation in the Republic's police and military services: 'The Defence Forces and the Garda are worthy and honourable callings. Dr Caird's men should get in. Women too.' The editorial concluded on an upbeat note: 'It is good to know from Dr Caird that the Church of Tone, Emmet and Davis is experiencing a revival.'[25] However, Donald was constrained to write in, contradicting a statement attributed to him that the situation in relation to mixed marriages was improving.

The reasons why Protestants didn't fulfil a bigger role in politics in the state were examined in depth in 'The Protestant Outlook', a two-part series in *The Irish Times* in December 1982, featuring contributions from a range of voices from the community. There was only one member of the Dáil from the Church of Ireland community whereas even the tiny Jewish community had three TDs. The question was asked, when Dean Victor Griffin and Bishop Poyntz in Cork were criticising the state's social legislation, were they reflecting the views of their flocks? And if so, why were the members of those flocks not within the political process? Why was most of the 'liberal running' left to Catholics such as Garret FitzGerald and Mary Robinson? Dr Fergus O'Farrell, president of the National Youth Council, asked why there was not more minority support shown for the 'constitutional crusade' declared by FitzGerald to dilute the perceived influence of the dominant religious ethos in the country's basic law. 'Is the political life of this country just that little bit grubby for Protestants and is duty done by mere vote and Sunday sermon? Or is there something that bit deeper, a hankering, a folk memory for the days before "their State" came into being?' the writer asked. Dean Victor Griffin of St Patrick's Cathedral offered the view that, while the younger Protestant would have the same zeal for his country as his Catholic counterpart, he might not think it disloyal to join the British forces as his grandfather had before him. Such an attitude could seep into political thinking and he might not get so worked up about getting into the Dáil.

The piece featured a contribution from Donald, who noted that the main political parties (principally Fianna Fáil and Fine Gael) traced their origins to the civil war of 1922–24. If those parties still maintained their identities on that basis, Protestants might regard politics as an irrelevancy for them. 'Some Protestants might regard the state as a Roman Catholic one. They might feel that they like living in the South, that they have been here for hundreds of years and why should they now disturb the situation by entering into public attention.' He believed that such a view was mistaken, however. Elsewhere, the article quoted Trevor Matthews, a member of the Church, as saying that he had specifically joined the Fianna Fáil party because 'it was the Republican party, not because it was nationalist, Green and RC.'

The decimation of church membership which had occurred as a result of two world wars was noted by Bishop Poyntz, a loss evident from the rolls of honour to be found in many a country church. The loss of local connections, which occurred with children in scattered rural Protestant communities having to go away to boarding schools of their denomination, was pointed out by Ivan Yates, the sole Church of Ireland TD: Catholics in day schools do not have the disadvantage of returning to their rural areas as 'black strangers' after years in such places as Kilkenny College or King's Hospital.[26]

In 1984, it seemed earlier Protestant republican 'revivalist' optimism in the spirit of Tone, Emmet and Davis had been premature. In a profile interview with Deaglán de Bréadún in *The Irish Times*, Donald again bemoaned the weakness in engagement of the southern Protestant community with Garda, Army and Dáil. Asked for the reasons for this, he put a hand on either side of his face, saying:

I'm always thinking about this. They probably have opportunities in business and the professions, on the land etc. I think another reason is the enormously high profile of the Roman Catholic Church in state enterprises.[27]

Being Protestant in Ireland was the theme of a Social Study conference[28] in Kilkenny the same year, featuring addresses by a range of speakers from North and South. *Protestantism and National Identity* was the title of an address given by Donald. He suggested that, like the constitution of the state, the definition of national identity should be left as broad and comprehensive as possible, granting as wide a freedom as possible to those who lived in the country to claim fellowship with their neighbours, acceptance of and pride in the common traditions of the country, and commitment to the welfare of the people in a changing environment. Such characteristics constituted the true claim to national identity rather than the narrow ethnic and religious aspects which had so often in the past been defined as the necessary qualifications, and which in Ireland had made, over centuries, many Irish men and women strangers in their own land.

He criticised rivalry between the Christian churches as impeding the progress of ecumenism, and in the Irish context, decried the tendency on the part of churches on both sides of the border to align themselves with particular strands of national identity: 'where the emblems of power and authority of one church ... are used to evoke a chauvinistic spirit ... then a disservice to ecumenism is being done.'[29] In the past the religious element in the formation of the sense of national identity had largely been divisive and contentious. However, this should be increasingly less the case provided Ireland kept within the world movement towards greater understanding between the churches.

In a profile of the dioceses in *The Church of Ireland Gazette* also in 1984, the question was posed by Donald, in relation to Meath and Kildare, of how church members were to live in the [wider] community with grace and Christian charity as members of a church which in the past had enjoyed a position of privilege and ascendancy which although removed may linger in the memory, and when the view was still fostered in the community that to be Anglican was to be unpatriotic, and also how to deal with the 'unequal terms' imposed by the Roman Catholic Church in the case of mixed marriages.[30] These would continue to be themes which preoccupied him.

Although willing to direct such challenging observations to his own Protestant community, where necessary, Donald was also anxious to see his church community portrayed in a fair light in media commentary. He took issue, along with some other Church members, at a series of articles on the Church of Ireland by Kevin Myers in *The Irish Times* in January 1980. In a letter to the editor, he criticised a focus on weak parishes in sparsely populated dioceses without balancing this with reference to strong suburban parishes and country churches which were thriving and well-filled. He bemoaned the view presented of the church as 'the last vestige of a displaced and dying ascendancy, stranded by the tide of history and unable to adapt to the changing social and economic facts of twentieth-century Ireland' and the 'distorted and barely recognisable likeness to the Church which I know and in whose ministry I am proud and happy to serve'.[31] He underlined the church's resilience, notwithstanding the depressed economic climate prevailing, in his 1982 diocesan synod address. He pointed to the extensive restoration of St Patrick's Cathedral in Dublin, a renovation of Christ Church Cathedral and the recent completion of St Anne's Cathedral in Belfast (which had been an ongoing work since the first decades of the century). In his own dioceses, there was the ongoing restoration of St Patrick's Cathedral in Trim, the reopening of the round tower at St Brigid's Cathedral in Kildare, refurbishment of other churches, building of new parochial schools, restoration of rectories and the development of Wilson's Hospital school.

The Church of Ireland was subjected to close scrutiny in a Partners in Mission Consultation exercise in 1984, with Anglican representatives from Canada, the United States, Spain, the Sudan, Wales, Singapore and other places working with local representatives to examine its life and state of health. In their audit of the church, the partners noted the great commitment by people and communities, while stating that there was perhaps too much emphasis on local church building and the need to keep it going at all costs. This gave cause for reflection. Donald mused at his synod that 'perhaps there was myopia in relation to our perspective of the wider church. We were infinitely better off than we realised'. One of the main problems identified by the partners was that of secondary education and the onerous and costly responsibility of maintaining boarding schools. Donald told his synod that the Partners-in-Mission thought the Church of Ireland had not progressed in the area of practical ecumenism as other parts of the Anglican communion had done, and had urged the Church to 'free itself from all commitments of a sectarian nature'.

The announcement of the intention of the distinguished Archbishop of Armagh George Otto Simms to retire in early 1980 was greeted with 'a sense of sadness and impending loss' by the whole Church of Ireland, Donald said. Simms had sought to give a lead to his community by showing an interest in Irish national life. Recalling from his own days in Trinity the 'young, gently handsome clergyman who looked as young and often younger than the undergraduates', Donald described his influence as Dean of Residence and sub-lecturer and examiner in the Greek New Testament on students: 'indelible and always for good'. His non-directive approach, 'gently nudging' others to talk out their problems until they themselves found the solution, was attested to. 'He sought to serve rather than be recognised for service.' His rapid rise through the ranks of the Church of Ireland to the Primacy in Armagh, which might have been 'unbecoming in an ambitious man eager for preferment' was always with the 'acclaim of the whole church, never with any trace of resentment on the part of his fellow clergy'. He had impressed at the 1978 Lambeth conference, explaining the problems of Ireland North and South to the overseas bishops with 'the scrupulous fairness of his judgement, by his ability to enter into the mind of those with whom he would most emphatically disagree'. Paying tribute to the work of Simms' wife Mercy with the Mothers' Union and Girls' Friendly Society, and her gracious hospitality, he wished the couple '*sláinte agus saol … go maire sibh i bhfad.*' (Health and vitality – long may they live.)[32]

Following the retirement of Simms, Donald's name featured in some of the speculation about his possible successor, along with Bishop of Ossory, John Ward Armstrong and a number of other candidates – Armstrong being the eventual choice.[33]

The Irish language

Influenced by his own early experiences on the Blaskets, in Cumann Gaelach na hEaglaise, and his early ministry in the North, Donald sought to present such Irish symbolism as St Patrick and the Irish language as possibilities for increased understanding rather than division. In a sermon preached on St Patrick's Day at St Columba's Church, Kells, and broadcast on RTÉ radio, he referred to the romantic legends surrounding Patrick. When these are dismissed, we find:

> the fifth-century saint would not have understood the reasons for the church's divisions as we find them today, and could not have even imagine many of the questions which later arose to divide Christendom ... We cannot use his name to support issues in theology or church government, of which he could not have conceived ... His faith was nourished by the Latin Bible ... and in his writing there is nothing which as Christians living at the end of the twentieth century we cannot wholly accept and with which we may argue.[34]

Leading an ecumenical act of thanksgiving and intercession during a Solemn Pontifical Mass held to mark the Silver Jubilee of the Gael-Linn organisation in October 1978, Donald said 'there is at present a real hope that, within the future, everyone who calls himself or herself Irish, whatever part of the country they come from, will feel free to learn and speak Irish without reference to job, religion, politics or personal ideology.' Men and women all over Ireland could speak Irish without any disloyalty to their particular heritage or without the implication of uniformity or 'orthodoxy' in matters of political or religious beliefs, or historical traditions.[35]

In 1981, the association of Irish-speaking Catholic priests, An Sagart, published a translation in Irish of the Holy Bible, *An Bíobla Naofa*. Msgr Pádraig Ó Fiannachta had undertaken this translation from Hebrew and Greek, and a copy was formally presented to Donald. This was the first substantial translation into Irish of the Old Testament since William Bedell's Bible, published in 1685 (the Church of Ireland's Canon Cosslett Quin had brought out his translation of the New Testament, *Tiomna Nua*, in 1970).

Douglas Hyde, son of the rectory, renowned Irish scholar and co-founder of the Gaelic League (Conradh na Gaeilge), had been an inspiration to Donald since his student days. In March 1982, he preached at a bilingual service in Irish on the estate of John Wilson Wright at Coolcarrigan, near Prosperous in Co. Meath. The focal point of this estate is an attractive Georgian house, and on its domain is located one of the most picturesque little churches in the stewardship of the Church of Ireland. Coolcarrigan Church, consecrated in 1885 by Archbishop Plunkett, features a replica Irish round tower attached to the main church building. The church (surrounded by a dry moat) is entered by passing through one of the very few lych gates in Ireland. Wright's grandfather Mackey Wilson had been a close personal friend of Hyde. Donald preached at a bilingual service of evensong, the service sheet featuring hymns such as Sean Ó Riada's *Ag Críost an Síol*, Hyde's *Álainn Farraige Spéirghlas* and *Tell Out, My Soul*.

In handwritten notes for this address,[36] Donald traced Hyde's link with Coolcarrigan. He was a close friend of Mackey Wilson at Trinity, and came to visit him at Coolcarrigan. The pair were boon travelling companions, visiting Scotland and the continent of Europe during holidays. Hyde was reputed to have been in love with Mackey's sister, although Donald expresses doubt about this. Decorative text in Gaelic script (though the words were in English) was painted by Hyde on the inside walls of Coolcarrigan church. When Mackey succumbed to tuberculosis and died in 1887, while still a young man, Hyde was overcome with grief: *'leagadh an Craoibhinn leis an mbrón …'* (An Craoibhinn collapsed with grief). Hyde's life was touched by other instances of tragedy: his brother Arthur had died in boyhood, and in September 1916 his daughter Nuala would succumb to tuberculosis.

In June 1982, Donald was invited to give an address at *Éigse de hÍde*, a festival in honour of Hyde, in Roscommon. His address, the first event of the weekend festival, was titled 'Dúbhglas de hÍde, Ball d'Eaglais na hÉireann' (Douglas Hyde, a member of the Church of Ireland). Published subsequently as a two-part series in *The Irish Times*, Donald focused on an aspect of Hyde hitherto given little attention: the significance in his life of his membership of the Church of Ireland. In order to gather some information for his address, Donald went to visit the veteran Cumann Gaelach na hEaglaise member Lil Nic Dhonnchadh, who, although in her nineties, Donald found to be still mentally sharp.

Lil, who had been a friend of Hyde for many years, was able to tell him that Hyde had always been an extremely loyal member of the Church, but he did not speak on such matters. *Tostacht*, or silence/reticence, was something which had served for him throughout his life as a place or state of sanctuary or refuge, in which he could hide the things most precious to him until stormy weather passed over. It was apparent from his diaries that he would withdraw behind silence at times when trouble was threatening him or when disagreement was about to break out between himself and somebody for whom he held respect or love. Donald speculates that this may have either been a trait inherent to Hyde or something which owed its origins to disagreements between him and his father about political or other matters.

The Hyde household had a long tradition of providing clergymen for the Church of Ireland, but disestablishment was looming in the late 1860s and this uncertainty may have made its presence felt in the family. Hyde was a divinity student at Trinity, and had won many prizes including the theological exhibition there. However, he was not attracted to the ministry. While he abandoned his divinity studies with some relief, he continued to worship God in accordance with the prayer book and spiritual tradition of the Church of Ireland. Although a member of the select vestry in his own parish in Roscommon, he had never served as a member of General Synod. Donald speculates that divinity as taught in the university at that time may have seemed cold, analytical and far removed from the devotion of the ordinary people who had captivated Hyde's poetic soul in the countryside. He expressed his spirituality more easily through poetry than through the abstractions of theology, but continued to cherish the Bible and attend church regularly throughout his life. Donald described Hyde as being a true ecumenist, before the term had even been invented – one who hoped to draw the two Christian traditions together through respect for the language and traditional customs.

Hyde was anxious to attract the support of members of his own Protestant tradition for the cause of the language. The early days of the Gaelic League, around the end of the nineteenth century and beginning of the twentieth century, had in fact seen substantial progress in enlisting Protestant support for the Irish language, both north and south on the island. For example, a Grand Master of the Orange Order, Richard O'Kane had been a strong supporter of the League. In a letter to his friend, the Rev. J. O. Hannay (the novelist, George A. Birmingham) dated 3 November 1906, Hyde reported: 'I have just come back from Belfast where we had a great highly "respectable" meeting and where I found great growth of the Gaelic League spirit amongst Protestants.' In other correspondence with Hannay, Hyde had expressed the view that the only way to check undue ecclesiastical power in Ireland was to give the country home rule, when the eyes of the country would be centred on their lay representatives.

While a critic of Roman Catholic clerical influence in the country, Hyde had not hesitated in weighing in against members of his own Protestant tradition who manifested animosity towards the language or Gaelic culture; in 1899 challenging J. P. Mahaffy of Trinity College who had expressed the view that nobody could find a text in Irish which was not silly, overly religious or laughable: 'knowing Dr Mahaffy's genuine interest in all intellectual movements I shall not despair of his sympathy if he ever succeeds in mastering from the inside the bearing of this and other native Irish questions.' Hyde also took issue with a leader writer in *The Church of Ireland Gazette* who had attacked the work of the League in

1904. He strongly supported the holding of Irish language services, and the work of the Cumann Gaelach na hEaglaise, contributing articles to its journal *The Gaelic Churchman* throughout the period of its publication. Donald summed up Hyde's contribution in his closing paragraph:

> *D'fhan sé dílis dá thír is dá Eaglais. Bhain sé aoibhneas as áilleacht na tíre. Bhain sé aoibhneas as cuideachta a charad Gael. Bhain sé aoibhneas as ceol na teanga. Bhain sé aoibhneas as seana gacha dighe agus nua gacha bidh, agus thug sé adhradh do Dhia.*

(He remained loyal to his country and to his Church. He rejoiced in the beauty of the country. He rejoiced in the company of his Gaelic friends. He rejoiced in the music of the language. He rejoiced in the freshest of food and the oldest of wine and he gave glory to God.)

Like his father George before him, Donald was anxious that his children would pass school examinations in Irish, and took them on a trip to Inis Oírr in August 1983 on the *Naomh Éanna*. His son John recalled the experience:

Ann, myself and Helen, I think. We stayed in Conneeley's guesthouse. Cóilí was still there. We were there certainly a week and we brought our Irish books – my father was trying to 'beat' Irish into us ... We sat there every day for an hour to an hour and a half to go through the books. The *módh coinníollach* (conditional tense) or something! I did the Inter Cert in 1984 and Ann did the Leaving Cert in 1985. We would walk around the island and see the Plassey.[37] I had a voracious appetite. There was one shop there and you would buy cans of Club Orange and stuff. There was a little airfield where a plane would land ... Cóilí's son ran the water supply system for the island I think, and I remember going up to inspect the reservoir and pump station on the island ... I remember we would be on the beach and the *Naomh Éanna* anchored offshore and the farmers would get their livestock off, they would harness them and tow them with a currach, and the animals would be kicking fiercely. A harness would be lowered from the deck of the ship and a crane. Horses and cattle were lifted out of the water. It was fascinating. That was the last time I was there, I would love to revisit it. At nights, I think we had books and read. I don't remember watching television there. My dad fell asleep on the deck of the boat on the way out. They wanted to make sure all the passengers were on board to set sail before the tide dropped [this was after a stop en route at one of the other islands], and they couldn't find him. He'd fallen asleep on the top deck. They just squeaked out with the tide – we had nearly been stranded – they were fuming! I said my dad must have gone off the boat ... he was asleep upstairs all the time and came down to this kerfuffle.

During a brief period from 1977 to 1980, it so happened that the three most senior bishops in the Church of Ireland were Irish speakers: George Otto Simms as Archbishop of Armagh, Henry McAdoo as Archbishop of Dublin and Donald Caird as Bishop of Meath and Kildare. This led Lil Nic Dhonnchadh, one of the founders of Cumann Gaelach na hEaglaise, to remark:

> Má tá fonn ar bhuachaill óg dul chun cinn a dhéanamh in Eaglais na hÉireann, ba choir dóibh an Ghaeilge a fhoghlaim!
> (If a young man wishes to progress in the Church of Ireland, he should learn Irish!)[38]

Mission abroad and Uganda visit

The diocese of Meath had commitments to overseas missionary aid including the maintaining of a doctor at St Columba's Hospital in Chota Nagpur, India (which had been founded as a result of the Dublin University mission to the region in 1892). There was general support for the missions from all parishes and some had their own missionaries in the field.[39]

In February 1985, Donald undertook a three-week visit to Uganda as the Church of Ireland representative at a Partners-In-Mission Consultation along with representatives of many other member churches of the Anglican Communion. He took with him gifts from the Church of Ireland Bishops' Appeal to the 3.8 million member Ugandan church, and from the Mothers' Union in Ireland to its sister organisation in Uganda. A focal point of his visit was the honouring of a martyr of the Ugandan church, Archbishop Janani Luwum, who had been murdered in 1977 for voicing criticisms of the régime of dictator Idi Amin.

The consultation was housed in Bishop Tucker Theological College in Mukono, about fourteen miles east of Kampala, and Donald wrote a detailed account of his visit for *The Church of Ireland Gazette*.[40] The external partners visited various dioceses in the Ugandan church (Donald visiting East Enkole diocese), and reported back to the consultation. Among the key themes identified in the report to the plenary session of the consultation were the need to train clergy and lay workers for the work of mission and to enable them to make use of means of communication such as radio and television; the extension of Christian stewardship; the development of the potential of women in the church and especially in its ministry; and the need to supply transport for the clergy at parish level (motor cycles were recommended and a loan scheme suggested).

The issue of human rights proved a thorny problem among the external and internal partners, but they managed to agree on a statement for inclusion in the joint report of the consultation. An exuberant 'jubilation with the wonderful rhythmical singing and handclapping with which the Ugandans celebrate' followed the agreement of the final report. Donald preached at the service of thanksgiving which concluded the conference, taking the opportunity to refer to the many clergy from the Church of Ireland who had served the Church of Uganda, especially as lecturers at Bishop Tucker Theological College.

A closing reception was held in the 'magnificent' Kampala Conference Centre, Donald noting that this was in fact the same building in which the martyred Archbishop Luwum had had his fatal meeting with Idi Amin:

> We were met in the reception area by a number of young civil servants, impeccably dressed and groomed, wearing dark suits, white shirts, sober ties and elegant shoes. We, who numbered well over one hundred and twenty, were conducted to a fine conference room of impressive proportions, with a deep green carpet from wall to wall. White coated waiters attended tables covered with white cloths, on which cool drinks stood, and were very welcome in the heat of the evening. The Police band played unfamiliar and yet easily memorised Ugandan music. The various members of Dr Obote's cabinet, senior civil servants and senior army officers, then joined guests and mingled most cordially, and spoke to everyone present openly and affably. The band suddenly ceased playing familiar hymn tunes … and struck up the Ugandan National Anthem. This marked the arrival of the President. He toured the room, speaking individually to everyone. He was dressed very much as the young men who met us on arrival, and he carried an elegantly carved walking stick which seemed to be a symbol of status as well as a support.

Donald attended a memorial service for Archbishop Luwum the following day at Namirembe cathedral. The service, attended by the President and his cabinet, heard an account of how the Archbishop and two lay members of the church (one of whom was a Minister of State) who were with him had met their deaths. It so happened that the Church of Uganda was celebrating in that year the centenary of twenty-five other young Ugandan martyrs (men and boys) who had refused to renounce Christ in the reign of Kabaka Mutesa in 1885: 'It was a most impressive service and everybody was deeply moved, especially as the Archbishop's family and the families of the other martyrs were at the service.'

The following day, Sunday, 17 February, the partners attended the elaborate enthronement ceremony of Bishop Kauma, the new Archbishop of Namirembe, at Kampala Cathedral:

The service commenced at 10:30 a.m. and was still in progress at 2:30 p.m. There were fifty or sixty bishops present. The vast cathedral was packed. The choir, including the world-famous Gagaza Girls' Choir, were magnificent. The service was in English and Luganda, the sermon being translated, which added time to the service. One was surprised and impressed by the fact that though the church of Uganda by the standards of the Church of Ireland is very 'low and evangelical' in theology and general way of life, the ceremony in the enthronement service was very elaborate and ornate, and nearly all the bishops, except of course the Irish representative, wore all the elaborate panoply of mitres, copes and albs. One felt that Anglicanism was alive and flourishing in Uganda.

Donald noted the difficult situation faced by the new Bishop – the previous May, the diocesan theological college at Namigo had been attacked by the military on suspicion that 'terrorists' were hiding there, and the principal and a number of other members of staff were killed, while several students were wounded. Following the enthronement service, an elaborate feast (to which five or six hundred guests were invited) was held in the playing fields of a neighbouring school. Members of the Mothers' Union 'dressed in their handsome long white elaborate dresses with deep cummerbunds in the dark blue of the MU' acted as hostesses.

Donald spent the final week of his visit at the Church of Uganda Guesthouse in Namirembe, affording him a chance to see the day-to-day life of the church in the surrounding dioceses – visiting a hospital and taking home a 'shopping list' of aid and necessities required. He also had an opportunity to meet a group of Irish Franciscan Sisters who were running a hospital in Kampala: 'They came from all over Ireland, from Antrim to Cork, and were delighted to meet a Church of Ireland Bishop and to send back through him greetings to Ireland.'

Accompanied by a young clergyman of the diocese, Donald paid a memorable visit to Kabaka's Tomb in the Kampala region,

a compound of six native houses built in the circular fashion of Uganda with conical thatched roofs, with a very large building of similar design in the centre. The vast building is completely dark inside where a Stygian gloom presides. Only slowly as one's eyes become accustomed to the darkness does one become aware of wraith-like figures sitting or kneeling on the rush mats that are strewn on the earthen floor. These are the old retainers of the last Kabaka, King Freddie, and various collateral relatives of his, who keep constant watch day and night by the Kabaka's Tomb hoping and praying for the return of his dynasty. Many of them are blind or nearly blind from their constant vigil in the darkness. It is a sad experience to see them in their hopeless quest. Their amazing loyalty is heart-breaking to witness. They represent a very sad bye-way of history. The Kabaka was expelled in 1966. They remind one of the vain hope kept alive in the Highlands of Scotland for so long in the eighteenth century for the return of Bonnie Prince Charlie, '*An Buachaill Beo*' of many an Irish and Scottish poem.

On his final Sunday in Uganda, Donald preached at two of the many newly-built churches to packed congregations.

Each church had a splendid robed choir. The people are generous in their contribution to the church … 'It is our numbers which make it possible for us not only to survive but to expand as a church,' one of the rectors remarked, 'even though we are very poor.'

Donald had kept a journal of his experiences and impressions of the country and its people, noting the ubiquitous bicycle:

Bicycles are everywhere … a symbol of family prosperity. Each bicycle at the present rate of exchange costs about £400, that is three years' work wages for an average person, largely. [The bicycles are] British made, strong, nothing fancy, with a 1920–1930 appearance, made for hard work and it is hard work they get.

He recalls the enthusiasm of the life of the church in Uganda. Summing up in his account for *The Gazette*, Donald struck a hopeful note for the future:

The Church of Uganda has passed through the crucible of fiery trial and is entering a period of peace and triumph with a deep sense of thanks-giving to God and commitment to Jesus Christ.

Moving on

When Donald's old mentor, Henry McAdoo, the Archbishop of Dublin, was obliged to retire after suffering heart trouble, the electoral college meeting to select his successor (comprising fifty-two episcopal, clerical and lay persons) was set for 11 June 1985. Dublin was the most numerically significant diocese in the southern province of the Church of Ireland and had a significant status in the Anglican communion internationally.

The three candidates tipped for the succession in media speculation were Donald (the Bishop of Meath and Kildare holding the next most senior position after Dublin among the bishops), the Bishop of Cork, Samuel Poyntz (although his outspokenness was adjudged by some to be a possible disadvantage) and the Bishop of Derry and Raphoe, James Mehaffey (although his diocese included parts of Co. Donegal which were in the Republic, his mainly northern experience was felt to militate against him). The range of responsibilities and challenges which would confront the new Archbishop were detailed by a writer in *The Irish Times*:

> responsibilities in connection with many aspects of church life including the training of candidates for ordination in the theological college and in TCD and of national teachers in the College of Education; the central administration of the Church of Ireland at the representative church body officers in Rathmines; and endless correspondence, councils and committees – but also a Primate of Ireland, who must be a public figure who can speak for the church in the Republic on issues of national importance.[41]

Donald was elected as the new Archbishop of Dublin. His promotion would see him take up a role as the premier voice of the minority tradition in the Republic at a time of accelerating social and political change North and South – and a historic transformation in the ministry of the Church of Ireland.

CHAPTER SIX

Archbishop of Dublin and Bishop of Glendalough
(1985–1996)

Election and Enthronement

The United Dioceses of Dublin and Glendalough comprise the greater Dublin area (with a population of approximately one million people), together with Co. Wicklow and part of Co. Kildare. In the city itself, there are two cathedrals of medieval foundation in the custody of the Church of Ireland: Christ Church Cathedral (the diocesan cathedral, where the Archbishop has his *cathedra*), and St Patrick's Cathedral (designated since 1871 as the national cathedral of the Church of Ireland). The headquarters of many national Church institutions are located in the city, and much of its administrative business carried out there, it being a convenient meeting point for people coming from different parts of the island. The Theological College (now the Theological Institute) and Representative Church Body Library are based in Braemor Park, Rathgar, and the College of Education in Rathmines. Several secondary schools under Church of Ireland management are located in the dioceses, as well as numerous national schools at parochial level.

The reaction to the news of Donald's election in 1985 as the fifty-eighth Archbishop of Dublin and the sixty-ninth Bishop of Glendalough, Primate of Ireland and Metropolitan was positive, but there were almost immediately hints of the social, ecumenical and political controversies to come. His old friend and colleague on the Christological group and the interchurch standing committee on mixed marriages, Catholic Archbishop of Dublin, Dr Kevin McNamara, congratulated Donald on his appointment, stating that he looked forward 'very much to renewing my collaboration with him in the work of serving the people of the archdiocese we share.' Dr Caird responded that he looked forward to working with Dr McNamara because of their long-standing friendship. He made it clear however that he did not share some of the views expressed by his Catholic counterpart, citing his belief that it was an 'inalienable right' of parents to plan their families, and his view that individuals could not be denied the civil right to divorce, although, as a

Christian, he hoped they would not resort to it. He paid tribute to his mentor and model, Archbishop Henry McAdoo saying he was sure the archdiocese had been well looked after by his predecessor and he would be slow to make changes (as well as McAdoo, another retired predecessor, George Otto Simms, also lived in the dioceses). Addressing his own priorities on assuming the Archbishopric, Donald pledged to continue to work to improve ecumenical relations on such issues as mixed marriages, underlining however that he would work for the acceptance of 'total equality of the partners'.[1]

The Archbishop was a major figure on the diplomatic circuit in the Republic's capital city of Dublin, the order of precedence for senior clergy being the Roman Catholic and Church of Ireland Archbishops of Armagh; followed by the Roman Catholic and Church of Ireland Archbishops of Dublin. In terms of the network of connections available, the post of Archbishop of Dublin was probably the most 'interesting' position in the Church of Ireland, and Donald attended at many state occasions, including the inauguration of President Mary Robinson in Dublin Castle in 1990, a state reception for visiting Archbishop of Canterbury, George Carey, in 1994 and the state dinner for the official visit of Prince Charles in 1995, the first official visit to the Republic by a senior member of the British royal family since independence.

In an editorial, *The Irish Times* praised the 'exemplary choice', made by the electoral college, noting that Donald followed in the steps of Dr Simms and Dr McAdoo in being at home in both Irish and English. The leader writer noted that

> the appointment of the Church of Ireland Archbishop ... is still a matter of some general interest outside his own denominational community. In the city of Dublin itself, with all its state and civic functions, he becomes a well-known personage ... it is not a political appointment, but it carries political and social implications. His advice is likely to be sought at government and official level ... and in this age of much movement in social and sexual mores, he will find it hard to step aside from thorny questions.[2]

Donald's enthronement ceremony at Christ Church Cathedral, was fixed for the 29 September – the Feast of St Michael and All Angels, just as it had been for his consecration and 'sending out as a Bishop in the Church of God'[3] in the same cathedral fifteen years earlier.

The ceremony, which for the first time was transmitted live on RTÉ television, was attended by an array of civic and religious dignitaries[4] including President Hillery, Archbishop McNamara and Archbishop Methodius of the Greek Orthodox Church. Having struck, in time-honoured fashion, the south-west door of the cathedral with his episcopal staff and been duly admitted, Donald declared: 'Mr Dean, we are come here that I may be openly enthroned into the archbishopric of Dublin.' Responding, Dean Tom Salmon replied 'Most Reverend Father in God, all things are prepared for the installation to take place.' The installation service featured the reading of the Lord's prayer in Irish by Dáithí Ó Maolchoille of Cumann Gaelach na hEaglaise, and Donald in his sermon noted (in Irish) that while many languages have been heard in the cathedral, Irish has been used in every age and still today services are held there in that language.

It was a proud occasion for the new Archbishop's family, as they looked on from their seats in the congregation: his wife Nancy, daughter Ann (18) who was embarking on her study of medicine at Trinity; son John (17) and younger daughter Helen (13), both still pupils at King's Hospital, Palmerstown.

Following evensong, Donald ascended the pulpit to deliver his sermon, noting that he could trace his antecedents in the city to the eighteenth century. He referred to the public debate under way on the issue of divorce, declaring his belief that 'the state's function must surely be to mark by its legislation the broadest limits of choice proffered to its subjects, while the choice would be freely exercised by the individual guided by his or her accepted teaching authority within his or her community of faith or belief.' His plea was essentially that the state would leave to the consciences of its citizens the task of making judgement on matters of social mores which did not command consensus.

His enthronement sermon also heralded some themes which would fail to be addressed in the time ahead, such as the problem of unemployment and its threat to the stability of society (while noting grounds for hope that economic tides might return to lift boats as they had in the 1960s), the difficult path of ecumenical understanding ('but the search continues with an openness and mutual commitment not experienced for five hundred years') and the common social concern of the churches in Ireland on such issues as alcoholism, drug addiction, housing and environmental pollution. These were all matters on which the churches had conducted joint studies, 'but the churches cannot be content to rest there. A joint programme of action in conjunction with all the agencies of the state must follow'.

Reaction in the media to his sermon was positive. The lead writer in *The Irish Press* took up the question of ecumenism more generally, noting the historic divisions in Ireland which were compounded by the Northern Troubles, and demands by some for dramatic gestures: 'The new

Archbishop was a practical man "with his feet firmly on the ground": "his philosophy, if one may be so bold as to sum it up, is *Festina Lente*".[5] In an upbeat editorial headed 'Cheer and Courage', *The Irish Times* quoted a notable passage in the Archbishop's sermon:

> Committing ourselves to the guidance of the Holy Spirit whose promise is to lead us into all truth and seeking the best available scientific knowledge for our day, we as Christians have to face towards these problems not in fear but in hope, cautious and questioning, but always concerned to distinguish potential good from evil, learning to differentiate and distinguish and not meeting the new, unfamiliar and often overawing with blanket condemnation.[6]

Representatives from rural parishes in the Glendalough portion of the dioceses attended a liturgical reception for him in St Saviour's Church, Rathdrum, in late October. As Archbishop of Dublin, Donald also had a stall assigned to him as of right as Prebendary of Cualaun in the national cathedral of St Patrick (where he also exercised, by statute, the office of Visitor), and he was duly installed there on the third of November 1985 by Dean Victor Griffin.

The 1988 Lambeth Conference and ecumenical affairs
As Archbishop of Dublin, Donald attended the 1988 Lambeth Conference of bishops in the Anglican Communion (he had attended his first in 1978, as a 'baby bishop', when in Meath). This is the gathering – every ten years – of bishops from churches around the world, many of which had their origins in the missionary outreach of the Church of England within the British Empire, but are now fully-fledged national churches or 'provinces', as well as some newer churches. The Archbishop of Canterbury is the focus of unity as *primus inter pares*.

Donald, addressing his diocesan synod in 1986, had conveyed the wish of the Archbishop of Canterbury, Robert Runcie, that all the bishops would 'bring their dioceses with them' to Lambeth. He announced a consultation process, and signalled some of the key themes for the 1988 conference, including the ordination of women to the priesthood and Anglican responses to the Agreed Statement of the Anglican/Roman Catholic International commission.

Unlike the 1978 conference, the wives of the bishops resided with their husbands in 1988 on the campus of the University of Kent, during the week-long programme held for spouses (their husbands remaining on for a further two weeks in conference). Discussions at the Lambeth

Conference 1978 were structured under a number of key themes, such as *Ecumenical Relations, Christianity and the Social Order, Mission and Ministry, Dogmatic and Pastoral Concerns*. Each theme was further subdivided for discussion into a number of working groups consisting of some ten to twelve bishops each.

Donald was assigned to one of the working groups discussing ecumenical relations, with a particular focus on Anglican–Lutheran relations, along with bishops from a variety of countries including the United States, Uganda, Australia Papua New Guinea and some African countries. Each section agreed resolutions for forwarding to the plenary session of the Lambeth conference, where they would be discussed and voted upon, for inclusion in the final conference report. The resolution on Anglican–Lutheran relationships adopted by the 1988 conference restated the goal of full communion, commended work previously done in this area[7] and recommended to member churches, subject to the concurrence of the Lutheran World Federation: (1) a deepening of relationships including interim Eucharistic sharing and joint common celebration of the Eucharist; (2) regular meetings of church leaders for prayer and consultation, 'thus beginning joint episcope'; (3) mutual invitation to synods, with the right to speak; (4) common agencies where possible; and a number of other initiatives to further pastoral and spiritual cooperation.[8]

With customary wit, Donald reflected on Lambeth 1988 and the organised chaos that sometimes seemed to characterise inter-Anglican discussions, marked as they are by the absence of a teaching magisterium:

> The poet T. S. Eliot remarked of the Anglican Communion that it insisted on washing its dirty linen in public and added cryptically that at least we know that it is washed. It was anticipated in some quarters, not least I think in some parts of the Anglican Communion itself, that this year's Lambeth conference would be the scene of such a ritual ablution that the communion might wilt under the gaze of public scrutiny.

He went on to say that this had proved not to be the case, praising the openness and frankness with which discussions were conducted. He noted the strong endorsement of the conference for the final report of the first Anglican/Roman Catholic International commission (of which his predecessor Archbishop McAdoo had been co-chairman and which had produced agreed statements on *The Eucharist* and *Ministry* and *Ordination with Elucidations*), and the encouragement given to its successor, ARCIC II, in its ongoing work. The fact that for the past ten years, women had been ordained to the priesthood in various provinces (member churches) of the Anglican Communion had not seriously damaged dialogue between it and the other great Christian churches (though he himself would subsequently, in the debate over women's ordination in the Church of Ireland, see it in terms of a breach of catholicity). The lack of a cohesive teaching authority within Anglicanism was a problem, and the conference had agreed to the establishment of a committee to discuss the development of structures and instruments of unity, to be headed by the Archbishop of Armagh, Robin Eames:

> The Lambeth conference is alive and well and taking measures to improve its fitness to deal more effectively with the modern world. And to this end the Church of Ireland is making a significant contribution.[9]

Donald sought to be reassuring in the wake of adverse reaction to the visit made by Robert Runcie to Pope John Paul II in Rome in 1989. During this visit, Runcie had attended a Papal Mass, and agreed a Common Declaration[10] with the Pope. This declaration, while recognising the difficulties for their dialogue presented by the admission of women to the priesthood in some provinces of the Anglican communion, highlighted the 'certain yet imperfect' communion the churches already shared, grounded in the Trinitarian belief, common baptism, the scriptures, creeds and centuries of inherited tradition. It noted that 'Even in the years of our separation we have been able to recognize gifts of the Spirit in each other.' Separate to the declaration, there were reports of Runcie saying that, in a reunited church, the Pope might exercise a primacy of service. This led to protests from some Protestant clergy, including the Rev. Ian Paisley, who flew out to Rome specially for the purpose. Donald counselled people to read the text of statements, which if read carefully could be seen to be within previously agreed positions between the churches: if people were clear as to what was actually said, they would not 'run away frightened and dejected'. Remaining differences with Rome outlined by him included Papal infallibility, dogmas relating to the Blessed Virgin Mary and problems on the Catholic side relating to the ordination of women. He welcomed a statement from Archbishop Robin Eames reiterating that the Lambeth Conference and its standing committee, the Anglican Consultative Council, was a consultative, rather than a legislative, body and that only the General Synod of the Church of Ireland could determine the church's position 'in all matters of faith and doctrine and relationship with other churches'.[11]

In 1994, Donald visited the Spanish Reformed Episcopal Church in Madrid in Spain to take part in celebrations of the centenary of the consecration of its *Catedral del Redentor* and to preach at its special service. The Church of Ireland had historical associations with the Spanish church, its first bishop having been consecrated by an Archbishop of Dublin, William Conyngham fourth Lord Plunkett (concordats between Spain and England prevented the involvement of the established Church of England there).[12] Donald unveiled a ceramic plaque in the north-west aisle of the cathedral in Madrid which marked the association of the two countries' churches, and was given one to bring back to Ireland, to be placed in Christ Church Cathedral. A Roman Catholic representative attended the Spanish celebrations, expressing fraternal fellowship with the Spanish Reformed Episcopal Church – Donald saw this action as sealing the assurance that things had changed radically for the churches in Spain since the era of General Franco.[13]

Donald also enjoyed strong ecumenical relationships on the interpersonal level. Both he and his successor as Archbishop of Dublin, Walton Empey, were friends with Cardinal Tomás Ó Fiaich, the warm and gregarious Roman Catholic Archbishop of Armagh. Ó Fiaich was a distinguished Irish language scholar and a strong nationalist. Empey recalled 'great soirées' at the Cardinal's residence, Ara Coeli, in Armagh attended by both himself and Donald. Donald recalled receiving 'the most kind reception' at evening gatherings held for the Cardinal's 'Gaelic-speaking friends'. On one occasion, he gently ribbed the Cardinal:

> I know how the Roman Catholic Church rules the world now, you come into the room full of people, some of whom may be opposite to your point of view. You draw out of your pocket this vast pipe, you fill it with tobacco, and in a few minutes none of them can breathe, and this is how you are suppressing the intellect of the opposition!

Donald recalled admonishing the Cardinal at one stage: 'you do too much', noting that Ó Fiaich, 'a heavily built man', had acquired a bicycle at one point, and would ride it around Armagh. The Cardinal died of a heart attack while leading a diocesan pilgrimage from Armagh to Lourdes in 1990 and Donald, who spoke of his death as a 'personal loss', represented the Church of Ireland at the funeral. Reflecting on their friendship, he said: 'We had great fun, I liked him and I think he liked me and was always delighted to see me.'[14]

Donald enjoyed good personal relations with Ó Fiaich's successor, Cardinal Cahal Daly. In Dublin, he had known Archbishop Kevin McNamara (who presided over the Catholic Archdiocese from 1984 until his death in April 1987) for a number of years through the Christological group and held him in warm regard. Donald recounts that, on the night before he died, Archbishop Kevin McNamara telephoned him, to say that he knew he was dying, and that he wanted to say what a great pleasure and joy it was to have had fellowship with Donald for a number of years. A special memorial service was held for the late Archbishop in Christ Church Cathedral, Donald emphasising that 'this is not an exercise in ecclesiastical diplomacy ... but the genuine, spontaneous heartfelt tribute of Christian friends to the memory of a friend.' He was also friendly with McNamara's successor, Archbishop Desmond Connell, a fellow philosopher,[15] whom he entertained to dinner at the See House. Both Archbishops of Dublin exchanged greetings in their respective diocesan magazines, *Church Review* and *Link Up*, in 1994.

Evangelism and Mission

The proclamation of a Decade of Evangelism for the 1990s was the headline initiative which emerged from Lambeth 1988, and the diocese was recognised as the primary unit for its promotion.[16] Determined efforts were made to see it bear fruit in Dublin and Glendalough. A committee was formed to devise a strategy for the Decade, and proposals for a conference on pastoral care emerged from the annual conference of clergy. The Rev. Ricky Rountree was appointed as director, with the task of coordinating the diocesan programme. *Faith Alive* was the title given to the diocesan response to the call of the Lambeth conference, Donald noting the 'forbidding undertones to the title' (a reference to some of the more extreme manifestations of charismatic worship associated with the description 'evangelical') but reassuring his people that *Faith Alive* will reveal 'none of these characteristics'. The Church of Ireland would be responding in its own way, fashioned by its own history, scholarship and sense of identity.

Initial proposals from the diocesan clergy included a year of preparation in formulating plans, the issuing of a prayer card, the holding of 'rudder' focusing days for clergy, a Lenten course and a youth conference. *Faith Alive* ran in three year cycles, and at an early stage, visits to Dublin by the Primates of the Episcopal Church in the United States and in Brazil, and from Archbishop Desmond Tutu of South Africa gave added stimulus to local efforts. The Bishop of New York, Richard Grein, whom Donald had met at the Lambeth Conference, also visited Dublin in 1992, addressing clergy and laity on the topics of *Making a moral decision* and *The nature of commitment* in Taney parish centre and preaching at the annual Citizenship Service at Christ Church Cathedral. The introduction

Donald Caird as Archbishop of Dublin.
(Copyright courtesy Beryl Stone)

A family group in the See House in Dublin. Standing behind Donald
and Nancy are Helen (left), John (centre) and Ann (right).

The Church of Ireland house of bishops in 1986. Donald is seated in the first row, fourth from the left, with the new Archbishop of Armagh, Robin Eames, to his right.

With Archbishop of Canterbury, Robert Runcie (centre), and Bishop Samuel Poyntz of Cork at the British Council of Churches meeting in Cork, April 1986.

Donald (second from left) and other senior clergy greet Queen Elizabeth II at the opening of Partnership House, headquarters of the United Society for the Propagation of the Gospel (USPG) in London, 30 October 1987.

Donald enjoying a sing-song with local people at a function of the Liberties Association in Dublin, 1987.

Minister for Labour Bertie Ahern TD with Donald Caird at the opening of the SPADE enterprise centre in the former St Paul's Church, September 1990. (Copyright courtesy *The Irish Times*)

Donald in Aran sweater and relaxed mode on holidays in 1992, with his son, John, and their Airedale dog, Ben.

Donald in October 1992 with the Bishop of New York, Richard Grein (left), as he is received by the Lord Mayor of Dublin, Gay Mitchell (centre).

Donald (third from left) following the receipt of an honorary degree from the National Council for Educational Awards in November 1993. Pictured are his daughters, Ann (far left) and Helen (second from left); his wife, Nancy (to the right of Donald); Professor Eda Sagarra of Trinity College, Dublin (second from right) and Donald's son, John (far right). (Copyright courtesy Lensmen)

Dáithí Ó Maolchoille of Cumann Gaelach na hEaglaise (left), Donald as Archbishop of Dublin, and Canon Cosslett Quin at the launch of a book of collects in Irish to accompany the Church of Ireland's Alternative Prayer Book in 1994. (Copyright courtesy Lensmen)

Archbishop of Canterbury, Dr George Carey (left), Cardinal Cahal Daly (centre) and Donald during the Archbishop of Canterbury's visit to Ireland, 15–19 November 1994. (Copyright courtesy Pacemaker)

Donald at the SPADE enterprise centre with the Archbishop of Canterbury, George Carey, during the latter's visit to Dublin in 1994. (Photograph courtesy Frank Fennell)

Donald as Archbishop of Dublin pictured with
President Mary Robinson (right) at a function.

A happy family group in retirement. Donald is pictured on the right holding one of his grandchildren. Standing behind him is his son, John, and standing to John's left is Richard Greene. Richard's wife, Ann (Donald's daughter), is seated second from the left, while John's wife, Julie, is seated to the far left. Donald's younger daughter, Helen, is seated in the centre, and her mother, Nancy, is to the right. The adults are surrounded by Donald's grandchildren.

Donald and Nancy in retirement.

Donald (second from right) pictured on one of his regular walks on the pier at Dún Laoghaire, in the company of other retired gentlemen. Pictured also are Mr Bill Murphy (far left), Mr Brendan Matthews (second from left) and Mr Enda Whelan (far right).

Donald with the author outside the old Ó Guithín homestead, Great Blasket Island, August 2008.

Donald pictured outside Kilmalkeader Church of Ireland Church in Corca Dhuibhne, August 2008. The church has been closed since 1980, but it was there in the 1940s that Donald attended a service in Irish on one of his first visits to the Gaeltacht.

of a diocesan cycle of prayer and *Faith Alive* prayer for use in churches kept the Decade of Evangelism to the forefront of worshippers' minds week by week.

Following on the need for an informed laity identified ten years earlier in his sermon at the General Synod service, a new educational initiative for the laity was launched in 1988 'in response to many requests from parishes and individuals for systematic instruction in theology in support of an informed and deeper faith':[17] the Archbishop of Dublin's Course in Theology. Originating as a proposal from the Council for Mission for the dioceses, Donald declared: 'If the ghost of doubt stalks our faith, there was only one way to lay a ghost: face it in the light. This course of lectures and seminars will enable us to face the ghosts of doubt about our faith.'[18] The initiative, launched in 1988, coincided with the announcement of the Decade of Evangelism.

Of two years' duration, the course (presented by a panel of distinguished theologians in the form of seminars involving dialogue and exchange of views) was designed to cover systematically a wide range of theological topics, broadly grouped under the titles: *Creation, Christ, the Spirit* and *the Church*. Featuring end-of-term project work by each course member ranging from essays to recorded interviews on particular subjects, the initiative was a great success and was heavily over-subscribed. Thirty-five people successfully completed the course in May 1990 and in October were to receive their certificates from the Archbishop.[19] In the years following, several further cycles of the course were held.

In the summer of 1992, some one thousand people gathered in Glendalough for an open-air service as Donald called for the Decade of Evangelism to 'come alive', recalling the history of Glendalough and the life of St Kevin. The same year saw the establishment of the charismatic CORE (*City Outreach through Renewal and Evangelism*) project at St Werburgh's in the south inner city, headed by the Rev. Willie Stewart, with an emphasis on informal and enthusiastic forms of worship using modern communication methods. Its launch was accompanied by reassurances from the Archbishop that this would not lead to the displacement of traditional patterns of Church of Ireland worship (such charismatic initiatives in worship were widespread in the Church of England).

In 1994, an *Enquirer's Pack* was launched for persons interested in finding out more about the Christian faith. At his diocesan synod address in October 1995, Donald congratulated the organisers of *Faith Alive*, which had involved 'nearly all of the parishes in a renewal of interest in new ways of Christian nurture for children and adults', through working groups in Christian nurture, worship and lay involvement. Other initiatives included a conference on *Worship for the whole church family* and the production of a hanging library for parents to share their faith with young children, to be distributed by the Mothers' Union.

Another aspect of the dioceses' missionary outreach was the *Flying Angel* centre, located in Alexandra Basin in the North Wall extension to Dublin Port. Run by the church's Mission to Seamen (now the Mission to Seafarers), the centre, based in a portakabin, offered to sailors the opportunity to make telephone calls to their homes all over the world, tea and coffee, a chance to watch television, and a copy of the Bible or New Testament in their own language. Noting that volunteers already included a retired sea captain, radio officer, steward and many others, Donald appealed for volunteers who could be free during the day to visit the ships. His brother Jim's experiences over many years on ships may have been in his mind as he observed that the sailors

> come as lonely men looking for friendship, worried men looking for guidance, bereaved men looking for comfort and sympathy, often harassed men looking for advice or even protection ... The majority come from the Third World. They would have met the *Flying Angel* in most of the large ports, where they have put in to load or unload, so that they don't come as strangers, they have learnt what to expect in the way of kindness, understanding and Christian fellowship.[20]

Mission to those outside was accompanied by the affirmation of the church's community in its different age groups. The importance of offering support and hope to youth was a repeated theme in the Archbishop's public addresses and pronouncements. Unemployment and the often accompanying dangers of alcohol and drug abuse were a threat, and he emphasised the role of organisations like the Boys' Brigade, Girls Brigade, Girls Friendly Society, scouts, guides and youth clubs in the formation of moral character and in giving young people a sense of direction and order in their lives. They offered 'a fulfilled and balanced life in the tradition of our church'.[21] In summer 1995 Donald visited the diocesan youth camp being held at Gurteen Agricultural College to affirm the team of young people who organised and ran the annual event, and its leader, the Rev. Anne Taylor.

However, clergy and church institutions were frequently seen as remote from the daily preoccupations of teenagers and young adults. A Church of Ireland Youth Council forum held at St Patrick's College, Drumcondra, in January 1996 heard strong criticism of the church's leadership from young speakers. The brainchild of the Archbishop of Armagh, Robin Eames, the forum featured the presentation of indictments against the church in the form of a trial, with nine of its bishops sitting in the 'dock'. Pressures on young people ranging from the influence of the media, the music industry and 'how you look', to temptations offered by drugs and sex were starkly illustrated by a sketch in which a teenage boy and a group of girls flirted while about fifty young people in the background chorused in a loud whisper 'sex, sex, sex'. 'Church of Ireland youth finds its clergy largely irrelevant' was the sobering *Irish Times* headline on 8 January 1996, Eames saying the bishops had heard 'a genuine cry' from young people.

The Mothers' Union in 1987 celebrated the centenary of its foundation in Ireland (by the wife of the then rector of Raheny, Anabella Hayes). Donald said the MU afforded women the opportunity

> in the fellowship of the church to learn and discuss those concerns which were perhaps so close to them that they did not articulate them and view them in a wider context: that is, the family and Christian marriage. Over these hundred years, which had seen great social changes, particularly in relation to the place of women in society, one might have thought that the significance of the Mothers' Union would have diminished; but in fact we find that [it] has more than kept pace ... and is as relevant and influential today as it has been at any time in its history.

Nor were the concerns of older members of the community neglected: the Commission for the Care of the Elderly established by the Archbishop made a detailed analysis of the various retirement homes in the diocese, and representatives of the residents were able to bring issues of concern to them for discussion in a Council of Homes.

In 1985, the Taoiseach Garret FitzGerald turned the first sod for the building of twenty-five self-contained units at Brabazon in Sandymount, so that single and married people could enjoy 'privacy as well as warmth and security of communal life when they require it'. Such provision for the elderly, who suffered isolation and loneliness, was, as Donald put it, work 'worthy of the church'.

There was some rationalisation of resources, the Northbrook home re-establishing itself within the complex of Brabazon House in 1990.

In a sermon preached in St Patrick's Cathedral in relation to the Gascoigne home, Donald noted that the home

> is a symbol of what our faith is about – the love of God in creation and redemption, our response to his grace, the expression of thanksgiving in

the support of those who do not enjoy our strength of body, of mind and of the good circumstances of our life.

Population shifts, church closures and redeployment

The question of what to do with long established churches and parishes in the inner city which were suffering from dwindling congregations as a result of movements of population to the suburbs, was one which exercised Donald during his tenure in Dublin, as it had his predecessors. Indeed, in his address to the Dublin and Glendalough diocesan synod in the first year of his tenure, Donald pointed to the work of a 'vigourous committee', the Parochial Organisation and Development Committee, which was addressing itself to the question of the most beneficial deployment of churches which were falling into disuse.

One of the most venerable of these, St George's in Hardwicke Street, finally faced closure in April 1990, its spire having been surrounded by scaffolding owing to its dangerous state of disrepair for the previous ten years. Once the parish church of one of the most fashionable residential districts north of the Liffey, the parish experienced a slow decline, which accelerated after the First World War, people moving to the suburbs but, up to the 1960s, frequently returning for services as accustomed members of its congregation. At the final service, attended by a large congregation, Donald pointed out that all of the great cities of Europe were facing the same problem of congregations moving from the inner city to the suburbs. In his diocesan synod address in 1998, Donald said that to concentrate on such closures and not look to developments in the suburbs (including a new centre in Kill O' The Grange, a parish centre in Bray, a new school in Malahide and seven other new schools in the pipeline) would be a distortion. In private however, at the closure service of St George's, the diocesan communications officer Valerie Jones recalled him looking 'down' and wistful, remarking 'I'm very dubious about all this.' Indeed, some of his fears were subsequently realised when the church became a nightclub, although its intended function at the time of sale had been for offices for a charity.

However, there was also a more positive side to the redeployment of church buildings. Inner city churches which found new uses after closure included St Andrew's Church on Suffolk Street (now a city centre tourist office) and St Kevin's Church on South Circular Road (which became part of the National Rehabilitation Centre). A cause of worry for some time had been the fate of a prominent symbol of the Church of Ireland in the city: the old Synod Hall situated atop St Michael's Hill, opposite Christ

Church Cathedral and linked to it by a covered bridge. The General Synod had not met there since May 1982. In the early 1990s, a body titled The Medieval Trust, under the chairmanship of businessman Craig McKinney of Woodchester Bank, undertook to convert the hall into a heritage centre, *Dublinia*, which would present 'a historically accurate portrayal of life in Dublin in medieval times'.[22] This initiative would secure the maintenance of the outward features of the building, and prove a boon to Christ Church Cathedral, with many of those visiting one of the attractions crossing the bridge afterwards to see the other.

St Paul's Church in North King Street, which closed in November 1987, was developed from 1988 as an enterprise centre, the *Saint Paul's Area Development Enterprise* (SPADE). In his sermon at the closing service in St Paul's in November 1987, Donald highlighted the necessity to look beyond regrets and a sense of loss:

> It cannot but be sad to close a church where faithful people have learned the ways of God, where they worshipped God, where they had been baptised into his name, where they had been nurtured as children in his faith, where they have been confirmed in that faith, where they have taken the marriage vows, and kept them, where they had seen their children brought up to worship God as they had learned to do, where in the fullness of years they had been laid to rest 'in the sure and certain hope of Resurrection to eternal life'. ... But the faith of Christ still triumphs ... George Berkeley was deeply concerned about the economic state of Ireland in his day, for he maintained that no country can be strong or secure while part of its population is weak and deprived. He wrote a very perceptive book, *The Querist*, in 1735, criticising the present economic policy in Ireland ... Berkeley was a clergyman with a deep sense that religion had to do with the whole of life, including the work life of ordinary people – God was not confined to the altar. I believe that it would rejoice his heart to learn that the select vestry of this parish petitioned the Archbishop of Dublin in 1987 formally to close this church, and to allow the church to become an enterprise centre to help the unemployed in Ireland in the 1980s ... As this parish was renowned in each century for its charity and concern for the poor and distressed, it will still serve the needs of those who are less fortunate in a very practical and constructive way, for 'Behold, I make all things new.'

SPADE was officially opened in September 1990 by the Minister for Labour, Bertie Ahern TD. By late 1991, Donald was able to report to his synod that twenty-six units were in operation giving employment to about sixty people, and some one hundred people had found employment over the course of the development of the project. Examples of enterprises which had been set up included cake and confectionery outlets and a fashion design unit. In 1995, an extension to the project was officially opened.

Since 1979, in an era of recession and high unemployment, the Diocesan Employment Bureau had operated drop-in centres in the parishes of Monkstown, Dawson Street and North Strand, registering over one thousand jobseekers by late 1988, and finding job placements for 'hundreds'. In his synod speech of that year, Donald paid tribute to the key drivers of the bureau: businessmen Frank Luce, Ronnie Osborne and Alf Keatinge.

In April 1988, Donald took issue with a report in *The Financial Times* stating that there were barely two thousand members of the Church of Ireland in Dublin – assuring his flock in his letter in the diocesan magazine in April 1988 that they numbered some thirty-two thousand in Dublin, while Dublin and Glendalough combined had in excess of forty thousand members. He also noted the growth in suburban parish population to balance decline in the inner city. This combative defence of the position of the Church of Ireland was also evident in his challenge to figures in the 1991 census, which had indicated a decline of 13.1 per cent in the number of Protestants in the Republic.

He stated that the census did not reflect experience within the Church, and suggested that those who had reported their religious affiliation as 'Anglican', as well as some of the group who describe themselves as 'Protestants' could also be claimed as part of the Church of Ireland number. He believed that some people in making their census return would regard the question of denominational affiliation as an intrusion, and cited the building of new schools, school extensions, new parochial halls and parish centres, and the refurbishment of churches as conveying an impression of growth rather than decline. He had his staff carry out a separate diocesan census, which indicated a figure of some thirty-one thousand Church members known to rectors in Dublin and Glendalough.

The Church of Ireland Gazette reported in May 1994 that, as a result of the strong stand taken by the Archbishop, the Central Statistics Office was obliged to issue an amended estimation of its figures, revising downwards an earlier published decline of 13.1 per cent in the Protestant population to one of 6.5 per cent. In the 1981 census a category of unspecified Protestants had been included with the numbers given for the Church of Ireland population, and its exclusion in 1991 had created a false impression of a greater decline than had actually occurred. The 1991 census recorded 89,187 Church of Ireland (including 'Protestant'), 13,199 Presbyterian and 5,037 Methodist, in a total population of 3,525,719.

Dublin county (which was only part of Donald's dioceses) had a Church of Ireland (including 'Protestant') population of 28,326.

Media and communications

By tradition, and in virtue of his metropolitical role as Primate of the Church of Ireland's southern province,[23] it fell to the Archbishop of Dublin to be the prime spokesperson for the Church in matters concerning the Republic of Ireland.

There was a concern among key individuals with an overview of the dioceses such as Gordon Linney (Archdeacon of Dublin), John Paterson (Dean of Christ Church Cathedral) and Canon Desmond Harman (editor of the diocesan magazine *Church Review*) around 1989 that not enough media coverage was being given to the Archbishop and diocesan developments. This was felt to stem from a couple of factors. As the debate on the Anglo–Irish agreement and the tentative peace process progressed, there was an increasing focus on the position of the Archbishop of Armagh. Robin Eames's Anglican Communion involvements internationally brought a lot of press attention, notably from England (arising out of the 1988 Lambeth Conference, with him being appointed to chair the Communion's commission on Communion and Women in the Episcopate). The Church of Ireland press officer, Liz Harries, was based in Belfast and much of her time was taken up with the role of the Primate, although she was answerable to the General Synod.

Allied to this were concerns about Donald's uneasiness with the media and the need to get an intermediary with a greater feel for such matters. It was felt that the state of the Church in Dublin and Glendalough at this time – with school extensions and new parish centres coming on stream, as well as a significant number of ordinations to the priesthood – deserved a higher profile. In his carefully (and cautiously) worded sermons and public pronouncements, Donald's philosophical training and methodology were often evident and the leading clergy felt they had something of a treasure in him, but that his light was being hidden under a bushel.

Gordon Linney approached Valerie Jones, a former teacher at Zion national school in Rathgar and one of the diocesan synod representatives for St Ann's, Dawson Street, who at the time was completing an M.Litt. degree. Jones knew Donald from serving on diocesan and General Synod boards of education, and also as a former pupil of Coláiste Moibhí when it had been based in Shankill. She agreed to take up the role of diocesan information officer in a voluntary capacity, the position subsequently becoming a paid part time one. In due course, the position of diocesan communications officer was made full-time, and Jones was appointed to the position. Donald maintained his attitude of wariness towards the media, seeming to feel that they were waiting for an opportunity to attack him. He once remarked to his Archdeacon that he didn't like the cut and thrust of the media: 'I'm not a fighter.' He felt also that the it displayed a tendency to build a person up one day, only to pull them down the next.

The picking out of the political and controversial aspects of his statements and addresses, to the neglect of spiritual points, seemed to mystify him. He was not well versed in the art of the 'soundbite', and expressed exasperation when the media picked only a few points out of a lengthy and closely argued sermon, which might run for ten to fifteen pages. He never understood that the media 'don't want the spiritual', observed Jones, who also felt that Donald did not understand the concept of saying to a journalist that something was 'off the record'. He needed advice on dealing with the media, including the basic precaution of walking slowly when a cameraman was present in order to prevent a fuzzy picture resulting due to the slower shutter speeds of the time.

Valerie Jones' extensive contributions of reports and photographs to *Church Review* earned praise from its editor, Canon Desmond Harman, as contributing greatly to communications in the dioceses, although the work was too much 'for even one full-time person'. *Church Review* played a vital role in the internal communications of the diocese. Paying tribute to Harman and Jones in his 1994 synod address, Donald called for greater support in the diocese to increase the magazine's revenue and viability, noting that about four thousand copies were sold monthly 'which is about one copy for every nine members of the Church of Ireland population of these dioceses'.

He was keen also that the church would exploit opportunities offered by the government's plans for independent local radio and television. Up to 1989, all national and local radio services were provided by Raidió Teilifís Éireann (RTÉ), although there had been for many years a vibrant 'pirate' radio sector operating outside the law in areas around the country. The Church of Ireland would, Donald declared in 1988, play a significant part at local level in promoting this, suggesting cooperation at the level of combined parishes in local areas: 'we should not merely accept but positively promote these new developments'.

Ordination of women to the priesthood

It was during Donald's term in office as Archbishop of Dublin that moves to effect a historic change in the ministry of the Church of Ireland by allowing the ordination of women to the priesthood intensified. The General Synod approved measures to allow the ordination of women to the diaconate in 1985 and the first candidate, Katharine Poulton, began her studies that year. This was inevitably seen, however, by protagonists of change as but a first step. Trinity College in Dublin hosted a conference on the ministry of women in 1986, the proceedings described by Donald in his diocesan synod address as excellent while contrasting its conduct with the recent behaviour of advocates of women ordination in Westminster 'where the legitimate authority of the Church of England was brought into public disrepute'. In advance of the conference, he had noted in his 'Bishop's letter' in the diocesan magazine the developments in relation to women in the diaconate, but warned that, in relation to ordination to the priesthood, the Anglican communion could not act as though it were in a vacuum. He himself conducted the first ordination of a female deacon in the Republic (Mrs Ginnie Kennerley) in June 1988. It was a heady time, and the sister Church of England had not yet approved the ordination of women to the priesthood.

The matter featured prominently in discussions at the 1988 Lambeth conference, with Archbishop Robin Eames being appointed to lead a commission on women in the episcopate, as mentioned earlier. Deep divisions appeared in Anglicanism internationally following the consecration of the first Anglican woman bishop in the United States in 1989. Views on women's ordination among senior church figures evolved over a period of years. The Bishop of Tuam, John Neill, had been among those opposed, initially, but his chairing of a discussion group on the issue at the 1988 Lambeth conference significantly influenced his thinking. Subsequent to this, he chaired the Church of Ireland's General Synod select committee on women's ordination, and it was he who, at the key General Synod in May 1989, introduced the resolution authorising women's ordination. This cleared the way for a bill to be brought forward the following year giving legal effect to the measure in the Church.

Donald, a cautious traditionalist, made an important contribution at the 1989 Synod, warning that a vote in favour would liken the assembly to a 'herd of lemmings'. Praising the work of those women who had been ordained to the diaconate the previous year, he felt that 'one year is a very short period in the history of our ancient church', and moving too quickly to sanction their ordination to the priesthood could be regretted.

> Indecision is not due to lack of ability to grasp the available facts, or to lack of determination or moral courage, but it is due to the great inherent complexity of the issue itself ... it is due to a conscientious concern that our actions should not jeopardise the status of our ancient Church in relation to other communions maintaining Catholic faith and order.

Noting that six provinces of the Anglican Communion, and the diocese of Hong Kong, had already ordained women to the priesthood, and one province had ordained a woman to the episcopate, he warned 'we must remember that we are Anglicans, and not lemmings, and we can still choose when to jump, or not to jump.' While some of the provinces which had moved to ordaining women as priests and which had committed themselves to consecrate them as bishops in due course, were among the numerically largest 'and temporally most powerful' provinces in the Anglican Communion, 'reception on such a vital issue ... must surely be indicated by the whole church Catholic and not only the Anglican Communion.' The communion was in official dialogue with both the Roman Catholic church and the Orthodox churches on the issue 'and our action in passing these resolutions would certainly be seem to pre-empt the conclusions of such negotiations'.

He did not think it was entirely fanciful to hope that other Christian communions which shared the orders of Bishop, Priest and Deacon might come to ordain women to the diaconate in the future, so that 'all the churches which share the Catholic orders of ministry' might be able to stand together on the basis of a commonly recognised diaconate with interchange of ministries at that level, 'as the first major movement towards unity by stages'. While he was not persuaded by arguments against ordination to the priesthood based on the 'intrinsic unsuitability' of women, he recognised the weight of tradition, and expressed concern in relation to relations with the neighbouring Church of England. There was the possibility that women priests of the Church of Ireland would not be recognised or allowed to minister there if that Church [which was then discussing the issue] did not end up taking the same step: 'I feel on this issue that we should not deliberately step out of line with the Mother church of the Anglican communion, however much we may disagree on lesser issues.' Though he saw no great division resulting for the Church of Ireland, 'a cohesive and close-knit community', if women were ordained, he was concerned for its relationship with other churches 'and I do not see it in the present context of the Church of Ireland [as] contributing to [its] specific mission ...'

Nonetheless, the resolution was passed, and the bill allowing women priests was finally made law at the General Synod in May of the following year. The Dean of Christ Church Cathedral, John Paterson, described the measure as 'totalitarian' because there was no clause allowing for conscientious objection by dissenting clergy. In contrast, deaconess Diana McClatchey, a member of the standing committee of the sister Church of England's General Synod, described the Irish vote as 'a great encouragement' to similar progress in England.

In his 'Bishop's letter' in *Church Review* the following month, Donald noted the assurance given by Archbishop Eames that, at next year's Synod, he would introduce a bill to safeguard the rights in conscience of those who disagreed. However, he emphasised that the church was a family, and the decision must not be accepted grudgingly, but in a spirit of 'rejoicing with those who rejoice' in a newfound ministry. In a sermon preached that summer in St Patrick's Cathedral, and again in his diocesan synod address that autumn, Donald called for sensitivity towards those who have difficulty or feel hurt by women's ordination. However, he stressed that he 'totally' accepted the decision and would shortly ordain the first woman to the priesthood in the diocese of Dublin and Glendalough, the Rev. Ginnie Kennerley. There were clearly sensitivities for the Archbishop, with the position of Dean Paterson and others to consider – which he had expressed in a conversation with Kennerley: 'Do you realise that by ordaining you I shall put myself out of communion with the Bishop of Chichester?' Kennerley herself had invited senior Roman Catholic clergy she knew to her ordination (in October 1990), *The Irish Times* capturing an iconic photograph of her embracing Father Romuald Dodd OP in the grounds of Christ Church Cathedral the following day.

While the Rev. Kennerley felt that Donald's lemmings speech in 1989 had been somewhat 'preposterous' and 'over the top', she did understand his feeling that the Church of Ireland was in danger of rushing over a cliff on a wave of 'women's libbery', and that if the Church of England did not ultimately follow, it would look pretty stupid and regret it. In regard to women proceeding no further than the diaconate, she felt that this was 'a big cop-out':

In England, they tried having permanent deacons, I think in Exeter Cathedral, in an attempt to demonstrate that this was a perfectly valid ministry ... For a start we went along with it but we formed the Women's Ministry Group in the mid-Eighties and after legislation was passed to allow the ordination of women deacons in 1984 we decided we should host a Conference to discuss their future ministry. We had Phoebe the deacon on the front of the leaflets and we invited Diana McClatchey, a senior deaconess from England ... and the Primus of the Scottish Episcopal Church, the Rt Rev. Alastair Haggart.

The Conference was held at Trinity College in April 1986, and Donald, as Archbishop, came to preside at the Eucharist. To the surprise of many of the women present, who were prepared to have the diaconate accepted by male clergy at the Conference as the limit of progression possible for women, many Church of Ireland clergymen stood up to say that a pile of women deacons would be no use to them; they needed help with the sacramental ministry, somebody to take the early morning service or to take over when they themselves were away. 'Stanley Baird was very strong on that, rooted in practicality. There was no point in ordaining somebody to do half the job.'

In relation to her own ordination as deacon in 1988, Kennerley recalled that a friend of hers had been very amused that Donald had attached his 'own gloss' to the prayer for her progression to the priesthood at the end of the ordination ritual, adding the words 'so far as the law allows'. She explained:

> The impression was that he was not committing himself, that he couldn't bear to pray that I would be called to the priesthood. He seemed to be implying, 'I'm ordaining this woman deacon; it doesn't mean I'm thinking of ordaining her as a priest.'

Although Donald had been absent when the bill introducing women's ordination was brought before the General Synod in May 1990 (he was attending the funeral of his friend Cardinal Tomás Ó Fiaich in Armagh), Kennerley thinks he was definitely there for the actual vote because 'twelve bishops all voted, nine for, three against … and we knew who the three were. It was filtered through and Donald was one …' However, the minority 'mostly came around very generously … Donald is a very loyal son of the Church of Ireland and accepted the decision without question'. When she herself came to be ordained on the October following this vote, she requested that Bishops John Neill and Henry McAdoo, both known supporters of women's ordination, should lay hands on her along with Donald, fearing that a 'deficit of intention' to ordain on Donald's part might be alleged by those still opposed:

> Donald never gave me to think he might do it with his fingers crossed behind his back, but I do know he experienced some reluctance, pointing out to me that by ordaining me priest he would put himself out of communion with the Bishop of Chichester … I did fear that some of the more extreme members of the Concerned Clergy might argue later that I hadn't really been ordained because Donald didn't really mean it.

So the fear was that a deficit of intent would be imputed to Donald by others, not that he would actually entertain such a reservation, she explained. There was considerable nervousness all round:

> Indeed the very next year, there was an attempt in General Synod to relativise the ordination of women by voting that ... clergy who could not and did not accept the ordination of women should in no wise be blocked from preferment on that account.

Kennerley argued that this was in effect to say that the recognition of women clergy was optional, and its effectiveness would be judged over time, allowing the possibility that the church might change its mind and 'go back on it'. This would place a question mark over women priests. 'It would have made us second-class priests.'[24]

She felt that Donald's full acceptance of women on a par with men in the priesthood was an incremental process: 'I think really it was "little by little". He first accepted women deacons, then that they could be priests, then that a woman could actually be rector of the parish. He didn't really think initially that that could happen in his diocese.'

Kennerley says that she was told by Donald in May 1993 that there was

> no way I'd get a parish in the diocese [of Dublin and Glendalough], but in June he was asking me would I accept a nomination to Narraghmore and Castledermot in Glendalough ... Then, less than a year later, when I was raising funds for a new roof on Castledermot church ... he came down and had obviously decided that women *can* do this! 'Here's this woman who's hardly arrived, and she's already nearly raised the money for a new roof!' ... I knew I was accepted when he got up and instead of [referring to] the Rev. Kennerley he said 'Ginnie'. I thought 'Ah, he respects me at last [as a priest], he can use my first name in public.' But before that, he had told one of my women students 'If you want to be a priest, you know, you'll probably have to go to Hong Kong.'

Considering this change in Donald's position, she recalls Daphne Wormell, who had been chair of the Women's Ministry Group and one of the first women lay readers in Dublin and in the country, saying to her,

'Donald is conservative and cautious, and he's against it now, but believe me he is a man who is willing to change his mind so we have to remember that.'[25] And he did change, she remembers.

> He wasn't obstinate ... Donald became a really good friend after that ... gradually. He would come down to Timolin, I would have him and Nancy

for supper and he'd do a harvest or confirmation service or whatever. Towards the end of his time as Archbishop, he'd be on the phone: 'Oh, Nancy and I are going down to Kildare, would you come out to dinner with us at the Red House?' [a local inn].

Noting that the Women's Ministry Group (WMG) group 'sort of faded out' once women's ordination was achieved, she felt that a support network for women clergy in the diocese was not seen as necessary by the 'next group of women' such as Gillian Wharton, who probably just wanted to 'get on with the job' and blend in rather than being 'in a group of mutually supporting women'.

The Rev. Gillian Wharton, who was ordained in June 1993 for the diaconate as curate assistant for Glenageary parish, recalls her final year of training for the ministry in the Church of Ireland Theological College. Parishes seeking new curates would contact the college, the candidates selecting from a list of three in which they were interested. Three rectors would then interview each candidate. Wharton recalls that there were three women in her year, of whom two were from Northern Ireland and therefore most likely to seek a posting to a parish there. As she was the only candidate without such a geographical restriction, Dublin came up for discussion, and the view expressed was 'Dublin [diocese] won't take anyone anyway because Donald Caird won't take a woman' (the Rev. Ginnie Kennerley wasn't in the full-time stipendiary ministry at this point). One of the parish rectors to interview her was Gordon Linney, Donald's Archdeacon and rector of Glenageary:

> I would have been aware of [Linney's progressive] views. I did the interview, and had pneumonia at the time. I got out of bed to do it and went back. The principal [of the college] then said 'Gordon Linney wants to see you in my study' so I got dressed again and went back down … I was shocked. Gordon Linney said 'you told me you weren't choosing a place, if you had the choice you were choosing a rector, so what's wrong with me (laughs)?' … I didn't think at the time this was Gordon Linney wanting to make the initiative [of having the first woman curate in Dublin] but now I know that was the case.
>
> After I'd been there for about a year or so, Gordon Linney said he felt he needed to bring the first woman stipendiary curate to Dublin so women would know it's okay to come to Dublin and Glendalough dioceses. He would be very close to Donald Caird. I don't know if it was ever discussed between them or not. I'd say Donald knew if Gordon Linney could, he'd bring a woman to Dublin at that time. I would say it was not even [directly discussed], Donald would know the way Gordon Linney would be [thinking], and probably not [be] surprised.

At the time, Ginnie Kennerley was lecturing in the theological college and was a non-stipendiary minister in Bray, while another woman, Margaret Gilbert, was also in the non-stipendiary ministry in the diocese, having been ordained deacon a year ahead of Wharton:

> It never crossed my mind that Donald might have any reticence about ordaining me to the priesthood … before that he would have been out in the theological college quite a bit, he and I would have known each other. He was Visitor to the college … once I was ordained, I never noticed any [difference in treatment from that given to men], never, to be fair to Donald.

She recalls Donald telephoning her in the summer of 1993. He replied to her greeting with 'hello, Archbishop speaking' and Wharton, thinking this was a prank being played by a friend, said 'X, would you ever get lost …!' Unruffled, this voice continued, 'how you coping with the Archdeacon being on holidays?' I thought, 'Oh Lord, it's Donald Caird!' She had been there about a month and he phoned to see how she was getting on.

In an interview with the author, Donald said that he was not 'put out' by the fact that Ginnie Kennerley had asked Bishop John Neill and former Archbishop Henry McAdoo to also lay hands on her at ordination – 'the more the better … I had accepted the decision of the church and went along with it wholeheartedly.' He missed the opening of the 1990 General Synod debate as he was attending Cardinal Ó Fiaich's funeral, but also felt that 'the Primate thought it would be kinder to relieve me of embarrassment, which I wasn't – but it was a generous and thoughtful act on his part. He was chairman of the Synod and couldn't go anyway.' Reflecting on his thinking on women priests, he states that his arguments were based on church discipline and tradition and that by embracing the measure, the Church of Ireland would place itself further away from 'the two great churches'. This he felt was unnecessary, when the other churches could have been approached with the very just argument that women be admitted to the diaconate. He recalled his predecessor Henry McAdoo, 'one of our best theologians' stating in the course of a presentation to the house of bishops that there was no way the church could deny ordination to the diaconate to women.[26]

Looking back, he said that some women coming in from 'all areas of life, who were always interested in the church' have brought with them great gifts:

> On the whole I have come round. I was very uncertain. I always held the
> view that a very good case could be made for ordination to the diaconate
> because St Paul talks of Phoebe the Deacon (not deaconess) in Corinthians.
> He was commending various members of the church.

He felt that there was never a very strong *theological* argument against
women priests. Opposition to it was based on the tradition of the
universal church, he said, noting that the Orthodox would not countenance women priests 'and they were not very keen on women deacons
even'. He did not subscribe to the Roman Catholic position based upon
the physical nature of men resembling that of God, 'that women were
losing out physically on an aspect that would have related them closer
to God. I don't think that is tenable. It is a pity that argument is still used
and I wouldn't use it.'

Walton Empey, in an interview with the author, recalled the late Henry
McAdoo advising that 'we must just think theologically in relation to
women priests' (rather than blindly accepting tradition). McAdoo had
ultimately persuaded Empey that the ordination of women would
happen in the course of time in the Roman Catholic Church, although
perhaps not in the Orthodox: 'as co-chair of ARCIC, he had some insight
into what some people thought on the Roman Catholic side.' Donald's
other colleague in the house of bishops, Samuel Poyntz, feels that a factor
in Donald's reluctance to countenance the major step of ordaining women
to the priesthood may have been his role as Archbishop of Dublin and
Primate of Ireland, a senior leadership position which required him to
take cognisance of the breadth of views in the church as a whole, and not
just his own dioceses.

Conversely, in an interview with the author, Robin Eames said that
while he had mixed feelings, he located his sense of responsibility (as
Primate of All Ireland in the chairing of the General Synod discussions)
as taking the steps that would reflect the mind of the Synod: 'I think
Donald's objections were rooted in the catholicity argument – that's fair.
Donald was knowledgeable about the Anglican communion [worldwide]
but not as involved in it – I was the opposite.'

John Neill thought that Donald probably sensed that the mind of the
church was moving in a certain direction, and that it would not be correct
to allow himself as bishop, or his diocese, to become a focus or totem for
those opposed to women's ordination in the Church of Ireland – in fact
there would be no episcopal focus for such traditionalists in Ireland.
Referring to the development of a theory of 'two integrities' in England,
whereby although women's ordination was voted through, detailed

provision was made for opponents (including separate episcopal oversight by traditionally-minded 'flying bishops'), Neill said the Church of Ireland recognised individuals who held differing views as valued clergy,

> but we never said we valued their *views* ... I remember once talking to one of the [English] flying bishops ... in my car, and he said 'John, it's terrible to be consecrated on a single issue, it means you can never change your mind.'

Gillian Wharton feels that the smallness and intimacy of the Church of Ireland, where so many clergy and people were personally known to each other, meant that the progression of women to the priesthood was not the 'faceless concept' it might be in a larger church such as the Church of England. Another significant divergence from the English experience was the fact that a large number of women deacons had not been built up prior to admission to the priesthood: the first woman deacon Katharine Poulton had been ordained in Northern Ireland in 1987, followed by Ginnie Kennerley in Dublin in 1988. There was no damburst of large groups of women being ordained all at once, and the progression was incremental.

Wharton maintained a strong bond of friendship with one of the most committed traditionalists, Dean John Paterson. Ahead of her ordination, she sent out the traditional Embertide card to people in the diocese, asking for prayers as an ordinand. She included Paterson in the mailing, with a covering note: 'I'm not sure if I should send this to you or not, I hope you won't be offended but I didn't want you to be the only person I didn't send one to, in the diocese.' She received by return a 'lovely letter' from Paterson, who said he had never been so moved by a letter, and assuring her that whatever reservations he had in relation to the ordination of women were completely put to one side when praying for anybody preparing for ordination. He would certainly pray for Wharton as he prayed for all candidates. He hoped to be present at her ordination, and if he felt that he could not bring himself to lay hands on her during the ceremony, that he would not then lay hands on any of the candidates, be they male or female – 'and I don't know if he did or not, it was like a scrum there!' Indeed, Paterson would subsequently appoint Wharton as the first woman priest vicar in an Irish cathedral.

Wharton recalled an anecdote some six years after she had been ordained, when Donald had retired as Archbishop. She and her husband were present at a dinner also attended by Donald and Nancy, as well as by Donald's successor Walton Empey and his wife Louie. The two bishops were wearing their clerical collars, while Wharton was wearing a dress. The host said 'I must take a photograph of Gillian with the two bishops', joking that this would serve for posterity when Wharton became the first woman bishop. 'The hilarious thing about this', responded Donald, 'is that [Walton and myself] were both opposed to the ordination of women – until we met you, my dear!' Amid great laughter, Wharton accused Donald of having swallowed the Blarney Stone whole.[27] She reflected in 2011:

> I never experienced anything from Donald but absolute warmth and [the] sense of him being my Father in God, and we would have a great relationship even now. He would come to retired clergy [events] in our rural deanery and [I experienced] nothing but warmth and affection for him and from him, and I think that speaks volumes.

Clergy

A few key appointments in the dioceses set the tone for Donald's time as Archbishop of Dublin, and brought to prominence a range of voices who would have a significant impact on the Church of Ireland in succeeding decades. In March 1988, the rector of Glenageary, Co. Wicklow, Rev. Gordon Linney was appointed Archdeacon of Dublin to succeed the venerable Roy Warke, who had been elected as Bishop of Cork (Cecil Price was Archdeacon of the Glendalough part of the dioceses, later succeeded by Edgar Swann). Linney, a Dubliner, had worked in a bank before entering training for the ministry in 1966. Having served a curacy in Northern Ireland, and been Dean's vicar of St Patrick's Cathedral group of parishes, he was a member of the Diocesan Council and the Glebes and Finance Committee, as well as having been honorary secretary of the diocesan Board of Education for a number of years.

In 1989, on the retirement of Tom Salmon as Dean of Christ Church Cathedral, Donald brought his old colleague from Kildare, John Paterson to Dublin as Salmon's successor. He had great regard for Paterson,[28] whom he described as 'very well read, a fine musician and good organiser', whose ordering of the services of the house of God 'will be to him not so much a solemn duty as a joy and challenge'.[29] In his diocesan synod addresses, Donald always made sure to pay tribute to the clergy, officers and committees who were vital to the administration of the church in the diocese, including the archdeacons, the diocesan secretary, the secretaries of the Synods, the Diocesan Council, the members of the

Glebes and Finance Committee and his personal secretary. One man – Walter Fisher – who had joined the diocesan office in 1928 was stepping down from the office of diocesan and provincial registrar after sixty-seven years, an 'astounding record of service'.[30]

Linney and Donald became close colleagues and collaborators in taking the work of the dioceses forward in the years that followed, and as contributors to public debate. They typically met on a Tuesday to discuss the business of the diocese: the agenda normally comprised a discussion of any 'crisis' which might have emerged, arrangements to be made for major diocesan events, issues concerning parishes (vacancies, and any problems or disputes), public relations, and matters concerning education and health. They were regularly joined by the Archdeacon of Glendalough and the Dean of Christ Church for these meetings.

In regard to Donald's role as 'Father in God' to his individual priests in the dioceses, Linney (who as Archdeacon worked closely with Donald in pastoral cases) recalled that Donald 'would be very distressed [whenever difficult personal cases arose], because he knew everyone so well'. However when he had to be, he could be strict and people would be left in no doubt as to the seriousness with which he would view a particular situation. 'For a small church, we knew each other very closely and you think of the wife and children, so issues were never easy to deal with.' Linney reflected that while the Roman Catholic Church was in a position to move priests around, for example in respect of issues which might arise from clerical celibacy, 'we're dealing with a more complex set of relationships and I think Donald found [it] at times very difficult because he did feel for the people involved; he had an extraordinary sensitivity.'

In the case of a priest in the dioceses who suffered from severe problems with alcohol, the provisions that Donald made for his care behind-the-scenes were 'extraordinary, and the public would not see this'. Problems with priests and alcohol amounted to a handful of cases over the years, according to Linney, who emphasised that there was a wider alcohol problem in society and the Church of Ireland clergy were no exception to this. To draw parallels with alcohol abuse among some celibate Roman Catholic clergy might distort the picture, whereas alcohol problems 'in the wider society of married people' might be a more relevant comparison. In one particular case, Donald resorted to direct personal action: bundling a priest into a car so that he would receive the necessary professional care.

While not great in terms of numbers of cases, Donald and Linney had to deal with some complex situations in regard to clergy discipline. There must have been enough, however, to give cause for the odd joke about the mysterious 'black book' of 'fellows who got into trouble' according to former diocesan communications officer Valerie Jones, who emphasised the discretion exercised by both Donald and his successor Walton Empey in such matters.

Adverting to a pastoral case of which he was aware, Bishop Paul Colton, who in Donald's time was rector of Castleknock parish, noted that Donald 'was there practically and meaningfully for that priest in that time of catastrophic need'. The capacity to take decisive action where required, balanced the more rarefied and thoughtful side of Donald's personality: this attested to the fact that he wasn't aloof ... 'in the same way that the witticisms [did] ... he was great company – at least I found him so – to be with'.

Individual priests have to bear a certain emotional burden of matters confided in them by the laity. Linney emphasised that, if something were confided in a priest, this was something he must not share with his wife or anybody else. 'That's always a temptation for married clergy but I'm very strict about it, if you're told something in confidence, that is what it means.' The burden of stress on clergy, their spouses and families, and the importance of providing support to them was emphasised by Donald in his diocesan synod address in 1995, as he announced the formation of a new clergy support group – the names of the support group members being sent to clergy and their spouses separately 'so that all clergy and their spouses would be free and independent ... should they wish to avail of the help of the group'. Donald welcomed the group as 'a great assistance to me and is an extension of my charge as pastor pastorum in the dioceses'.

Donald could sometimes convey an abstracted nature, and Walton Empey felt that some priests might feel there was little point in troubling him unduly – 'this in no way took from the warmth of their regard, but rather, with a smile, they would get on with it'. Colton responded to a question on Donald's 'approachability' for his priests:

> He wasn't alone in rathering that you wouldn't come to him on trivialities. I would find now that [with] a new era [of] a plethora of regulations and all of that, a terrible fear among the clergy [would arise] so that they come to you [as bishop] more readily. We [in our time as priests] wouldn't have troubled any bishop about something to which we might have been expected to find answers ourselves. He wasn't alone in that – I found him approachable, in some ways we were quite like-minded, he quite liked the lawyer in me so we got on. I think it is true to say that there were people who irritated him ... I know, visibly at diocesan synod when some people got up to speak, you could see him thinking 'oh no, not – here we go again.'

Colton found Donald 'very pastoral in his own way', recalling the thoughtfulness of a visit made by both him and Nancy to Colton and his wife Susan shortly after the birth of their twin sons, bearing a small gift, and Donald taking a service for Colton. 'Donald was very good with [the baby boys] and [he quipped] "well, there we are now, with Colton and Son and Son!"'

Shock and sadness visited the Archbishop, clergy and people of Dublin and Glendalough in early January 1990. The rector of Rathdrum, Glenealy, Derralossary and Laragh, Co. Wicklow, Rev. Stephen Hilliard, was tragically killed by an intruder in his quiet rural rectory in the early hours of a Tuesday morning. Hilliard was a young man of forty-two years of age, married to Betty and with a four-year-old daughter, Catherine, and had only been instituted as rector to the parish some six weeks earlier. He had previously worked as a journalist and subeditor at *The Irish Times* before entering the ministry (skills which he had fruitfully deployed in his very brief time as rector, in editing a book of essays contributed by older members of the Mothers' Union, and bringing out his single edition of the parish newsletter). He also had a deep knowledge and love of the Irish language, and Conradh na Gaeilge (the Gaelic League) wrote to Donald expressing sympathy. A man of remarkable personal charm, he was held in enormous affection by those who knew him. Large numbers attended his requiem eucharist at Christ Church Cathedral. Hilliard's widow Betty and brother Martin read the lessons, his mother Eithne being the other principal mourner. Nancy Caird sat supportively beside them in the pew.

The diocesan clergy conference in 1987 proposed a scheme for sabbatical leave, for the purposes of study, wider experience and spiritual refreshment, which would enable clergy who had spent ten or more years in their parish to get away for a period of about three months abroad, or to recognised institutions of theological studies in Britain and Ireland, so that they might benefit from wider parochial experience, more concentrated periods of study, or missionary work, and 'bring the benefit of this experience back to their parishes and the diocese'. Donald expressed an interest in the building up of a small fund to assist the scheme, to which clergy and laity could subscribe.

Some character sketches

The Church of Ireland Archbishop of Dublin is automatically the chair of the Board of Governors of Marsh's Library, situated in the close of St Patrick's Cathedral. Marsh's contains a collection of rare books and manuscripts collected by Archbishop Narcissus Marsh, an eighteenth-century predecessor of Donald's. Muriel McCarthy, for many years the library's Keeper, felt that Donald truly appreciated Marsh's, which was 'a scholar's library'. Narcissus Marsh was a polymath; a scientist and a musician, he was also interested in medicine. Donald's interests, ranging over the Irish language, religion, philosophy and history, would have made him a kindred spirit:

> There was a book here with Ben Jonson's motto [in Latin] in it and I wasn't sure what it meant. One day I met Donald Caird on the street and immediately he knew what [it] meant. He took his role as governor very seriously and never missed a meeting.

Samuel Poyntz, who sat beside Donald at meetings of the standing committee of General Synod for over ten years, recollected that occasionally 'I'd get a Limerick passed to me about what someone had said, or a portrait etched of someone ... he'd lost attention [due to] someone waffling away! But he could think very deeply when he wanted to – this kept him sane!' Robin Eames, in emphasising Donald's capacity to be a good listener, highlighted one gesture made by Donald whenever he thought he had driven a point home successfully in discussion: he would rub his hands vigourously together in a kind of expression of glee, evincing a boyish enthusiasm: 'Walton [Empey] and I would remark on that, 'You know, Donald has won the case, he's rubbed his hands!' He recalled that, at meetings, Donald would appear to have 'a sort of faraway look', leading an observer to think he had lost the thread of the discussion: 'but what in fact was happening [was], that he'd seen another dimension to what was being discussed. He would then come back to the exact point, and that was the philosopher at work rather than the activist.'

Gordon Linney recalled an occasion where a discussion on the question of authority in the church was being held after lunch. Donald appeared to fall asleep (or so everybody had assumed):

> One of the younger bishops proceeded to speak about the importance of the office of Bishop, and how the General Synod ought to legislate to give them more power. When it concluded, Donald rubbed his ears ... shook himself, and said 'I agree', then proceeded to disagree, saying 'our fore-fathers gave us a constitution which was very wise in that it restricted the powers of bishops. If you look at the modern Roman Catholic Church, problems arise because bishops have too much power.' This was just before he retired, and on the way out the door, the chief officer of Church House said, 'we're going to miss that man'.

Donald's handwriting, in letters to Eames, clear and easy to read, conveyed to the latter a sense of openness and warmth. He could, however, evince a stubborn streak, once he had made up his mind on a matter.

Gordon Linney recalled the 'brilliantly funny' caricatures drawn by Donald at meetings, which he would immediately tear up, and none of which have survived. One anecdote has it that a rector's wife telephoned Donald at short notice to inform him that her husband was very ill and would not be available to take services on Easter Sunday. Donald got onto his Archdeacon, asking 'what will we do, I've been going through my list here' and proceeded to read out three or four names, only to be greeted by negative responses from Linney such as 'he's not working etc.'. Donald finally mentioned the name of a particular Canon, X, and said 'we should ask him!'. Linney replied: 'I think you'll find he's dead, Your Grace.' Donald replied: 'oh, we must tell people they are getting Canon X – and you'll find the church will be packed for his resurrection!' Gordon Linney observed, affectionately, that Donald was 'not very good on technology – there was a joke among the clergy that if you got a blank piece of paper, that was [a fax] from the Archbishop!'

On encountering one of his priests, Paul Colton, smoking a pipe at a clergy conference, Donald exclaimed 'how wonderful it is to see a man with a pipe, it's a sign of a quiet mind, a still mind!' Donald's sense of humour was expressed in such quips and maxims, but in a gentle 'old school' fashion, containing no barb. Linney recalled another occasion at a Synod meeting. It seems that a particularly long-winded contributor had stood up and said 'Your Grace, I have three points I wish to make.' She then laboured through the first point (to general sighs), followed by the second and then paused. 'Oh, your Grace,' she said, 'I'm afraid I've forgotten the third one.' Donald very quickly wrapped matters up, saying 'thank you very much!'

Samuel Poyntz recalled attending his final meeting of the Standing Committee of General Synod before stepping down. The Primate (Robin Eames) made a farewell speech, and asked if the Archbishop of Dublin wanted to say something. Donald stood up and made remarks to the effect that the first time he had heard Poyntz's name was from the touchline at Portora, little 'urchins' yelling 'come on, Sam, get stuck in, give them hell!' – the entire committee erupting with laughter. When silence descended again, Donald delivered the punchline: '... and you know, he's been giving us hell ever since!'

Widely known and loved for his gentle courteous and humorous nature, Donald would not be human if there were not other dimensions to his personality. These were occasionally evident to those who got to know the man through deeper acquaintance. Valerie Jones felt that, with huge demands on his time as Archbishop, he could evince some signs of stress in private. She recalled a meeting with him when she was new to the job as diocesan information officer: 'I talked, he talked, and then he lost his diary in the middle and went up and down the house, and I realised this man is stressed … He was never a man to say "I am working Monday to Friday, and then stopping all day Saturday to take a rest. I need creative time/downtime …".' Occasionally, before a function, he would say to Jones 'I don't want to go to this', and yet, at the function, he 'would be the last out!' revelling in the occasion and the company, yet perhaps not measuring how much he should be giving to it – which may be a virtue in many ways, and yet a defect in terms of balance.

Donald felt keenly the history and fate of the church he loved, liking to draw the tapestry of a community's history together occasionally at the conclusion of a service in a church which might be a few hundred years old: 'go forth in peace, in remembrance for [all] who worshipped here, for all people baptised, married … a wonderful drawing together, I never knew another Archbishop to do it …' As with the closure of St George's Church referred to earlier, Jones recalled the closure of the Irish language secondary school Coláiste Moibhí coming as a great disappointment to Donald personally. Robin Eames recalled saying to Donald, at the height of some dispute in his diocese concerning the closure of a church or the appointment of somebody, 'I'm sorry you have to face this', and seeing for a moment a flash [of expression] that convinced him 'it was hurting him' – this was one of the first occasions in which it appeared to Eames that there were was another side to Donald, a shyness or sensitivity, and a possibility that he could be easily hurt.

Donald had an old-fashioned, almost quaint formality of character. He always addressed Gordon Linney as 'Archdeacon', even on informal social occasions. Even the children in Linney's parish would call the Archdeacon 'Gordon', but not Donald. Linney, in turn, addressed him only as 'Archbishop', which he saw as Donald's way of preserving the status and independence of the office, 'so that when dealing with issues he could be the Archbishop – a figure of authority', and reflecting a generational difference on the part of the older man. Valerie Jones recalled that Donald as Archbishop would confer with her as diocesan communications officer across a desk, in contrast to some of his successors as Archbishop, who would simply sit on a chair close by, and use first names. Whereas Donald liked to be addressed in the traditional style as 'Your Grace', his immediate successor Walton Empey preferred 'Archbishop', and John Neill 'would let you call him John'. Donald was 'good with people', smiling and greeting people at the door after church services. 'It's lovely to see you' was a characteristic warm and friendly greeting to familiar faces.

Jones recalled that Donald could go into 'modes': wearing at times in more relaxed settings, his Aran hat, and yet having an almost Victorian approach at other times – this may, of course, simply reflect the varied cultural experiences of the man and his sensitivity to setting. She recalled Archbishop Eames at a pre-General Synod press conference opening his remarks by thanking the press for coming: 'I always know it's summer when the Archbishop of Dublin is wearing his white jacket and his straw hat.' Paul Colton also refers to a certain 'sartorial quality' which Donald had, recalling vividly encountering him in the department store, Brown Thomas: 'we were both in there looking for new Panama hats ... Even after retirement, I remember seeing [him] on Merrion Road walking to Dún Laoghaire from the centre of town, with [a hat] ... stepping out sprightly.'

Liturgy and Churchmanship

Donald, in the view of his colleague Walton Empey, had a spirituality 'all of his own ... not along any traditional lines, more philosophically, and systems of thought'. Liturgically, Donald was conservative, and rooted in the middle-of-the-road, slightly low church tradition[31] of the Church of Ireland. He was however, quite a stickler for the keeping of rules, he would not like to read in the newspaper that there had been a visiting preacher from another diocese in one of the parishes, without his prior consent having in sought to preach or associate. 'He saw it as a function of protecting the church from the extremes', observed Paul Colton, who said Donald was an avoider of extremes both theologically and ecclesiologically:

> He was very suspicious of low church things, but also of anything so high that it contravened the canons. The canons were the established mores, and often at the end of the clergy conference, when he was briefing us on something of interest, he would say 'oh and just one more thing, I would like you all to keep the canons, keep the canons, they are the yardstick.'
>
> He was thoroughly Church of Ireland ... but that is not to say he was entrapped or enclosed by that, don't forget he was married to an American, so it is not as if he was insular! He had a family who were very expansive and exploring other disciplines. If you want to get him to [do something], ideally you need to get him to think the idea was his, so you planted the [seed] and he'd ideally come back and say 'I was thinking ...'.

This seemed to represent the flip side of Donald's own methodology observed by Gordon Linney: the philosopher reflecting on a seed of thought implanted by another. In Linney's words:

He never issued diktats, rather he suggested lines of thought that encouraged people to think things through for themselves. He avoided controversy but planted a seed. He was not given to 'soundbite' ... I always thought of Henry Kissinger's definition of leadership, 'someone who leads his people to a place where they have not been.'[32]

Paul Colton mentions picking up a strong sense from Donald of 'once bitten, twice shy',[33] in the sense that when he had a particular [negative] experience, it 'coloured his methodology and strategy about that thing into the future', mentioning a practice Donald had in relation to lay ministers of the Eucharist, whereby he would only give permission for one such lay minister in each church, rather than allow panels from which rectors could draw. 'It did cause problems, because it was easier to pick five worthies than to pick one.' Colton feels this may have had its roots in some negative experience Donald had.

John Paterson, a high church Anglo–Catholic, would consult Donald if he wished to have somebody 'out of the [usual] run of things' preach in Christ Church Cathedral – 'I never objected.' The Archbishop, while a member of the Cathedral Chapter, never attended its meetings or intervened directly in its affairs: 'I had sensible deans and no need to attend like that.' Asked about his own style of churchmanship, Donald quipped: 'I never had much style!' In his dioceses, apart from St Bartholomew's, there were two other parishes noted for their high church tradition: All Saints, Grangegorman (near Phibsborough) and St John the Evangelist's in Sandymount (a trustee church outside of the normal parish system).[34] The incense, bells, vestments and other trappings of high church ritual, did not overly excite the Archbishop: 'I regard these things as trivial.'

Paul Colton observed that 'liturgically, you had to justify things to Donald'. The Chrism Eucharist on Maundy Thursday, where the priests of the dioceses gathered in the cathedral to renew their ordination vows, was reintroduced under John Paterson during Donald's time as Archbishop. Although this service had become commonplace in the Church of England, it was a rediscovery of an aspect of catholic tradition for the Church of Ireland

and Donald needed persuasion to allow it. Part of the persuasion was that there was [to be] a big long introduction justifying it. Donald was most keen that the rationale would be explained, that [the service] would be given a scriptural root, root of tradition, reasoning; so that it would not be thought of as a frivolous or vain innovation … I remember this long, long bidding [prayer in advance] … saying to John Paterson that what we were [now] effectively getting was a mandate for it to happen!

Under Paterson, and his predecessor Tom Salmon, Christ Church Cathedral had been growing a reputation as a centre of liturgical and musical excellence, as had St Bartholomew's in Ballsbridge, with attendant Latin choral settings and the use of candles. Although not a driver of such innovation, Donald was content to see this develop 'if that's what they want'.

Unlike Anglicanism in England, religious orders were not generally a feature of life in the Church of Ireland. However, there had been at one point two orders of Anglican nuns in the church: the Community of St Mary the Virgin and the community of the Sisters of St John the Evangelist.

I brought one of the communities back … because there were only two [sisters] left, and the work of running [St Mary's Home for the elderly, in Pembroke Park] was too great, so I saw the Mother Superior, a lovely lady but crippled with arthritis … and persuaded her to bring [the other sisters, who had gone to Wales] back and I think I raised some money, but I stopped them going altogether – [this was] just before I left [Dublin].[35]

Donald took the view that, within Christendom, churches were absolutely free to have orders of people living under their own rule [of life], people who 'may not wish to follow the normal course of marriage, they are perfectly entitled but they must not think the rules of their order are the sacred rules of the Church, or try to apply them outside'.

Northern Ireland Troubles

The Troubles in Northern Ireland continued to provide a tragic and gloomy backdrop to events in the South during Donald's tenure in Dublin, particularly in the first half of his time there, in the mid-to-late 1980s. Triggered by the deaths in 1981 of a number of republican hunger strikers including Bobby Sands, support in the Northern nationalist community for the republican Sinn Féin party increased steadily through the first half of that decade, giving rise to attempts by constitutional nationalist parties North and South to stem that support by addressing the disaffection and alienation in that community. This alienation had festered throughout the period of Unionist majority rule at Stormont since partition of the island in the 1920s (with attendant discrimination in areas such as the provision of local authority housing and the drawing of local electoral boundaries), and it survived the institution of direct rule by Westminster (briefly interrupted with the ill-fated Sunningdale experiment) since 1969. Republican and loyalist paramilitary activity, with a degree of latent support in each community, meant that during the 1970s and 1980s hardly a week went by without press reports of shootings and bombings in the North, and less often, in Britain itself.

Cardinal Tomás Ó Fiaich received a storm of criticism for remarks in July 1985 in the course of the interview with the Catholic newspaper, *The Universe*. In the course of explaining the reasons why some northerners voted for Sinn Féin, including the legacy of the hunger strikes and alienation from the structures of the northern state, the Cardinal stated that the IRA killed members of the RUC and Ulster Defence Regiment because they were members of the security forces, not because they were Protestant. He expressed the view that ninety per cent of religious bigotry was found among Protestants, whereas bigotry found among Catholics was mainly of the political sort. This provoked a hostile reaction from Unionist quarters, including many Church of Ireland members in the North. *The Irish Times* reported that the Church of Ireland accused the cardinal of 'insensitivity', and Donald expressed 'deep regret and disappointment'. In a subsequent interview, he noted that the cardinal had been a friend of his for some twenty years, but that 'we felt obliged to respond to his remarks as some people could've been very upset by what he said'. Bigotry was 'essentially a spiritual illness' and to attribute ninety per cent of it to Protestants was 'a bit much ...' However, some Protestant voices were raised in support of Ó Fiaich, including that of Dean of Cork, Maurice Carey.

A major initial step in efforts to address the sense of alienation among northern nationalists was the convening of the New Ireland Forum, representing nationalist parties North and South. Sinn Féin as an extra-constitutional party was viewed as beyond the pale of dialogue because of the IRA's continuing activities. The forum set out to forge a consensus in constitutional nationalism on the way forward. However, its three suggested 'solutions' – a unitary state, a federal/confederal arrangement or joint Irish/British authority (in the North) – were summarily dismissed by Margaret Thatcher in what became infamously known as her 'out, out, out' response. In the aftermath of this rebuff, Garret FitzGerald's government in the Republic embarked on a process of diplomatic persuasion. This painstaking work, which included lobbying of the United States administration, ultimately bore fruit in the groundbreaking Anglo–Irish agreement, signed at Hillsborough Castle in Co. Down in

November 1985. The agreement accorded the Southern government a formal right of consultation in Northern Ireland affairs for the first time, as effective interlocutors and guarantors for the Northern nationalist community. However, bitter Unionist resentment at this 'interference' in the North's affairs by the Republic, and a lack of consultation with them, escalated rapidly into full-scale opposition and large demonstrations on the streets. In Dublin, Senator Mary Robinson resigned the Labour Party whip in the Seanad in protest at the lack of consultation with unionism.

Church of Ireland attitudes to the Anglo–Irish agreement differed as between North and South. As prime spokesperson for the church community in the Republic, Donald appealed for the agreement to be 'given a fair try'. In his sermon at Christmas 1985, and in his 'Bishop's letter' in *Church Review* the following month, he acknowledged its imperfections, while reminding the two communities that it was open to them to seek to replace it by working out some mutually acceptable form of government evolving from agreement among themselves – something for which express provision was made in the agreement. Posing the question as to what members of the Church in the Republic could do for peace and reconciliation, he said that they could strive to understand the real hurt and concerns of many fellow members of the Church of Ireland community in the North and their sense of isolation and rejection, while encouraging them to look without prejudice at the 'very positive elements in the document, which gives assurance on the deepest issues of their concern. We are one church and we will be heard: our understanding and our friendship can help to heal and to reconcile'. The same month saw media speculation on Robin Eames (the young, articulate and urbane Bishop of Derry and Raphoe) as the likely successor to John Armstrong as Archbishop of Armagh. John Armstrong had held a broadly nationalist perspective, whereas Eames's more Unionist instincts were seen as appropriate for the times. The signing of the Anglo–Irish agreement (and its rejection by Unionist opinion) were seen as copperfastening his election as Primate.

As a student, Robin Eames had won a scholarship to Harvard to study law, but had opted for the ministry in the Church of Ireland (despite his Methodist upbringing). Donald, who chaired the meeting of the house of bishops to select the new Archbishop of Armagh, welcomed Eames's accession, saying the house could not have made 'a wiser and better choice'. Paying tribute to his personal qualities, he noted that as Bishop of Down and Dromore, and Derry and Raphoe successively, Eames had 'borne the heat and burden of the long, hard day of the Troubles in Northern Ireland, where his influence for good and peace has been constantly exercised often in grim circumstances'.[36]

The Archbishop of Armagh chaired meetings of the bishops, Donald recalling Eames's businesslike approach: 'there was little time lost, he knew what he wanted to do as soon as he sat down. The whole intention and energy of the meeting would be turned towards the agenda. He was very good.' Donald had experience of George Otto Simms and John Armstrong chairing bishops' meetings in their time: 'they were all very good men. George Otto Simms would never drive home a point as Robin Eames would.' Donald recalled somebody saying to him that Eames 'was born to become either Primate or Lord Chief Justice'.

On his election in February 1986, and despite his own misgivings concerning the Agreement, Eames stressed that the Church of Ireland should not 'back one political view' in relation to the North. He was a spiritual leader, and would work to win the trust of Church of Ireland people in the Republic. A group of Church of Ireland bishops had met with Taoiseach Garret FitzGerald early in the new year in 1986 (prior to Eames's election), where Donald had referred to the wide and general unease about the agreement in Northern Ireland. Samuel Poyntz had appealed to Northern Unionists to look carefully at what possibilities were contained in the agreement. After Eames had been elected Archbishop of Armagh, the group of bishops met with British Prime Minister Margaret Thatcher – ahead of a planned major Unionist protest rally for Belfast. Both the composition of this delegation, and the discussions at the meeting, reflected the tension in the house of bishops between Unionist and moderate nationalist tendencies (to a certain extent personified in the differing tone and emphases of its new Armagh and Dublin leaderships). For the meeting with Mrs Thatcher, Bishop of Meath and Kildare Walton Empey says the original intention was to have only bishops from the North present, but he challenged this on the basis that it was an all Ireland church, and southerners were added to the delegation. Empey was part of the delegation on both occasions (as was Donald), and felt that, of the two premiers, FitzGerald showed by far the most understanding of both traditions in the North. The Northern bishops expressed anxiety in relation to pressures on members of the Royal Ulster Constabulary as a result of the Unionist protests, and Eames conveyed the Ulsterman's sense of suspicion at secrecy and deals concluded 'behind closed doors'. Walton Empey recalled one particular exchange, concerning an upcoming protest march in a nationalist area. Mrs Thatcher turned to her secretary and asked 'isn't Mr Hume coming in to see us [later that week?]' On receiving a reply in the affirmative, she said 'well, would you please take a note to ask him to keep his people in [doors] on that day?'[37] Following the meeting, the bishops referred to planned Unionist protests, stressing that 'no act of intimidation, violence or coercion should be acceptable to people who were God-fearing'. Samuel Poyntz, who was part of the delegation, emphasised that despite differences of opinion in the house of bishops, they would maintain a united front when coming away from a meeting: 'this is part of the Church of Ireland … in Anglicanism, you can live with diversity.' In a subsequent note to Eames, Donald congratulated him on his conduct of the meeting.

In a profile interview in *The Irish Times* in April 1986, Archbishop Eames highlighted Unionist concerns and the dangers in the current situation, stating that there was a need to clarify what the relationship would be between the intergovernmental conference and a future devolved administration in Northern Ireland:

> The Irish government does not see progress in devolution as a clear indication that part of the agreement will self-destruct. Then we listen to the British Prime Minister and she tends to suggest that if we get on with the job of devolution then many of the things that are annoying Unionists … will be wiped out. That has to be clarified.

The Irish Times writer observed that Eames was 'more of an Ulster man than his predecessors' and expressed the confidence of members of the Church of Ireland in the Republic that he would take advice on political realities in their part of Ireland from the Archbishop of Dublin, Dr Caird.

The 1987 Remembrance Sunday bomb attack by the IRA at a ceremony at Enniskillen's war memorial catapulted an old Wesley fellow-pupil of Donald's, Gordon Wilson, into the world spotlight. His daughter Marie, a nurse, was fatally injured in the bombing and he held her hand and spoke to her as they lay under the rubble, his daughter's life ebbing away as she told him 'Daddy, I love you very much.' As Wilson recounted the story afterward, his words of reconciliation, absence of bitterness, and saying that he would pray for the bombers, made a powerful emotional impact, reverberating around the world in press coverage of the atrocity. Donald recalled that Wilson, who was over six feet tall and had been a powerful athlete in his day, 'seemed to bend over and become old' very quickly after the tragedy. Wilson had been a student at Wesley College in Dublin in the 1940s. The same morning as the bombing, the annual Remembrance Day service had been held in Dublin at St Patrick's Cathedral, with Donald in attendance, while Archbishop Robin Eames had been preparing for the remembrance service in the cathedral in Enniskillen at the time the bomb went off. On 14 November, at Donald's initiative, a minute's silence was held across the island for the victims.

The following summer, at Lambeth, alarm was expressed in Northern circles of the church at the wording of a resolution which came before the conference, referring to violence in the South African situation and its possible justification in response to oppression. Concerned that this could be interpreted as justifying republican paramilitary violence in Northern Ireland, Archbishop Eames and the Northern bishops spent the night in anxious discussion, resulting in what Donald described as 'a deeply effective plea to the conference to allow another resolution which would not allow the previous resolution to be interpreted or misinterpreted to supply support to terrorists of any complexion in Northern Ireland.'[38] Praising positive elements in the Anglo–Irish agreement, Donald noted in October 1988 that an upcoming review of its operation would present an opportunity to remedy the defect of lack of consultation with Unionists which had accompanied its original preparation.[39] Talks between Social Democratic and Labour Party (SDLP) leader John Hume and Sinn Féin leader Gerry Adams explored possible agreement on an analysis of the situation which might establish that the achievement of Irish self-determination could be pursued peacefully.

A Peace Chapel in Christ Church Cathedral was dedicated by Donald following evensong on 21 January 1990, and a practice was instituted of prayers for peace in Northern Ireland being said there at noon each day. Tentative signs of hope began to emerge the same year, with overtures to republicans being made by Northern Ireland Secretary Peter Brooke in statements encouraging debate within what he termed 'the terrorist community', Donald welcomed these developments in his Synod address in October 1990, referring to the first seven years of his ministry which he had served in Northern Ireland and the respect and affection he had for the people of both communities – 'our prayer is that talks may take place successfully after all these "years which the locusts have eaten".'

In an address at a service in Christ Church Cathedral in April 1991, Archbishop Desmond Tutu, while condemning 'all violence, from whatever quarter', added his voice to those then calling for inclusive talks in the Northern Ireland situation: 'let [all sides] be represented by those they regard as their authentic spokespersons, otherwise talks, as we have discovered at home, become an exercise in futility.' When primates of the Anglican Communion met in Belfast, Robin Eames arranged that they would be addressed by John Hume, leader of the SDLP, and James Molyneaux, leader of the Official Unionist Party (and a member of the

Church of Ireland). He requested that the Anglican primates would express concern not just about violence, but about its causes, and see diversity as a positive.[40]

There was much wariness among Northern sections of the church concerning ongoing political developments. Donald described as 'inopportune' the presentation of a report by the Role of the Church Committee for consideration by the 1991 General Synod which contained a section entitled 'The Anglo–Irish agreement and after – A Unionist perspective'. He underlined that this perspective did not represent the views of all of the members of the committee, a fact which was likely to be made quite clear when the report was presented and debated. In late summer 1991, Robin Eames was obliged to deny press reports that he was acting as an intermediary between Northern Republicans and the British government.

Reports of disagreements between Eames and Cardinal Cahal Daly (who had succeeded Ó Fiaich in 1990) concerning when Sinn Féin should be admitted to talks after violence had ceased surfaced in the press in January 1992 – Eames expressing the opinion that their democratic credentials would need to be tested over a period of time.[41] Because Unionist politicians were not prepared to become involved in talks, particularly in light of their perceptions of having been excluded from discussions over the Anglo–Irish agreement, Eames was a valuable conduit for the two governments in interpreting their concerns, and a barometer of likely reaction in the Unionist community to various suggested initiatives. While there were sometimes some irritation in southern church circles with a perceived emphasis on Unionist concerns on the part of Eames, this was tempered by a recognition of the important role he was playing in interpreting them to the two governments, and in counselling caution in relation to matters which he felt would not go down well. However, tensions were felt: because of the extreme sensitivity of the situation, some southern church people felt inhibited from saying what they felt from their own perspective for fear of 'rocking the boat'.[42]

Robin Eames sought Donald's advice in January 1992 following the publication of an article in *The Sunday Independent* by Shane Ross headlined 'The Politicising of the Primacy' in which he took Eames to task over an interview he had given to *The Sunday Times* newspaper, charging that he had commented favourably on the possible introduction of internment and changes to the rules of evidence, and expressed reservations about the Anglo–Irish agreement and dabbled in politics. Donald sought to be supportive in his reply, stating that it was nearly impossible to escape public misinterpretation while offering Christian leadership in the situation in Northern Ireland at this time, but that this was preventing much worse conflagration.[43] Later, he reported to Eames that Taoiseach Charles Haughey had responded positively to a suggestion that a government reception be held for members of the General Synod in May 1992, an initiative seen as helpful, presumably in the interests of demonstrating a commitment to inclusivity and pluralism by the Republic.

Bombings and shootings by Republican and Loyalist paramilitaries and actions by British security forces continued throughout the early 1990s. The Shankill Road bombing of October 1993 by the IRA, an attempt to kill loyalists believed to be attending a meeting above a fish shop, resulted on a busy shopping day in the loss of lives of nine civilians and the bomber himself and provoked widespread revulsion. Archbishop Eames, in a statement, described it as a 'blatant and totally sectarian attack' while Donald for his part characterised it as an act of 'naked barbarity'. Feelings of outrage among Unionists were exacerbated in the aftermath by media footage of Sinn Féin leader Gerry Adams as one of the pallbearers of the coffin of Thomas Begley, the bomber. Both archbishops joined soon afterwards in appealing for a day of prayer.

A key moment in the developing peace process was the signing of the Downing Street declaration by the British and Irish governments in December 1993, in which the British government expressly acknowledged for the first time the right of people on both parts of the island to exercise the right of self determination 'on the basis of consent freely and concurrently given, North and South, to bring about a united Ireland if that is their wish'.[44] Robin Eames was closely involved in discussions between the two governments as the peace process developed, and had a hand in the final draft of the declaration. In a statement faxed to government advisor (and member of the Church of Ireland) Martin Mansergh, Donald said the declaration was 'so balanced in its presentation that it is worthy of the most careful and open-minded study.'[45] Welcoming the 'warm and heartening document', which bore a message not unlike that of the angels to the shepherds in the Christmas story according to the Gospel of St Luke – 'peace on earth to men of goodwill!', Donald said that

> we may not have long to wait to see whether the paramilitaries in both communities in Northern Ireland are prepared to give peace a chance. A cessation of violence by all sides and on both sides of the Channel which divides us, for a period of three months would certainly give a good

indication that the invitation to the men of violence to enter the democratic political process was being seriously considered by them and the politics of the gun and the bomb was being superseded by rational argument, enlightened self-interest, mutual persuasion and common humanity without blind doctrinaire limitations.[46]

An important part of the peace process dynamic at the time was the communicating of clearer information to the public in Britain about the issues involved in the Northern conflict. The influential Church of England newspaper, *Church Times*, carried an opinion piece from Donald in the immediate aftermath of the Downing Street declaration, entitled 'The Churches' Task in a Changed Ireland'. Expressing cautious hope in relation to the declaration, he highlighted how the Republic of Ireland was 'not the same state that it was even ten years ago', and highlighted how liberal opinions were now heard in public discourse, how traditional voices of authority ecclesiastical and political had waned and how international interests were centred in the European union. The Church of Ireland had a role to play in helping both parts of the island understand each other, and in cooperating with leaders of the other main churches. He set out for readers of the newspaper the position of the Church of Ireland in the Anglican communion, its ties with other Anglican churches in the two islands and its involvement in ecumenical dialogue.

Progress in moving to a cessation of violence was painstakingly slow in the aftermath of the declaration, with requests for clarification from Sinn Féin and other teasing out of its implications being played out over several months. The IRA finally declared its ceasefire on 31 August 1994. Robin Eames issued a cautious statement, welcoming any step that could lead to permanent peace, but emphasising that the real value of the cessation must be judged through time. Donald, noting the cessation, called for understanding for those who expressed caution and suspicion, referring to the considerable hesitation displayed by paramilitaries when the Downing Street declaration had been presented the previous December.

The churches did their bit to contribute to peace process choreography and mutual understanding, and a landmark peace service was held at Christ Church Cathedral in November 1994 attended by President Mary Robinson, visiting Archbishop of Canterbury Dr George Carey, Roman Catholic Archbishop Desmond Connell and Donald. Church leaders washed the feet of four people who had suffered as a result of the Northern conflict, and prayers were said seeking forgiveness for wrongs done on all sides. During his visit, the Archbishop of Canterbury stated that the English needed to ask forgiveness for the 'often brutal domination and crass insensitivity in the eight hundred years of history of their relationship with Ireland'.[47] In his Christmas message of that year, Donald called for reconciliation – the only sure ground for lasting peace – noting that the past cannot be undone, and reconciliation required a willingness to seek mutual forgiveness and an honest facing up to injuries physical, psychological and spiritual 'which we have done to one another ... we are all called to be peacemakers'.

In an attempt to draw Sinn Féin more fully into the democratic process, given the cessation of violence, a Forum for Peace and Reconciliation was convened in Dublin in 1995, involving mainly nationalist parties North and South – the venture being seen as a successor to the New Ireland Forum of the 1980s (at which time Sinn Féin had remained excluded from talks because of the ongoing activities of the IRA). Groups in civic society, including the churches, made written submissions and direct presentations to the forum. The Church of Ireland highlighted the substantial decline in its population in the Republic since independence and analysed various factors which it saw as contributing to this. In a response to one its submissions, Sinn Féin criticised the Church's perceived silence on violation of nationalists' rights and its omission of British army and RUC violence. In its own submission to the Forum, Cumann Gaelach na hEaglaise recounted the history of Protestant interest in the Irish language, and supplied a reading list for forum members. It stressed that Irish was a vehicle for reconciliation and a unique part of Irish culture. The visit of Prince Charles to the Republic the same year was seen as a further step in rapprochement and building confidence.

Clouds were building on the horizon during that summer and autumn with the continued exclusion of Sinn Féin from talks with Unionist parties and the British government as a result of insistence on prior decommissioning of IRA arms, in what was known as the Washington 3 test. In March 1995, addressing journalists in the US capital, Northern Ireland Secretary Patrick Mayhew had set out three preconditions before Sinn Féin could be admitted to talks: (1) evidence of IRA willingness to disarm in principle, (2) the demonstration of an understanding of the 'modalities of decommissioning', and (3) a start on decommissioning some weapons as 'a tangible, confidence-building measure'.

In a statement at the end of summer, Donald asked whether it would not be possible to see a gradual decommissioning of arms, perhaps over a five-year period, supervised by a neutral source – 'the only way to get finally rid of arms is to ensure their need is rendered obsolete by the institution of fair and open government.' He set out his view starkly in his 'Bishop's letter' in the diocesan magazine in September: to allow this issue become a stumbling block 'would certainly incur the justifiable castigation of future generations in Ireland'.

The contrasting stances of the two primates over the question of decommissioning of paramilitary arms was highlighted in press reports that autumn. Proposing the establishment of an assembly in the North for the purpose of facilitating debate and discussion on the way forward, Robin Eames insisted at his diocesan synod in Armagh that there must be no fudging of the issue of the removal of the threat of arms, telling the paramilitaries that,

> for a community which is beginning to breathe again, the message is quite simple. Prove to us your good intentions. Once you do, then face up to the political reality of life. Be prepared to fight your corner not with threats but with the force of argument … We are told that a 'twin track' approach is receiving serious consideration. Whatever policy is eventually accepted, there must be no fudging of the issue of the removal of the threat of arms.

Donald, in his speech to the Dublin and Glendalough diocesan synod suggested that all-party talks could get underway on the understanding that there would be a gradual decommissioning, if each agreed element or institution in the overall political agreement were put in place. He praised the proposal made to establish an international commission to monitor decommissioning of arms 'which might be effected on this *pari passu* principle, which might avoid friction and prove to be thorough in operation'.[48]

Continued interparty wrangling in Northern Ireland, and lack of progress in proceeding to all-party talks, sowed an ever-increasing sense of foreboding. In his 'Bishop's letter' in *Church Review* at the beginning of 1996, he said: 'we stand before the New Year like a sculptor before a block of unworked stone. We must try to imprint upon it our own vision.' Referring to Ireland being a small island off the coast of Europe, and its upcoming holding of the presidency of the European Union, he expressed the hope that peace can be established, but 'hesitation and mutual recrimination have slowed the process to the point of standing still'.

In the last week of January 1996, *The Irish Times* carried news of Donald's intention to retire, in tandem with an article elsewhere in the paper from former Taoiseach Garret FitzGerald, advising the Irish government to reject British Prime Minister John Major's recently expressed precondition for starting all-party talks, which would require decommissioning to have already commenced: 'any reassurance that could give was always inherently negligible'. Confidence in progress was shattered with the explosion of a huge bomb in the Canary Wharf district of London by the IRA on 9 February 1996, killing two newsagents, injuring thirty-nine other people, and heralding the end of its ceasefire. Dominating television, radio and press coverage in the following days, the event seemed to crush all the burgeoning feelings of optimism that events leading up the 1994 ceasefire, and the resultant peace, had brought about.

Donald denounced the commencement of military activity by the IRA, 'if the killing and wounding of unsuspecting civilians can be regarded as military activity'. However, he was angry at the prevarication in political leadership, deploring the 'culpable delay in proceeding to all-party talks'. He pointed out that, in agreements between the British and Irish governments the understanding was 'quite explicit' that nothing would be agreed until everything was agreed, which context suggested that talks could have gone ahead while arms were kept at the 'existing strength'. Expressing support for renewed efforts by Taoiseach John Bruton to keep the peace process alive, he called for all-party talks to proceed, without, however, being dominated by the IRA and its supporters, 'for the nationalist interest would resist such domination as surely as the Unionist interest'.[49]

When Donald stepped down in April 1996, he expressed optimism that there would be a renewed cessation of violence in the North, despite hardline statements from the IRA. However, it would take over a year after his retirement, and the election of new governments in both the Republic (led by Bertie Ahern) and in Britain (led by Tony Blair), before a renewed cessation of violence would be declared and peace talks got underway.

As the two senior leaders in the church, North and South, the Archbishops of Armagh and Dublin had to form an effective working relationship against a backdrop, in the late 1980s and early 1990s, of a continually changing set of circumstances. Donald, having served time in the North as curate at Dundela and chaplain at Portora, was keenly sensitive to the particular context in which his Northern counterpart had to operate, recalling that Eames told him on one occasion 'I have just buried my 38th policeman today.'

In an interview with the author, Eames reflected that, during his time in Armagh, in so far as it corresponded with Donald's time in Dublin, 'we were going through hell here, terrible times'. He acknowledged a certain tension in the house of bishops, the church being an all-Ireland institution encompassing within it all shades of opinion from extreme unionism to radical nationalism 'and everything in between'. Eames said that he had to accept that a percentage of his people were against the Anglo–Irish agreement:

> But also in time, I hoped developments would show that it was right … you had to, as primate, balance the political and religious and the faith … Donald didn't necessarily have to do that to the extent he would have had he been bishop in Northern Ireland … One of the great periods was Albert Reynolds and Major and the Framework Document, and Donald was able to put [in] so much background for me by knowing the southern political mind. But he could in private be extremely critical of southern politicians … Based on his intimate knowledge of southern politics he was able to guide me through the minefield on many occasions.

Eames felt that Donald, being 'steeped in the Celtic culture' and his 'knowledge of the way the Celtic culture works', was a very valuable counterpoint to his own experience:

> If you say it's nationalist mind [that Donald understood], that would say I'm a Unionist. It's certainly not a political [thing] but living and working among these people, that was my culture. Donald was the same, but in his culture. Because we were able with maturity to talk from our own perspectives, and put ourselves alongside each other, [this gave] a tremendous strength to my primacy.

He recalls in the house of bishops saying to his colleagues from the South that the perspective they had south of the border 'is not the perspective we have in the North. The perspective we have in the North will not be yours in the South. How do we square the circle?' Pointing out that he had spent a lot of his youth in Dublin, and that his family had come from Cork (where they had been burnt out during the Troubles in the early 1920s), he knew that the bishops needed to be able to come to General Synod each year and present

> the moderate open-ended spiritually realistic attitude that I believe the Church of Ireland made as its contribution over the years, and I was privileged to be part of that. I knew with Donald that I could go to [him], phone him up, call at the See House, go for a walk and talk to him and say: 'Dónal, give me the perspective you have on this. 'What is it their perspective is, share it with me', and in the gentle open way of Dónal Caird, it was laid out before me like a book. I would say to Donald Caird, 'I'm going to have to face this crisis in the next month, now let me tell you why and warn you of the difficulties, and let me tell you how I think I'm going to do it. Now, when you hear me, tell me how that fits into your

perspective.' We had that sort of relationship as Primates. Yes, I did find his judgement was borne out as events unfolded.

Eames acknowledged playing a role in drafting parts of the Downing Street declaration [in 1993], being cast in this role of intermediary in the absence of Unionist political engagement, and feeling his role was to ensure that people in the North did not feel something was to be imposed on them:

> I simply fought the battle of saying to Albert [Reynolds, Irish Taoiseach] and to [British Prime Minister] John Major, 'look, you're going to be in a disastrous situation unless you give expression to consent for both [communities] – consent to be governed and consent to share government, and we had an awful battle over that, but eventually they agreed. There was a complete vacuum in politics here and that is why they came to me. I was up and down to Dublin to see Albert and [Irish government advisor Martin] Mansergh ... I kept Donald abreast of as much of that as I could. I wasn't necessarily doing that as Primate, I was doing that in a diplomatic role, because they weren't talking to any politicians, there were none to talk to! I got thrust forward and Donald showed such patience and understanding and if you read his speeches at General Synod, he made several very supportive speeches about me, even when I was sitting there, which meant a lot ... never once did Donald [attempt] to take the carpet away from under me. I always said to Donald, 'if you don't agree, tell me, but tell me in private.' My job was not only to do that sort of thing but also to keep the Church of Ireland united. And when I'm dead and gone, I hope they will say I did that, but it was very hard in those days.

The historian Alan Acheson referred to a risk that, due to the particularism of its leadership in Eames Caird, the Church of Ireland might evolve a tendency towards two autonomous provinces. Eames says that this proved not to be the case. Although fracture was an ever-present risk, the church's unity endured through the worst of the Troubles, including the period of the hunger strikes, the Anglo–Irish agreement, Enniskillen and (after Donald's retirement) Drumcree.

> The argument against that [is] were we honest enough, did we lose integrity? I'm a consensus person ... it's my faith, my belief, my personality. Because of that I had to be a constant listener and any step I took I had to be confident I at least knew the dangers. [Advice from] Donald was part of that. Looking back on that time, but for the grace of God, I don't know how we came through it. In those days, the Protestant people in Northern Ireland felt under siege by violent and political manipulation, and were besieged by a lack of confidence. In a book I'm

working on at the moment, I am trying to emphasise that this population, possibly unknown and unrecognised, lacks its own confidence, always being dependent on someone ... that's why friendships and confidences are so vital.[50]

He recalled Donald saying to him at one point 'your job is to hold the line' (presumably a reference to the value of Eames's reflecting of the concerns of the Unionist community): 'and then years later he said to me 'you held the line'. I got a bit emotional about it. He said that in retirement when we were reflecting on all that had happened.'

Civic engagement
Many of Donald's addresses and statements as Archbishop of Dublin comment on contemporary political affairs, both national and inter-national – evidence of his wish to represent the Protestant community's interest in such matters, as well as encouraging his community, through diocesan synod and the *Church Review*, to engage in public discussion. In speaking out regularly, Donald sought to give leadership by example.

There was a 'goodly heritage' to draw on. Preaching at a special law service in St Michan's church in November 1995 to mark its nine hundredth anniversary and its links with the nearby Four Courts, he recalled the church's illustrious history and links with many great figures such as Oliver Bond, the Sheares brothers, Edmund Burke and Charles Stewart Parnell. St Michan's represented the contribution of members of the Church of Ireland over the centuries to the cause of Ireland's freedom, as they understood it in their day, and to the establishment of the nation on the principles of freedom, tolerance and a pluralist understanding of nationhood:

> St Michan's is a memorial to brave men who transcended the common opinions of their class and creed, without parting company with the conviction of their fellow members, to reach a wider vision of nationhood and to envision a better future for their country.

The state established in 1922, he told his congregation (which included the President, Mrs Robinson; the Lord Mayor; the Chief Justice and other members of the judiciary), bore many of the distinguishing marks which such patriots had hoped to see – but there still remained marginalised sectors of society, those suffering the effects of marriage breakdown; the unemployed; those without reasonable access to third level education; those who resort to drugs to escape normal consciousness as too painful; the victims of the drug distributing underworld and other forms of violent crimes. The problems facing our society today in all these areas are daunting.[51]

In 1993, Donald had pointed out[52] that many members of the church – his father's generation – had come back from the First World War to a different Ireland. The Easter Rising[53] and War of Independence had intervened, and a newly independent state was bedding down, with a different ethos becoming apparent. There was a greater concentration on the life and structures of the Church of Ireland community itself among its members, 'and they did not march out into the larger community'. In the early years of the state, twenty Senate seats had been reserved for members of the southern minority tradition, and they had been encouraged thereby to stand for the Dáil. Subsequent decline in engagement represented an impoverishment for the nation, in his view.

Government cuts in education and other services undertaken by the Fianna Fáil government elected in 1987 in the face of deteriorating public finances, resulting in a 'bleak midwinter of the economy', were recognised as a stark fact in his letter in *Church Review* of November 1987. He acknowledged the view that there were hopeful signs for economic recovery in the very measures taken, since a firm hand would encourage investment. Our faith, he said, is that 'times of refreshing will come'. A series of scandals in public life in 1991 involving business people, semi-state companies and controversy surrounding land and commercial deals was accompanied by allegations of a 'golden circle' linking business and politics. Lamenting these events, Donald in his 1991 synod address counselled caution, thinking it likely that perfectly innocent people had been 'sucked into the vortex'. Insufficient attention had been given to such matters 'because in Ireland we have concentrated on other areas of ethical concern' – a reference to the traditional emphasis placed on sexuality in discussions of morality in national discourse.

On a wider canvas, he surveyed, in his diocesan synod address in 1989, developments in Eastern Europe following the fall of the Berlin Wall, and praised what he perceived as an orderly progression towards greater freedom, in contrast to the precipitous attempt to liberalise society in China which had had disastrous results (a reference to the tragedy of Tiananmen Square earlier that year, in which a large number of demonstrators were killed by the Chinese authorities in a forcible suppression of student-led protests for democracy in Beijing and other cities). A forthcoming visit by an ecumenical delegation of Christians from the Soviet Union to Ireland was seen as a sign of confidence on the part of the churches in Russia in the process of *perestroika* and *glasnost* (restructuring and openness, instituted by the reformist President Mikhail Gorbachev). For Ireland and for Europe, he noted signs of hope for the 1990s and beyond, referring to the construction of a new financial services centre in the docklands – the Custom House Dock Project. It was 'good to have this symbol daily before our eyes'.

In an address in 1990 assessing the contribution of the Church of Ireland to national life over the previous twenty-five years, Donald highlighted the public stances the church had taken in the abortion and divorce debates. He also outlined the position in relation to the church's schools, its various organisations, and the increase in the number of candidates for ordination. The church was no longer accepting its historically assigned role as 'the remnant of the garrison', but rather, was facing the future with renewed confidence. He continued in church circles to draw attention to the value of the work done by the National Army and wrote to the Minister for Defence and General Officer Commanding of the peacekeeping forces in 1988, congratulating them on the award of the Nobel Peace Prize to the United Nations – the Army had for many years played a distinguished role in peacekeeping abroad as part of the multinational UNIFIL forces.[54]

In August 1991, he reiterated what he referred to as his 'constant encouragement' of Protestants to take a prominent part in the civic life of the nation in the context of the local elections then taking place. He expressed satisfaction that the church in 'these dioceses is showing a fresh confidence in its capacity to public life'. Though scarcely an admirer of Charles Haughey, with whom he had jousted on a number of occasions in matters relating to education cuts, he paid tribute to him on his retirement in March 1992, expressing appreciation for the assistance that he had given to the Church of Ireland community on various occasions.

The southern Protestant community had a particular relationship with the office of President of Ireland, dating back to the selection of Douglas Hyde as the first holder of the office in 1938, and cemented in the alterations of the State prayers in the church's liturgy on the declaration of the Republic in 1949. From this time, prayers were offered in the Church's liturgy for the President rather than the monarch. The relationship was reflected in Donald's personal acquaintanceship with two presidents: Erskine Childers (who served briefly from June 1973 until his death in November 1974) and Patrick J. Hillery (president from 1976 to 1990), whom he had known from his Rathmichael days, as we have seen. A new memorial to former president Erskine Childers was dedicated in the nave of St Patrick's Cathedral in 1993, the address given by the Taoiseach Albert Reynolds and the blessing performed by Donald. This memorial complemented that in memory of Douglas Hyde nearby, while the single small bright tricolour hanging near the former presidents' memorials formed a counterpoint to the faded British regimental and Union flags laid up in the choir and north transept.[55]

Paying tribute to Patrick Hillery as he left office, Donald expressed the particular thanks of the Church of Ireland community to him for his attendance at many church events. When Mary Robinson, the first female president, succeeded him in November 1990, Donald paid tribute to her 'incisive mind, her enthusiasm, her charm, her political acumen and her skills as an advocate', assuring her that as president, she would be remembered in the Church's public liturgy. Robinson's husband, Nicholas, was a member of the Church, and her own legal career as an advocate for minority rights and pluralism, and as one of Trinity College's three senators meant she was well-known within that community. Her coming to office was hailed by Donald as a 'fresh flowering', which, along with the ordination of women, represented 'things we hardly dared to think of a generation ago'.[56] Performing the official opening of a £1 million parish centre for Taney in South County Dublin in November 1991, President Robinson, in the presence of Donald, clergy and public representatives, stated that it was 'appropriate for the President of Ireland and public representatives to be there and to affirm pluralism and space in modern Ireland'. When she attended the installation of new floodlighting at St Bartholomew's Church in Ballsbridge in 1995, Donald highlighted the lighted candle she had displayed in the window of Áras an Uachtaráin to reflect continued remembrance of the scattered Irish diaspora throughout the world, many members of which had their origins in emigration in the years after the Great Famine of the mid-nineteenth century. Robinson appeared at several similar church occasions in the dioceses, gracing the cover of a number of issues of *Church Review*.

Dublin city celebrated the one thousandth anniversary of its foundation in 1988, coinciding with the marking by Christ Church Cathedral of the nine hundred and fiftieth anniversary of its own foundation. In his address at the annual Citizenship Service in November 1988, Donald declared 'I am citizen of no mean city.' As part of the events to mark the millennium, a time capsule was buried in the ground, containing mementos of life in 1988 (to be opened a hundred years later). At the invitation of the Lord Mayor, Donald contributed a group of objects representing the life of the contemporary Church of Ireland: a

Church of Ireland directory, a copy of the booklet for the special millennium citizenship service, and a medallion of Christ Church Cathedral. Trinity College declared its intention of awarding leading Dubliners with honorary degrees to mark the anniversary – Donald being honoured along with poet Seamus Heaney, broadcaster Gay Byrne and actress Maureen Potter, among others. His wife Nancy, their three children and his half brother Commodore Jim Caird were present at the ceremony on 8 July 1988. The Archbishop was further honoured in November 1993 by the awarding of an Honorary Doctorate of Laws by the National Council for Educational Awards in Dublin Castle, where Professor Eda Sagarra of Trinity College drew attention to his linguistic interests, his ministry and his straightforwardness in hailing him as 'a man of tongues, a man of the word, a man of his word and a man of the Word'. In April 1995, a year prior to his retirement, Donald became the first Church of Ireland episcopal recipient of an honorary degree from the National University of Ireland.

Education

The Fianna Fáil government which entered office in 1987 sought to turn around the Republic's economy by achieving significant savings in areas of high government spending such as health and education, and as part of this proposed the introduction of a five-year cycle for secondary schools. Donald, as chairman of the Secondary Education Committee, protested strongly in public statements and in diocesan fora. The proposals would have a particular impact on Protestant schools, which would lose one sixth of their pupils and one sixth of their staff, meaning that the fees charged for remaining pupils must be increased due to economies of scale. He claimed that teachers in Protestant schools made redundant would not easily gain employment outside that sector. Secondary schools under Protestant management drew their pupils from a much wider catchment area of primary schools, because of the dispersed nature of the community – this made a six-year cycle all the more necessary to allow for a period of adjustment, given the pupils' varied experiences of primary education. A reduction in the number of teachers in a school would lead also to a reduced curriculum, lessening the school's educational attraction to many parents.[57] The schools under Protestant management were viewed by Donald as playing a vital role in 'maintaining our religious and cultural identity'. They were 'our most prized possession next only to our churches'. If their maintenance and protection was 'elitist', then he said, that term was to have changed its meaning.[58] They played a crucial role within the Protestant community in transmitting values to the next generation. Education, in his view, did not consist merely in the passing on of technical skills, but in gaining an appreciation of what was true and honourable.

The case was fought doggedly, and had a happy issue when Taoiseach Charles Haughey, officiating at the opening of an extension to St Patrick's Cathedral Grammar School in April 1988, intimated to the Archbishop that the six-year cycle would be retained, in the context of a three-year junior cycle, two-year senior cycle and a transition year.

The building of the first new secondary school under Protestant management on a greenfield site since Irish independence, East Glendalough Comprehensive, was seen as a major boost to the confidence of the minority. It was officially opened by President Patrick Hillery in 1989, Donald expressing thanks to the Minister for Education, Mary O'Rourke, and her predecessor, Gemma Hussey (who had turned the first sod on the site in 1986). He spoke of its importance to the community. The widespread building of new primary schools and extensions and additions to existing school buildings in the late 1980s and early 1990s formed a visible sign of progress to teachers, parents and pupils. To those who might criticise the church for spending money on bricks and mortar, Donald's answer was that, in his experience, those parishes which kept their buildings and facilities in first-class condition were also those which were most generous in contributing to need outside their own parish.

When the government proposed the establishment of local education authorities in 1994, with input from local public representatives on boards of management, this was seen as a threat to the Protestant sector. Many pupils at Church of Ireland-managed schools were either from a Roman Catholic or other non-Anglican background, the parents valuing the liberal system of education and strong commitment to academic success perceived there (the schools with their long history and distinctive traditions such as school assemblies also carried a degree of social cachet for some in Irish society). The secretary of the General Synod Board of Education David Meredith commented that the Church of Ireland was happy to provide a '*de facto* alternative system of education' for parents who do not want to send their children to Catholic schools, as long as majority Church of Ireland management was retained.[59]

Walton Empey recalled Donald fighting the Church's corner astutely in discussions with the Department of Education. He recalled one particular meeting when Charles Haughey was Taoiseach in relation to the block grant – a meeting arranged by Archbishop McAdoo in which Donald took a leading role:

Whenever we were in a slightly doubtful position, Donald would launch into Irish and Haughey would have to lean over to his secretaries to get straight what Donald was saying. It rattled Haughey! I had never seen this side of Donald before – astute, on the ball, right to the point, political with a small p ... McAdoo and the rest of us were left eating the dirt!

The Irish language

In celebrations held at French Park, Roscommon, in 1988 to mark the Golden Jubilee of the election of Douglas Hyde as first president of Ireland, Donald recalled the sense of 'mild gratification' expressed by older members of the southern Protestant community at his election in 1938. Referring to Hyde's seminal address *On the Necessity of de-Anglicising Ireland*, in which he had appealed for a greater development of, and pride in, native thought and customs, Donald interpreted this as an appeal for bilingualism and the recognition of pluralism, in the context of culture. It needed to be seen in the context of its time. He recalled that Hyde had departed the Gaelic League when it became more associated with nationalist politics, but that Lil Nic Dhonnchadh of Cumann Gaelach na hEaglaise had remained a member.

Hyde had criticised the Church of Ireland for its failure to identify more closely with the vast majority of the people of Ireland, and one of the fears that he had, if he were to be ordained a priest, was that he might be cut off from this vital contact with the life of Irish Ireland. Notwithstanding this, Donald noted how Hyde had remained an attender at St Andrew's Church and at St Patrick's Cathedral when in Dublin. Hyde's faith was expressed in the *Dánta Dé*, the folk songs and poems of the people, rather than through abstract theology. He had disagreed with his father, amongst other things, over the question of religion: 'I seldom talked to my father; I cannot bring myself to speak to him or keep up the conversation with him – that way at least, I have no rows with him.' Donald imagined that Hyde identified the Church with his father, disagreeing with each while still loving them.[60]

Preaching at St Patrick's Cathedral in January 1993, Donald stated that credit for the popular interest then emerging in Celtic Spirituality was largely due to Hyde. He had turned the lyrical gifts of the poet W.B. Yeats to Celtic themes and had awakened the mind of Lady Gregory (the playwright and founder of the Abbey Theatre) to the gifts of language and imagination among the rural peasantry which surrounded her. Speaking at *Éigse de hÍde* in Roscommon in June 1993, Donald said that Hyde was like the man in the gospel seeking a jewel. He found it in the place he least expected to, right at hand. The Irish language was a jewel for him – 'he discovered it joyfully and he spent his life polishing it and displaying it proudly to the world.'

Risteárd Ó Glaisne, in his book *De Bhunadh Protastúnach*, records that the aims and objectives of the contemporary Gaelic League (now known by its name in Irish, Conradh na Gaeilge) became a concern for Donald when he was invited to register as a member in advance of the organisation's centenary in 1993. One of the aims of the Conradh was that Ireland would be 'free and Gaelic'. Echoing Hyde's own concern about politics entering into language matters, Donald had discussions with Conradh na Gaeilge's president Proinsias MacAonghusa. He said his own wish was for 'comprehensive freedom' for the country, which for him meant freedom in all aspects of life. The clear implication was that freedom should not be interpreted in narrow jurisdictional or political sovereignty terms. Aspects of the national political culture which would appear to exclude non-nationalists from wholehearted participation in the language revival movement appeared to disturb Donald. When the aims of the Conradh were clarified to his satisfaction, Donald agreed to be present at important events during the celebration of its centenary in 1993.

As part of the celebrations, Cumann Gaelach na hEaglaise organised a special centenary service in Trinity College Chapel in May 1993, at which Donald preached. A commemoration service was also held in September to mark the ninetieth anniversary of the death of the Rev. Maxwell Close – another Church of Ireland language enthusiast, member of the Society for the Preservation of the Irish Language and of the Gaelic League.

On another occasion, the Archbishop attended an ecumenical blessing ceremony of a memorial plaque for Patrick Heaney (1881–1911), composer of the music for the Irish national anthem *Amhrán na bhFiann* (the words having being written in 1907 by Peadar Kearney). In Donald's personal notes, seen by the author, he has underlined three words of the English version of the anthem – references to the oath, a tyrant and rifle peal. Perhaps his concern related to the possibility that these might appear to be either blasphemous, offensive to Unionists or supportive of republican violence respectively. This vignette illustrates the complexity in this period surrounding symbols of the Irish State's revolutionary origins against a backdrop of continuing paramilitary violence in the North.

Donald liked to use Irish on public occasions, out of love for the language but also perhaps not unaware, in Valerie Jones' view, of its usefulness as an identifier – Jones recalled somebody remarking at an ecumenical event in which Donald had participated: 'why does the Protestant fellow always do the lessons in Irish?' At the service for the National Day of Commemoration at the Royal Hospital, Kilmainham (traditionally held on the Sunday in July closest to the anniversary of the 1921 truce in the War of Independence), Donald read the gospel in Irish. A highlight of the Irish language calendar in Dublin city was the interdenominational service held at Christ Church Cathedral during the Week of Prayer for Christian Unity in January each year, an annual fixture instituted in the 1970s in the early years of the Troubles in Northern Ireland. As Archbishop, Donald was a faithful patron of this service, which united his ecumenical instincts and his love for the language. He also celebrated other services for Cumann Gaelach na hEaglaise from time to time as his schedule permitted.

An Irish translation of the Church of Ireland's *Alternative Prayer Book* (1984) was launched in Power's Hotel, Kildare Street and in 1985, the Representative Church Body authorising the translation 'subject to the approval of the Bishop of Meath and Kildare' (although by the time of publication Donald had in fact been transferred to Dublin). In 1989, he was present at Áras an Uachtaráin, when President Hillery was presented with a new history of the Irish language in the Church of Ireland, *An Ghaeilge in Eaglais na hÉireann*, along with Dáithí Ó Maolchoille and Leslie Bryan (respectively, Treasurer and Secretary of Cumann Gaelach na hEaglaise), and the author, Risteárd Giltrap, Principal of Coláiste Moibhí. This work set out, for the general reader, a chronology of the Church's contribution to Irish in three successive stages since the seventeenth century: evangelical, antiquarian and revivalist. Giltrap in his foreword expressed appreciation for Donald steering him towards valuable sources of information, and observes of his leadership in relation to the language that 'a good example was better than goodwill'.[61]

At Buswell's Hotel, Dublin in 1992, Donald spoke at the launch of a reprint of the Bible in Irish, *An Bíobla Naofa*, produced by *An Sagart*, the Roman Catholic priests' organisation. The Church of Ireland in its Irish language services frequently made use of this Irish translation of the Bible (particularly in view of the fact that no other modern translation of the Old Testament was available. Canon Cosslett Quin had produced a translation of the New Testament – *An Tiomna Nua* – in 1970 (published by Cumann Gaelach na hEaglaise). The basis of *An Bíobla Naofa* was a painstaking translation of the scriptures from Hebrew and Greek. Originally published in 1981, the 1992 reprint contained some revisions of spelling and standardisation ('*ceisteanna litrithe agus caighdeáin*', as Msgr Pádraig Ó Fiannachta, the main driver of the project, put it).

Commending the publication, Donald said that he himself used *An Bíobla Nofa* each day to read the reading for the day from the Old Testament. He referred to the fact that he and Ó Fiannachta knew the same Gaeltacht area [in Kerry] well, and indeed had slept 'in the same bed' – adding, after a well-timed pause, *'ní rabhamar ann ag an am céanna'* (we were not in it at the same time), which led to a roar of mirth among those assembled.[62]

1994 saw Donald officially launch two publications produced by Cumann Gaelach na hEaglaise to further the development of the Church's worship through Irish: a set of collects to accompany the Irish translation of the *Alternative Prayer Book*, 1984 (Donald teasing the translator, Canon Cosslett Quin, that he had forsaken the 'lovely Irish of the great Blasket' for the Donegal dialect), and a book and cassette tape of sung worship material in Irish for choirs, *Ceol Diaga do Chóracha*.

Cosslett Quin, born in 1907, was a classical scholar and linguist who had served for some time as Professor of Biblical Greek in Trinity College. He made a renowned translation of Brian Merriman's *Cúirt an Mheán Oíche* into English. In his biography *Cosslett Ó Cuinn*, Risteárd Ó Glaisne recounted an amusing incident during Quin's final illness. Donald had spoken very loudly to him, and Quin wrote on a piece of paper 'I am dumb, but I'm not deaf!' He died in 1995, and in an obituary piece written for *The Irish Times*, Donald paid tribute to his 'broad and receptive mind and large and generous heart'. His wife Doreen had provided a 'sure ballast' in the journey of life. Irish was Quin's 'first and abiding love', and Donald painted a vivid picture of him 'with his pipe in his hand as he strove to bring out the exact quality of a word catching the subtlety of the sound'. Noting that Quin had felt himself at home with people of many religious and political traditions, Donald described him as a true patriot.[63]

The closure of Coláiste Moibhí, the only Irish-medium secondary school under Church of Ireland management, in 1995, came as a bitter disappointment to Donald, who as Archbishop had chaired its board of management. The school, referred to earlier, was one of the last survivors of the preparatory school system established in the early years of the independent state, to ensure students intending to train as teachers in primary schools had a sufficient standard of Irish. Coláiste Moibhí at this stage was taking in pupils who were in their fifth year of secondary education, and it was a juniorate of the Church of Ireland College of Education, with which it shared a campus in Rathmines. Dáithí Ó Maolchoille recalled that a visitor to the campus in that era would customarily hear the students conversing in Irish. The author recalls a letter writer to *The Irish Times* at the time recalling its pupils chatting in the language on the Rathmines bus.

The school had survived for some decades longer than its Catholic preparatory college counterparts, and Donald had the impression that the Department of Education took the view that, by the 1980s, it 'should have completed its work and it should by then have been as easy for a Protestant to learn Irish [without this special provision] as a Catholic'. He expressed strongly his opinion that the school should be kept open to ensure a good supply of Protestant students with a high standard of Irish for training in the College of Education. In the period prior to its closure, most of the students training to be teachers were coming from ordinary secondary schools and only a minority from Coláiste Moibhí.[64] There were some concerns in Church circles at the limited curriculum which could be offered in a small school of some thirty pupils.

Speaking in the Dáil on 4 July 1995, Education Minister Niamh Bhreathnach placed on the record that

> the first proposal for closure came, in 1981, from the Church of Ireland authorities. At the time, however the Department of Education asked for the juniorate to remain in operation so as to ensure an adequate standard of Irish among Protestant candidates for primary teacher training. A review … was initiated by the Department in the early 1990s. The outcome of that review was that the Department accepted the need to phase out the juniorate as its continuation could not be justified on either financial or educational grounds.[65]

Agreement was reached between the Department and the College of Education that that College would establish an extra lecturer in Irish and develop an Irish language enrichment programme. Donald's strong personal regrets at the closure of the juniorate were conveyed in newspaper reports, and in his 'Bishop's letter' in *Church Review*, where he expressed the hope that the closure would not mark a point of decline in the Protestant community's interest in the Irish language. However, in his book, *Coláiste Moibhí* which examined the history of the school, Risteárd Ó Glaisne said that it was difficult to look at the closure in any other way, there being no evidence of a growth of interest among Protestants in the language at that time. He also questioned, given the Department's view that it was too costly to keep the school open, whether the generosity demonstrated by the State to the Protestant community since 1922 was at an end.

The Past Pupils' Association of the College of Education had empathised with Donald's views, but expressed regret at the lack of open discussion of the future of Coláiste Moibhí at the General Synod Board of Education, or within the wider Church community.[66] Preaching at the closing service of thanksgiving for the school in June 1995, Donald outlined his long connection with it over many years, and stated that every one of its scholars stood as a memorial of the life of the school and the training and faith given there. However, his diocesan synod address that autumn sounded a hopeful note: the College of Education had registered a record number of candidates – thirty-four students – and the Irish language enrichment programme 'looks hopeful'.

Socio-sexual liberalisation in the 1980s and 1990s

The late 1970s and early 1980s saw increasing public discussion on questions of law and morality in the Republic, and demands for liberalisation on socio-sexual issues such as divorce and contraception, which had through the years of the State's development since independence been influenced by Roman Catholic moral teaching. The Church of Ireland began to articulate ever more strongly its stand on the right of people to decide these matters in accordance with their own conscience and beliefs rather than have it enforced by law.

I. CONTRACEPTION: 'Contraception an inalienable right, says Bishop Caird' was the stark headline over a report carried in *The Irish Times* on 18 October 1979, of a diocesan synod address given by Donald as Bishop of Meath and Kildare shortly after the Pope's visit to Ireland. Noting that the Pope in his visit, though addressing Catholics specifically, had been expressing the concern of the whole of Christendom on the topics of abortion, contraception and divorce, Donald restated traditional Anglican teaching that sexual intercourse outside marriage constituted (in the language of the time) 'fornication or adultery' and as such was sinful. However, he explained that the 1958 Lambeth Conference, in stating Anglican teaching on responsible parenthood, had noted that the 'inalienable' right to plan the family had to include consideration of the health of the mother, the welfare of the children and responsibility to the wider community, in the fulfilment of which some methods of contraception acceptable to both parties were permissible. He also underlined that 'we would not link abortion to contraception as its necessary sequel, while we would deplore as heinous sin the deliberate destruction of a viable human life capable of fulfilment'. Speaking in 1994 on the Year of the Family, Donald made the reasonable observation that abortion could not be considered in isolation from the availability (or otherwise) of realistic and effectual means of contraception.

II. ABORTION: Prior to the general election in 1981, a group of anti-abortion activists sought commitments from various political party leaders to introduce an amendment to the constitution, explicitly recognising the right to life of the unborn child. This proposal met with strong backing from the Roman Catholic hierarchy. Fianna Fáil leader Charles Haughey, and Fine Gael's Dr Garret FitzGerald, committed themselves to introducing such an amendment, and a wording was subsequently prepared by the government led by Mr Haughey, which took the precaution of consulting the churches, including the Church of Ireland. The Archbishop of Dublin, Henry McAdoo, played a role in having the wording finessed, to reflect strong concerns about certain situations in which the life of the mother might be placed in danger as a result of having to carry a pregnancy to full term, the matter having been discussed in detail at meetings of the Church of Ireland house of bishops.[67]

The final text of the proposed Amendment to Article 40 of the Constitution contained a balancing paragraph recognising the equal right to life of the mother:

> The State acknowledges the right to life of the unborn, and, with due regard to the equal right to life of the mother, guarantees in its laws to respect, and as far as practicable, by its laws to defend and vindicate that right.

Reacting, the standing committee of the General Synod set out the Church of Ireland's position: while emphatically rejecting abortion, the Church 'admitted' that there were cases in which medical necessity required the termination of a pregnancy.[68] Expressing grave doubts as to the wisdom of using constitutional prohibition in this particular area, the standing committee stressed the obligation on all citizens, once the wording was published, to examine it fairly and critically. The 'attempt' to take account of the position of the Church of Ireland and other churches was recognised.

The Church of Ireland Gazette however accused the Taoiseach of being guilty of the 'most shameless political opportunism' in calling the referendum (presumably meaning he was seeking thereby to burnish his anti-abortion credentials with conservative catholic voters), claiming that 'an overwhelming majority of citizens of whatever religious persuasion are reasonably satisfied with the present position of the law' (whereby abortion was prohibited under the 1861 Offences Against the Person Act). In November 1982, a new government comprised of Dr Garret FitzGerald's Fine Gael party, and Labour, came into office. *The Irish Times* reported on 31 January 1983 that the Church of Ireland had now joined the Presbyterians and Methodist churches in reiterating its opposition to the proposed amendment. The standing committee's statement of November 1982 was reissued: the amendment would 'not alter the human situation as it exists in the country, contribute to its amelioration or promote a responsible and informed attitude to the issue of abortion'.

In the face of bitter disagreement in public debate, the coalition prepared a revised wording for the constitutional amendment, which would merely state that no law would be declared unconstitutional by virtue of the fact that it prohibited abortion (something that would prevent a challenge to the existing Offences against the Person Act 1861 on the basis of some countervailing constitutional right being argued, for example in the area of bodily integrity, but which would not prevent the enactment of any future legislation introducing abortion). This was viewed more favourably by the standing committee, which in a statement in March 1983 expressed its feeling that the onus for legislating in this area should remain vested in the Oireachtas: 'We consider this to be preferable to an amendment, the wording of which, it has been suggested, might lead to the necessity of interpretation by the courts.'[69] However, the revised formula came under strong attack from the pro-life lobby as being inadequate, and the changed formula was defeated in the Dáil. The original wording would be the one put to the people by Garret FitzGerald's government, notwithstanding its misgivings about it.

The debate was a fractious one. The Archbishop of Armagh, Dr John Armstrong, said that any amendment imposing a complete ban on abortion would be the imposition of the theological thinking of only one church on all the people – 'this is the Mother and Child Act all over again'. While the coalition government's revised wording had been a little more 'specific', the original Fianna Fáil wording

> was too vague ... For instance, when does the foetus become a living thing that can be aborted or not aborted? That might have to be decided in court. Is it from the beginning or is it after a few days? Doctors seem to be having difficulty in interpreting it.[70]

Dean Victor Griffin of St Patrick's Cathedral criticised the 'unedifying spectacle' presented by a serious moral issue being exploited for party political and electoral advantage. He was criticised for this by Michael Woods of Fianna Fáil – this was an unwarranted attack on public representatives: 'nothing could be more unedifying than the killing of the unborn.' The pro-life movement was not sectarian, and Protestants were at the forefront of it in the US, in Northern Ireland and in the Republic. Woods also stated that 'Archbishop Armstrong speaks as Primate of All Ireland, and his views were sought before framing the pro-life amendment we put forward.'[71] In fact, there were some Church of Ireland voices raised in favour of the amendment, including the Rev. Cecil Kerr, founder of the Christian Renewal Centre in Rostrevor.

In the closing weeks of the referendum campaign, there was a cooling of the rhetorical temperature, the Church of Ireland archbishops, Dr Armstrong and Dr McAdoo, restating their position that a decision by voters was a matter for individual conscience:

> The Church of Ireland's position has been consistent throughout the debate – it is that the Church of Ireland is opposed to abortion, save at the dictate of strict and undeniable medical necessity, but has drawn attention to the possible medical and legal difficulties that might arise from the intended form of wording.[72]

The Roman Catholic hierarchy for its part, while stressing its strong support for the amendment, had also in a statement towards the end of the campaign acknowledged that voting was a matter for the individual conscience.

An editorial in *The Irish Independent* noted that the statements from both churches meant that voters could now cast their ballots 'free from any fear of moral opprobrium':

> The Catholic Hierarchy have felt obliged to point out that among the anti-amendment campaigners, there is a body of pro-abortionists. While this is undoubtedly right, we feel it is also right to point out that the vast majority of those opposed to the amendment also oppose abortion. The Church of Ireland bishops drew attention again yesterday to what they describe as 'the medical and legal difficulties that might arise from the intended form of wording'. The Catholic hierarchy, in common with the Pro-Life Amendment Campaign protagonists, are satisfied that these difficulties do not exist. We feel that therein lies the nexus of this debate and voters will have to make up their minds on the basis of how they conscientiously and responsibly resolve these two opposing positions.[73]

The Eighth Amendment to the Constitution was carried by a strong majority in the referendum in September 1983, but would have significant repercussions some years later. Donald appealed for reconciliation after the divisive debate which had characterised the referendum, warning against the exploiting of the victory by conservatives:

> If having achieved the added security of a constitutional prohibition of abortion, this advantage should be exploited further to interfere in the area of essentially private sexual morality, one can see that the tenderest scars of recent conflict could easily be opened again and the public subjected again to perhaps an even less edifying display of vituperation which though finding occasion for its expression in the debate on the subject of abortion, did not always find its origin there.[74]

The passing of the referendum inserting the pro-life amendment, along with the defeat of proposals to introduce divorce early in Donald's term as Archbishop of Dublin, paradoxically took place at a time when the overwhelming influence of the Roman Catholic Church on the laws and civic mores of the Republic were probably weakening somewhat, some years after the Papal visit. In a profile interview headlined 'The Thinking Person's Bishop' in *The Irish Times* in May 1984,[75] Donald when Bishop of Meath and Kildare had observed:

> I'll probably be shot if you print this, but I think the Irish people have had as much religion as they can stomach [for] a very long time and I think we're just getting back to normal ... Someone said on television recently that we have accepted as normal the tremendous interest in religion that began probably in the 1860s and went on into the 1960s. You had practically every Roman Catholic family turning out a priest. We were affected by the same syndrome in the Protestant churches. But that was not normal. Now we're returning to normality – and we think it's a disaster. In fact it may be a very healthy thing ... I have, I suppose, this very Protestant attitude that the institutions of the church, while very important, are not everything in the Christian faith. There is also the relationship of the individual to God.

Controversy over abortion erupted again in his time as Archbishop of Dublin. In 1992, the Attorney General made an application to the High Court to restrain a young girl who had been raped and was pregnant, from travelling outside the state to secure an abortion. The application was made in the context of an understanding that the state had a constitutional obligation under the 1983 amendment to vindicate the right to life of the unborn, without qualification as to where the perceived threat to that life might occur. Evidence was given to the High Court that the young girl was suicidal, and the matter was appealed to the Supreme Court.

In what became known as the 'X case', the Supreme Court gave a decision holding that suicide was a threat to the life of the mother, that abortion was permissible in these circumstances, and overturned the injunction. There were contrasting reactions, with liberals on the one hand appealing for legislation to set out the precise parameters within which abortion might be lawfully made available within the state (and for guarantees of the right to travel abroad for abortion services, which might not necessitate another constitutional referendum), and from conservatives on the other, who appealed for a fresh referendum to insert a new provision ruling out suicide as a justification for permitting an abortion.

The standing committee of General Synod made a statement, recalling its position in respect of the 1983 amendment. Donald appealed for legislation rather than a new referendum, warning against attempting simplistic solutions to the constitutional problem which had arisen and urging legislators to define the limited circumstances in which abortion would be permitted, in order to prevent the judgment being used to open the floodgates to abortion on demand. He recalled the views expressed by the standing committee of the Church of Ireland in 1983:

> In the strongest terms Christians reject the practice of induced abortion or infanticide which involves the killing of a life already conceived (as well as a violation of the personality of the mother), save at the dictate of strict and undeniable medical necessity.

Donald stated that this implied clearly that there can be circumstances in which termination of pregnancy may be required. The Supreme Court judgement appeared to conform with the views expressed by the standing committee in 1983, and with Church of Ireland anxiety at the time to ensure that the amendment wording contained a balancing reference to the right to life of the mother.

However, even the securing of the balancing reference in 1983 had not amounted to Church of Ireland endorsement of the amendment at that time (the standing committee having confined itself to expressing its opposition to such morally complex and divisive issues being inserted into the constitution). There was evidence of confusion as to what the Church of Ireland view of 1983 was, as the then Primates Armstrong and McAdoo seemed to have been consulted when the wording was being prepared. A member of the church, Trevor Matthews, defended former Taoiseach Charles Haughey, who he said told him that the previous Archbishop of Dublin (McAdoo) was shown and approved the original wording of the anti-abortion amendment – which was (perhaps not unreasonably) interpreted by politicians as Church of Ireland approval at the time.[76]

The Irish Bishops' Conference (of Roman Catholic bishops) issued a statement deploring the judgement in X and reiterated its stance that human life begins at conception and warning that legislation permitting abortion, even in restricted circumstances, rapidly leads to abortion on demand. A new amendment was passed in December 1992 declaring the right of citizens to travel abroad to avail of services lawfully available in another state, notwithstanding other provisions of the Constitution. However, no move was made by the Oireachtas to fill the legislative gap highlighted by the Supreme Court, in setting out the parameters in which termination of pregnancy might be lawful within the state, until 2013, following controversy surrounding the death of Savita Halappanavar, a pregnant woman in hospital in Galway.

III. DIVORCE: In Donald's time in Meath and Kildare, divorce remained subject to a ban under the 1937 Constitution. Annulment of marriage, which rendered it capable of being declared void *ab initio*, and which was accepted by the Roman Catholic tradition in certain circumstances, was also frequently the only means available within the law of the land to deal with the vexed question of marriage breakdown. In light of substantial public resistance to the removal of the ban on divorce, and the stance of the Catholic Church, there were suggestions that extending the grounds whereby a marriage could be annulled in law could represent a way of dealing with the problem of marriage breakdown. It was a remedy viewed with unease in the Church of Ireland tradition.

In 1976, Archbishop Buchanan had declared that government proposals to amend the law on nullity of marriage were so geared to the teaching of one church that it was sure to be adjudged to be sectarian. Grounds for nullity might include an incapacity to form a stable relationship and also ignorance of the full meaning of that relationship:

> Surely these were artificial? No man or woman was completely capable of such a relationship or knowledge at the time of marriage. Some were more mature than others, but could one really draw a hard and fast line between the mature and the immature? In any case, marriage was more than just a contract; it was a growing lifelong relationship.

Noting that a marriage could be annulled after many years, he warned about the danger of 'manufactured evidence' on one side or the other – could any marriage be accounted secure?[77] In 1979, Donald warned in his address to the diocesan synod that proposals to extend the traditional grounds for legal annulment risk the danger of falling into a 'medieval morass' which seemed to undermine the whole fabric of marriage as an institution.[78]

Two referendums on a proposal to remove the ban on Irish courts granting a dissolution of marriage (divorce) in the Constitution of Ireland were held during Donald's tenure in Dublin, one near the beginning, and the second towards the end of his term. The first was held in 1986, during the lifetime of Dr Garret FitzGerald's Fine Gael–Labour coalition government.

In his enthronement service in September 1985, Donald referred to the acrimonious public debate which had taken place two years earlier on the abortion referendum, expressing the hope that this would not be repeated 'in form or content' in relation to divorce. He observed that the Christian churches were frequently represented as being in 'implacable conflict' on such issues whereas in reality the differences between them, while significant, were not extreme.[79] This was presumably a reference to a tendency in media coverage to present the Church of Ireland's more ostensibly 'liberal' position on socio-sexual issues as a useful foil to the more conservative and traditionalist pronouncements of the Roman Catholic hierarchy. Indeed, on the very day following his enthronement, newspaper reports juxtaposed the divergent views on divorce expressed by Archbishop Caird and by Archbishop Kevin McNamara respectively, over the same weekend.

McNamara, addressing a meeting of the Knights of St Columbanus, deplored a tendency 'in chat show discussions, for speakers of little or no qualifications to parade with confidence the most varying and contradictory opinions'. Saying that there was no time for a 'so-called pluralism' which would claim to embrace both traditional and liberal views at once, Archbishop McNamara underlined the Catholic hierarchy's view that the removal of the constitutional prohibition on divorce would, however wellmeaning, be 'inescapably a choice to undermine the institution of lifelong marriage and inflict irreparable harm on the family'.[80] Donald took the view that the church had to temper discipline with compassion: marriage should be lifelong and exclusive, but even the best intentions may be frustrated by human weakness.

McNamara criticised a perceived media bias in favour of divorce, but the Church of Ireland was also criticised in other quarters for not taking a more active role in the debate. Following the publication of a pastoral letter from the Roman Catholic bishops in *The Irish Times*, the editor of *The Church of Ireland Gazette* asked whether the Church of Ireland bishops were letting the position on divorce go by default through their silence. The latter did not presume to direct their flock in how to vote, but rather attempted to give guidance on the issues involved, Donald stressing that it was not desirable 'that we enter an open contest with the Roman Catholic Church' – divorce was a matter for the civil authorities. He did however note that the faith of members of the Anglican communion in some thirty seven countries had not collapsed as a result of divorce being available there.

Proposals were made during the referendum campaign for an extension of the civil laws on nullity of marriage, as a possible alternative to divorce. The legal position on civil nullity, Donald noted, was being developed by case law, and he feared that if this continued, a situation could be reached whereby the validity of a marriage depended upon the opinion of a psychiatrist informing a Judge. This would tend to be 'much more destructive of marriage' than the introduction of divorce, in his view.

The proposal to remove the ban was defeated by a substantial margin in 1986. Reacting, Donald noted pointedly that the views of the minority had been taken into account, and then rejected by the electorate: 'Ireland now stands with Malta as the only [other] European country which does not allow for divorce. That is the league we are in.' He was, on the other hand, deeply critical of media selectivity in relation to views expressed by the Church of Ireland in the campaign (highlighting arguments tending to support the removal of the constitutional ban, in juxtaposition to the views of the Roman Catholic Church), saying he was grateful to have the diocesan magazine available to present a more rounded (and nuanced) picture. Speaking at his diocesan synod, he described the referendum as a 'courageous attempt' by the government to face the growing problem of marriage breakdown and the consequential personal, social and legal difficulties which arose:

> The debate prior to the referendum at no point constituted a contest between the churches concerning the nature of marriage or divorce. The Church of Ireland had been criticised for not speaking out more strongly but it had made its doctrine on marriage and divorce plain and had stated that it was a matter of the degree of freedom of the individual citizen under the Constitution ... a matter of civil rights.

The second referendum on divorce was held in November 1995, during John Bruton's term of office as Taoiseach, leading a three party 'rainbow' coalition of the Fine Gael, Labour and Democratic Left parties. A number of statements were made by Donald, articulating the views of the house of bishops. In formulating public statements, the bishops took legal advice and also received submissions from within its own membership. The Mothers' Union, as we have seen, had a tradition of opposition to divorce. Extensive briefing material on the Church of Ireland's expressed views on divorce over the years was provided by the diocesan communications officer to the Archbishop.

Speaking to his diocesan synod a month before the 1995 vote, Donald referred to the advice of St Paul to the Philippians, chapter 3 verse 1: 'to repeat what I have written to you before is no trouble to me and it is a safeguard for you', and set out the key points made in a statement by the standing committee of General Synod the previous month:

(1) the church's teaching that marriage is a lifelong union, coupled with recognition that marriages do break down, and that this had increased in recent years,

(2) the recognition that even the best intentions of those who marry may be frustrated through human failure and weakness, and that discipline must always be tempered with compassion,

(3) the tragedy involved in divorce for the married couple, their children, relations and friends, and for society, which was based on the stability of the family as its basic unit,

(4) the impact on children of marriage breakdown, separation, annulment or divorce, and subsequent marriages entered into by either party,

(5) the major difference between the proposed referendum in 1995 and the previous referendum in 1986, in as much as many of the social issues which caused disquiet in regard to the rights of partners, children, and the distribution of property, had been the subject of legislation in respect of separation in the intervening period.[81]

When speaking at the service to mark the nine hundredth anniversary of St Michan's Church (previously referred to), Donald referred to the upcoming vote – in considering the issues involved, 'heed might be given to the biblical injunction to avoid "straining at gnats and swallowing camels"'. How any individual might vote was a matter of personal conviction based on a fair review of the social issues involved. It was, he said, essential that this choice would not be affected by pressures of any kind. Days ahead of the vote, he noted the difficult position of Protestants in the Republic in the absence of civil divorce – unlike Catholics, they had no recourse to a church annulment procedure, while the limited civil annulment procedure was 'extremely expensive', leaving Protestants in broken marriages more restricted as a minority. Stressing church teaching on marriage as a lifelong union, he said the basic question is whether one regards divorce as 'totally corruptive of society as we know it'. In the circumstances of Ireland with its 'very strong majority who would not have recourse to divorce', it was difficult to be persuaded that its introduction would have such a deleterious effect on society as those campaigning against it anticipated. He would not 'insult the intelligence' of church members by telling them how to vote, noting that this had been tried in 1912 when some bishops urged the General Synod to vote against Home Rule – 'probably the last time that ever occurred, and I hope it would never occur again'. Reflecting some exasperation with the tenor of public discourse on the matter, Donald stated that people must grow up – 'our people are grown up, they are of age and they make up their own minds. I regard this as a largely civil issue.

The electorate finally voted in November 1995 to remove the divorce ban. Noting that the voice of the Irish nation had now spoken, Donald reiterated the necessity to redouble efforts to support the institution of marriage. He expressed the hope that the people's decision would not give rise to recrimination and vindictiveness, but that 'we may be able to settle down again to the peaceful tenor of our ways and get on without pressure with living our usual lives' – reflecting a relief that the intense public focus had lifted.

There was a view that many Protestants in the Ulster counties of the Republic (Donegal, Cavan and Monaghan) would have voted no in the first divorce referendum, but there was never any substantial correspondence in *The Church of Ireland Gazette* criticising the somewhat more liberal official line taken by the Church of Ireland. There may have been a certain element of people not wanting to be seen to be on the same side as the Roman Catholic hierarchy, which was vocal in its opposition to divorce.

Donald had made a number of important interventions in the debates surrounding the two referendums on the matter – although a number of his contemporaries felt that his heart wasn't totally in it in the sense that his traditionalism would have led him to regret the necessity (which he fully recognised) to face up to the reality of marriage breakdown. The first referendum in 1986 had been a divisive experience and he was slightly more cautious in approaching the matter the second time around. His colleague on the bench of bishops, John Neill, remarks that striking a balance between accommodating the reality of marriage breakdown and upholding the church's traditional understanding 'always leads to a personal dilemma for those with a fairly traditional view. That was true for a lot of us in that time'. He was not conscious of any strong division among the bishops on the matter, characterising discussions as a process of 'wrestling' with the issue rather than marking strong divisions.[82]

IV. HOMOSEXUALITY: Homosexual acts between consenting adults remained prohibited by criminal law in the Republic until 1993, when Justice Minister Máire Geoghegan-Quinn introduced legislation, prompted by an increasing clamour for reform as well as a judgement of the European Court of Human Rights in a case brought by Trinity College Senator David Norris, a noted public campaigner for gay rights (and member of the Church of Ireland), assisted by his counsel, Mary Robinson. It was, however a matter on which the house of bishops of the Church of Ireland had not pronounced, the silence forming a stark contrast with the profile of the Church in other areas of liberal social reform. Without referring to any specific bishop or diocese, Paul Colton, in an interview with the author, felt the whole approach in the 1980s and early 1990s to homosexuality in the Church was one of 'don't ask, don't tell'. If somebody got into trouble, the criminal card might be played and it said to the person 'this is a matter of law'. As with other social issues, there was a practice of exporting problems and even clergy, to England. Ginnie Kennerley believes that, in the 1990s, there must have been clergy in the diocese of Dublin known to be gay. The question of homosexuality began to gain traction in Anglicanism internationally in the run-up to the 1998 Lambeth conference, after Donald had retired. In retirement, he remarked to Gordon Linney one day that he would really like to 'study' the topic of homosexuality some more. This, in Linney's view, reflected the philosopher in Donald, wrestling with the instinct from tradition (that this was not right), but questioning that tradition (does that still hold true, today? I'd like to think about that). Linney credits this as a source of encouragement to him in speaking on the issue of homosexuality during John Neill's time as Archbishop.

V. THE MEDIA AND THE 'LIBERAL AGENDA': In an interview with journalist Patsy McGarry in 1989, Donald expressed resentment in relation to the phenomenon whereby liberal Catholics were 'quite prepared to use us' instead of standing up for themselves in their fight for more illiberal laws on divorce and abortion. They 'set up' Protestants who often don't want divorce and abortion. In a profile interview for *The Irish Times* in 1990,

Donald said that, during the referendums on divorce and abortion, people thought they were going to 'slay Protestant dragons', whereas there was only 'a mild intelligent Protestant voice'. Some interventions in the debate around the new Tallaght Hospital (see below) were also on his mind. His interviewer noted that his eyes blazed for a short time, when he expressed irritation at portrayals of the Church of Ireland in relation to sexual ethics, as if it only had two doctrines – on divorce and abortion: 'we aren't constantly thinking about abortion or tubal ligation or divorce. These things are peripheral to our lives, just as they are to everybody's life except, presumably, the media's.' He had another blast at prominent Catholic liberals, saying that if they were depending upon Protestants to voice their position, 'the answer is they've got to voice their own position'.

Walton Empey shared some of Donald's irritation at perceived 'media dragooning' of the Church of Ireland in support of the 'liberal agenda' in the 1980s, recalling in an interview with the author that he had said publicly that the Church was 'about much more than contraception, abortion and divorce'. This was a riposte to Jeremiah Newman, the Catholic Bishop of Limerick, who, in 1990, had queried the meaning of the 'Protestant ethos' in discussions on Tallaght Hospital (see below). Kenneth Milne recalled one of Donald's predecessors, Archbishop Buchanan, saying once how 'weary he was of it all' (referring to the debates on such matters as divorce and contraception). John Neill makes the observation that this period [of the 'liberal agenda' in the 1980s and early 1990s] was the first in which the views of the Church of Ireland house of bishops were being actively solicited by the media on issues other than ecclesiastical. In decades prior to this, views sought from the Church would relate largely to doctrinal issues and its responses to matters such as the 1950s promulgation of the Roman Catholic Church of the dogma of the Assumption of the Blessed Virgin Mary.

Tallaght Hospital

The transfer of the Adelaide Hospital to a new merged hospital complex in Tallaght, along with the Meath and National Children's Hospitals, became an issue of concern for the Protestant community which Donald as Archbishop had to contend with. Dublin city was served by two major hospitals with a Roman Catholic ethos: the Mater Hospital on the northside of the city, and St Vincent's on the southside. The Church of Ireland was anxious that the small Adelaide Hospital's distinctive Protestant ethos and tradition be maintained, and its fate had not yet been decided by the time that Donald became Archbishop. His immediate predecessor, Henry McAdoo, had set out concerns for the tradition's future at the Adelaide nurses' prize day in 1981:

> Whatever emerges for the Adelaide hospital during the years ahead, there are many people in our community who desire to see the Adelaide School of Nursing continue in any new arrangement, and we would wish to have reassurances on this. Far from being a separatist [issue], it is motivated by a real partnership and by a democratic spirit which permits all sections of the national community to give of their best in its service.

Discussions on the merger of the three hospitals had been ongoing since the tenure of Barry Desmond as Minister for Health in Garret FitzGerald's coalition government prior to 1987. However, in 1989, there was concern that previous assurances that an agreed quota of forty places would be reserved for the recruitment of nurses from the Adelaide tradition were not being honoured. Gordon Linney, a member of the board of the Adelaide, told the General Synod that

> there were two levels on which this issue should be judged: the first was that of medical ethics and our status in the future of doctoral and nursing training. The second, the political, relates to the value of the assurances given by different political parties to all minorities on this island as to the security of their traditions for the future.

Donald warned in April 1989 that the future of the Adelaide 'is of concern to us' and 'may require our voices to be heard loudly, clearly and publicly', recording the long and intimate association of the hospital with the Church of Ireland. There was hardly a parish that had not at some time had a nurse trained in its nursing school.

The General Synod was informed in May 1990 that, in a meeting with Donald, Robin Eames and other Protestant leaders, the Taoiseach Charles Haughey gave assurances in relation to maintaining a key role for the Adelaide tradition in the new hospital. However, there were reports that members of the boards of the other two hospitals intended for the merger, the Meath and National Children's hospitals, did not welcome moves where they might find themselves in a minority on a new joint board dominated by Protestant members. The Adelaide issue entered into ongoing talks surrounding the Anglo–Irish agreement and peace in the North. It was raised at the General Assembly of the Presbyterian Church in Belfast and by Northern Unionists who demanded that the controversy be put on the agenda at Anglo–Irish talks. Press reports indicated that, as a result of pressure from the minority in the Republic and adverse criticism from within Northern Ireland and from Britain, the government might in fact abandon entirely plans for the new hospital (thus retaining the Adelaide).

In 1991, Donald served warning that if the ethos of the Adelaide could not be guaranteed in arrangements for the new hospital, the proposals for the merger with the Meath and National Children's Hospital would have to go back to the drawing board. A working group was established to steer negotiations, under the chairmanship of David Kingston, chief executive of Irish Life. Donald spelled out the demands of the Adelaide: its position as a focus for Protestant participation in the health services and its particular denominational ethos must be continued in the new hospital in Tallaght, and all forms of treatment which were legal within the state should be available there.[83] In May 1993, agreement was finally reached guaranteeing a minimum quota of nurses from the Adelaide tradition in the new hospital, and affirming the religious character of the new institution. It was recognised that religious welfare was part of the total welfare of every patient, and would be supported by chaplains of each major denomination.

In the public discussion surrounding the proposed new hospital at Tallaght, there had been some difficulty in arriving at an exact definition of the 'Protestant ethos'. The conservative Bishop of Limerick, Jeremiah Newman, in May 1990 publicly queried the meaning of the term. Claiming that the essence of Protestantism was to protest, he said that 'if Catholic ethics were not respected, then other ethics are.'[84] Donald was exasperated at the Adelaide becoming a football between proponents of liberalism on the one hand and conservatives on the other. In a profile piece in *The Irish Times* in October 1990 (referred to earlier), he expressed resentment at the expectation of some Roman Catholics 'that I'm always going to be opposed to them', saying that Protestants looked at legislation and its effects rather than the source. He felt that the religious nature of the Adelaide tradition was being somewhat eclipsed in the debate, asserting that this tradition was 'religious in the same sense as a major Roman Catholic hospital'.[85]

The Irish Times, in an editorial entitled 'Republican ethos'[86] and in reports, attempted a definition. Under the Protestant ethos, 'it is the individual consciences of patient and doctor and nurse which determine the outcome of the reputed discussions, rather than the dogma of one particular religious denomination or another.' There would be no ethics committee in the new hospital, and all services, including tubal ligations, vasectomy and sterilisations, would be decided privately between doctor and patient. All services lawfully available within the state would be provided, without prejudice to the rights of conscience of individual medical and/or nursing staff. This was to be a central objective of the revised charter for the hospital, and it was also implicit that abortions could be performed there if the law of the land so permitted.[87]

The Church of Ireland Archbishop of Dublin would be president of the new hospital, and have the right to nominate six board members (for formal appointment by the Minister for Health), while the Minister would make a further two independent appointments. The Adelaide's board would appoint a further six members, the Meath six and the National Children's Hospital three, thus ensuring a majority for Protestant interests on the twenty-three-member board. Special arrangements were to be made to ensure continuity of board membership in the early years of the hospital. These arrangements would provide for nominal equality of representation among the various traditions represented in the merger, while the addition of the Archbishop's nominees would secure the maintenance of the 'Protestant ethos'.

Once this beachhead was secured, it was felt on the Church of Ireland side that matters could evolve naturally. Linney lauded the 'quality people' Donald appointed to the board as the first president. Among these was Kenneth Milne, who served for a term of six years, and recalled the enormous logistical challenge of transferring some three thousand staff 'from doctors to cleaners' out to Tallaght. Donald had been cautious in his public pronouncements on the matter, leaving most of the media running on the issue to Gordon Linney. The latter referred to Donald's dislike of the concept of 'Protestants beating drums', demanding rights and complaining about their treatment in the Republic, interpreting this as a wariness about being seen to be an oppressed minority, and thus giving ammunition to Northern Unionist critics of the southern state. Linney felt his own (slightly younger) generation to be less burdened by this, and therefore more forthright in its articulation of minority concerns.

Concerns over HIV and AIDS

The spread of Acquired Immune Defiency Syndrome (AIDS), caused by the Human Immunodeficiency Virus (HIV), was a significant source of concern in the late 1980s and early 1990s. A great deal of fear and ignorance surrounded public discussion of the topic. The use of condoms in the fight against AIDS was not countenanced by the Roman Catholic Church, which emphasised sexual abstinence outside marriage as the surest way to prevent spread of the HIV virus. The position was not terribly different in the Church of Ireland: in December 1986 Donald stated that he could not support any action which would promote sex outside marriage – which was 'adultery and fornication'. In the fight against AIDS, he said, the church must 'do its part to teach our people that sex is for marriage alone'.

In February 1987, in comments accompanying a statement by the Church of Ireland house of bishops, he warned adults who were exposed to a misuse of sex or drugs to consider carefully the 'terrible cost to themselves and to society', emphasising 'self-control and fidelity within marriage' as the only sure way of limiting the spread of the HIV virus. He referred (in the bald terms which then had currency) to the risk groups identified, including 'promiscuous homosexual males, drug users, haemophiliacs'. Christians, he said, must show compassion but reserved the right to 'censure those false prophets who misled untold numbers of young people into believing that there is no moral limit to human freedom'. He emphasised that there was no risk of contracting the virus through use of the common chalice at communion services.

By April 1991, however, he was making a more nuanced observation, reflecting maturing public discussion and advances in understanding and prevention of HIV. Public health campaigns were placing a strong premium on the more widespread availability of condoms. Reiterating the church's teaching on sexual activity outside marriage, Donald regretted the necessity the government perceives 'to require this urgent departure from the current arrangements in relation to the accessibility of condoms', but balanced this with an expression of confidence that 'they are acting on the best available advice'.[88]

The Right to Die case
A distressing and emotional case involving a forty-five-year-old woman who had been in a persistent vegetative state in hospital for some twenty-three years reached the courts in the summer of 1995. The woman had been in this condition since undergoing a minor gynaecological examination under general anaesthetic at the age of twenty-two. The Supreme Court delivered a judgement upholding an earlier decision of the High Court to allow the feeding tube to be withdrawn with the consent of her family. There was intense reaction to the judgement, with disquiet expressed as to its implications for other cases, and fears that it might lead to euthanasia becoming widely available.

In response to questions from the media, Donald issued a statement, emphasising that Christian reflection must always include a real sense of our own fallibility, saying that this was why, in the liturgy of the Church of Ireland, petition was made for all in authority in the State, including the judiciary. A moral judgement was always a judgement, and could never reach the degree of certainty of a mathematical 'demonstration', because it dealt with concrete personal issues with all of the contingencies actually involved, rather than with contingency-free abstractions. He questioned whether the term 'life' as used in Article 40 of the Irish constitution was to be understood as 'mere existence or as life in all its fullness', citing the Gospel of John, chapter 10, verse 10. Donald deplored responses which had characterised the decision as 'legalised murder', and which sought to compare it to Hitler's programme of extermination of the unfit, while he recognised fears that those who would press for euthanasia might make use of the case to support their campaign: 'we can recognise public disquiet in this issue as we are told that there may be as many as twenty similar cases at this time in the country.' The court had reached its decision in the specific circumstances of the case before it, and had taken it with great sensitivity for the woman and her deeply distressed family. The judgement had specifically stated that it should not constitute a ground for argument in relation to any other similar issue which might arise in the future. Each case presented unique circumstances which would require consideration and treatment, and Donald expressed the hope that legislation would be enacted to cover such cases. Concluding with a reminder that life was a gift from God, and one had to accept the imperfection of life within that wider perception, he said that 'medical science should always be used to protect life and to enhance life, but not merely to prolong the process of dying.'

It should be noted that an element of the anxiety surrounding the Supreme Court's decision related to the extent to which some of those in apparently vegetative conditions might continue to have an inner life undetectable to others, and to the question of how a true judgement could be made.

Family life and the See House
The See House was a detached Georgian house located on the quiet Temple Road in the leafy suburb of Rathmines – a change from the busy street on which the Cairds had lived while at Leixlip. Ann lived there with her parents on starting university in 1985, John joining them a year later after leaving King's Hospital. The kitchen was at the heart of the Cairds' home there. Although Donald's office was located in the house, he was frequently out attending events, and returning late at night, when he would delight in relaxing and chatting with family members in the kitchen.

While he did not watch very much television, two programmes he did enjoy were *Dad's Army* and *Yes, Minister*. His daughter Helen recalls her father's pleasure in taking Ben (the Airedale dog they had while in Dublin) out for walks.[89] Ben came into the Cairds' possession after the twelve-year-old Irish terrier they owned was killed on the road after chasing another dog while momentarily off the lead. Donald travelled up to Belfast to collect the new dog just a week after this incident. 'I couldn't imagine life without dogs.' Asked whether having a dog or cat teaches one Christian values, Donald said that he didn't know, 'but we should always exercise Christian values in relation to them and treat them with kindness and respect. They give good service, especially in companionship. They have to be treated as animals, however, and not as vicarious human beings.'[90] The quietness of Temple Road in Rathmines came as a change from his previous episcopal accommodation, and the change was felt in both human and canine experience: 'We have actually had to send one of our dogs away because in the quietness here he could hear all the dogs barking from miles around and it drove him crazy barking in reply to them.'[91]

> For the past twenty-five years, if one rang the See House to speak to the Archbishop between the hours of 10:30 a.m. and 4:30 p.m., from Monday to Friday, the telephone was answered by a charming voice which combined in its tone courtesy, efficiency, patience, friendship and a readiness to help, while at the same time being flexible enough to deal effectively with those interlocutors who by their tone suggested that their business was trivial, inappropriate, too persistent, aggressive, or just plain eccentric. That was the voice of the Archbishop's personal secretary, Miss Patricia Hastings Hardy, who retired from office on June 29,

wrote Donald in his 'Bishop's letter' published in the diocesan magazine in July 1990. She was 'the essence of discretion', in Donald's description.[92] He fondly recalled:

> We always stopped [work] at 1pm for lunch and I would always eat a very light lunch. I can't eat [too much during] the day, digestion! I always loved a toasted cheese sandwich, and a bottle, half pint of Guinness … Then about 1:30 p.m., I would get into my chair for a sleep, and always try to wake up before [Miss Hastings – Hardy] would return. I could hear her car on the gravel. But often I was too tired, and she would knock on the door and say that there was 'a very urgent message' – she didn't like Archbishops sleeping at lunch hour! I had probably been up since 7:30 a.m., and might not have got back from some outlying parish before 1 a.m., getting to bed maybe at 2 a.m.

The See House being the venue for many church-related events, Nancy had a busy time as hostess, eschewing active roles in areas such as the Mothers' Union. She reflected on her role, seeing her particular gift – indeed, her ministry – as that of affording hospitality and in that way being a help to her husband: 'I loved gathering people from all strata of society to a church property, making it an inclusive and welcoming place.' Described by her youngest daughter, Helen, as a perfectionist, she paid keen attention to detail in organising the many receptions in the See House. As many as sixty guests might be present at a buffet supper, and Nancy was punctilious about introductions, finding the provision of nametags a helpful strategy when a group of strangers were gathered together. Donald, as official host, enjoyed giving a practical hand in preparations as circumstances allowed. In addition to the formal entertaining, Donald and Nancy enjoyed having neighbours to dinner.[93] Among the many guests entertained at the See House on various occasions were the British Ambassador and his wife, and the Catholic Archbishop Desmond Connell. A special reception was held for visiting Archbishop Desmond Tutu of South Africa, with President Mary Robinson in attendance. The Archbishop also traditionally hosted a buffet dinner for bishops and their wives, after the Eve of Synod service – a tradition started by George Otto Simms, and continued by his successors. There might be up to fifty people present at such receptions, and Nancy would call on some assistance to help with catering.

To relax, she would take Ben, the Airedale dog, for a long walk in the Cruagh Woods in the Dublin mountains, let him off the lead and he would chase rabbits and deer: 'this was my exercise and space … about one and half hours and then come back down.' The Cairds had kept up their old friendship with Cyril Patton (Donald's old schoolmate at Miss Guilgault's) and his wife Philippa, who now lived in Mount Merrion, Dublin. Nancy enjoyed occasional walks in the mountains together with Philippa. Cyril Patton recalled: 'as Archbishop's wife, Nancy couldn't talk to just anyone, but she got on like a house on fire with Philippa and they loved each other's company. They had known each other before all that.'[94] Philippa also helped Nancy with catering in the See House.

Nancy would also accompany her husband on some of his late evening walks in Rathmines down Temple Road, along Cowper Road, up Palmerston Road. She enjoyed an interest in art, building up over time a small family collection of pictures which appealed to her. The demands of hosting a large number of events over a period of ten years at the See House must have been onerous. Reflecting on her parents, Helen referred to her overwhelming feeling of pride in her father as 'a human being with a fantastic font of knowledge about Irish history, heritage and language, and philosophically … My mother is a wonderful person. I'm sure there must have been times she didn't feel like entertaining, but [she brought] a wonderful sense of life and character'. The family continued to enjoy time spent at their house in Kerry (Donald usually managing a month there around August, the rest of the family staying a few weeks longer), with a visit traditionally paid to the Guithín brothers during their stays there at Christmastime.

During Donald's time as Archbishop of Dublin, his three children embarked successively on new stages of life, moving on from boarding at their secondary school, Kings Hospital in Palmerstown (they spent the summer months from June to September at home with their parents, and might go with them to Kerry) and embarking upon their careers: medicine in the case of the two eldest, Ann and John (medicine being a strong tradition in the family of Donald's mother Emily); and in the case of the youngest, Helen, teaching followed by a change of career to art.

Pre-retirement

In January 1996, when Donald announced his intention to retire the following April, many tributes were paid to him by his colleagues in the church. Media assessments noted his recent achievement in securing the position of the Adelaide interest in the new Tallaght hospital, and highlighted his role as leader of the southern minority in a time of change. *The Church of Ireland Gazette* reported on the appointment of Walton Empey as Donald's successor, one of its writers observing that the fact that Donald 'made light' of the onerous nature of his duties shouldn't obscure the fact that the role of Archbishop of Dublin 'is far too big a job for one person'.[95]

On 21 April 1996 in Christ Church Cathedral, following the service of evensong, a presentation of a set of luggage, a cheque and a bicycle pump was made to Donald, who quipped 'I can now become properly inflated in my retirement!' Warm tributes were paid to Nancy, who in turn thanked the organisers and those with whom she had worked in the See House. She paid tribute to Donald as a wonderful marriage partner and remarked that Dun Laoghaire will 'either be a second childhood or a second honeymoon'. As they left the cathedral for a reception at nearby Dublinia in the old Synod Hall, Donald closed a chapter as a serving bishop and key spokesperson for the southern minority which had lasted just over twenty-five and a half years, a time of constant flux in the life of church, state and community in Ireland.

Archbishop Robin Eames paid tribute to Donald for giving 'faithful and patient leadership to the clergy and people of the southern province, while earning the respect of all traditions. The Church of Ireland has been the richer because of this gentle scholarly servant of God.' As he relinquished office, Donald was optimistic about the state of the church, stating that a decline in its numbers had halted, and the church was a 'confident minority'. He expressed a parting wish for the nation:

> I hope and pray that there will be a permanent peace in this country. This is my greatest desire and wish and I really believe that it is possible. I believe that my successor will see this peace in his tenure and I look forward to it.[96]

CHAPTER SEVEN

Retirement

Family life in retirement

An attractive early nineteenth-century house on Crofton Avenue, a tranquil location off the main seafront road in the south Dublin coastal borough of Dun Laoghaire, would become Donald and Nancy's base in retirement. The couple purchased the property in January 1995, but did not move in until May 1996, shortly after Donald retired. The little house at Camp in Kerry, however, had originally been envisaged as their retirement base. 'None of the other places we lived in belonged to us,' reflected Ann. 'I became aware of this as I got a bit older in Limerick. Kerry was the one constant. We moved relatively often.'[1]

However it quickly became apparent to the family that, while short stays in Kerry were very relaxing, longer stretches at the house in Camp, particularly in winter, could prove quite bleak; their parents would not easily adjust to living in retirement outside the cosmopolitan milieu of Dublin, where they enjoyed attending many cultural and social events. The Church of Ireland community in West Kerry was small and dispersed. However, Kerry remained the favoured destination for short breaks. Since 1970, both Donald and Nancy had been members of Cumann Seandálaíochta Chiarraí (Kerry Archaeological and Historical Society), which held occasional meetings on the Blasket Islands, with sometimes up to one hundred people making the journey out.

The Cairds' daughters, Ann and Helen, recall the transition to retirement being somewhat difficult for Donald, who had been so used to dealing with many people in the course of his work as Archbishop. The sudden change in tempo meant that, initially, their father 'sank a little bit'. Nancy experienced more relief at retirement. In Helen's assessment, while she had enjoyed the life enormously, and had thrown her heart and soul into hospitality at the See House, it had been a demanding role to fulfil, particularly as the years went on. The prospect of going as Visiting Professor of Anglican Studies to the General Theological Seminary in New York the following year gave Donald a new lease of life, and exercised his mind for the first winter of retirement, as he devoted himself to preparing his series of lectures. He became a familiar sight in Dún Laoghaire through his early morning walks on the pier, enjoying the company of other retired people engaged in the same activity.

Only a month after he had retired, there was cause for celebration in the family: Ann, the eldest daughter, married Richard (Dick) Greene[2] (originally from south Roscommon, whom she had met in her college days), in early summer 1996. The wedding took place in Kilgobbin Church, Camp, Co. Kerry. Ann and Dick live in Cork city, Dick holding the position of Professor of Obstetrics and Gynaecology at University College Cork while Ann is a general practitioner and partner in a medical practice in Carrigaline. They have three children. Ann's brother, John, is a Consultant Paediatric Neurosurgeon working in Dublin. Married to Julie, who is a general practitioner, the couple have five children. Donald and Nancy's youngest daughter, Helen, having determined that teaching was not for her, studied art at Galway Regional Technical College (later, the Galway and Mayo Institute of Technology) in 1997. She lives in Galway and is a member of an art co-operative group.

In the autumn of 1997, Donald and Nancy travelled to New York, and Donald took up the position of Visiting Professor of Anglican Studies in the General Theological Seminary (GTS) in Michaelmas term. The invitation had come about as a result of his making the acquaintance of the Bishop of Kansas, Richard Grein, at the Lambeth conference in 1988. Grein had shared the section to which Donald was assigned, dealing with ecumenical relations, and the pair hit it off well. As we saw earlier, Grein came to Dublin in 1992 (he was then Bishop of New York) to give a talk during the Decade of Evangelism, and it was subsequent to this that he extended the invitation to Donald.

Located in the Chelsea neighbourhood of Manhattan, GTS is the oldest seminary of the Episcopal Church in the United States. Its campus, called the Close in the manner of the enclosed areas of property surrounding cathedrals, was built on the Oxford model, its buildings facing onto a central quadrangle. Although located in the heart of Manhattan, with its skyscrapers and modern urban buildings, the Close features a row of neo-Gothic buildings and tree-shaded lawns. The Chapel of the Good Shepherd was the focus of liturgical life at the seminary. Embarking upon his series of lectures, Donald stated:

> My wife and I look forward greatly to this period of fellowship, spiritual and social, which we know that we shall enjoy and by which we shall be refreshed and enriched. It comes to us like a second spring, since I retired

from the Archbishopric of Dublin and the Primacy of Ireland in April 1996, when I left the routine that had sustained me in the ministry for forty-six years.

His lectures ranged over his own background, as well as touching briefly on Nancy's American connections. He outlined the various phases of his ministry, as curate and teacher in Northern Ireland and Wales, and then as rector, dean and bishop successively in the Republic. He went on to trace for his students the nature of the two jurisdictions inhabiting the island of Ireland, and their development since partition in the 1920s, including the Troubles in Northern Ireland since 1969. His lectures took in the full span of Irish church and political history, ranging over St Patrick, St Brigid and St Columba and the early Christian church (detailing the various folklore and legends surrounding the key figures), the Viking raids, the medieval period, the Norman invasion and the long history of English involvement and conquest through the centuries. The lectures took in the Reformation, the dissolution of the monasteries, frequent battles and rebellions, the Flight of the (Catholic) Earls, the foundation of Trinity College, the plantation of Ulster, the Penal Laws, the Act of Union, the disestablishment of the Church of Ireland in 1871 and its aftermath. He also painted a picture of the modern Church of Ireland and its contribution to the southern state, including the two members who had held the office of president, Douglas Hyde and Erskine Childers.

In his lectures, Donald came down heavily on what he perceived as the unjust treatment suffered by Roman Catholics in Ireland under the Penal Laws of the eighteenth century:

Roman Catholics in Ireland, particularly in the north of Ireland, think back with undoubted historical justification to the eighteenth century in Ireland when the Protestant Nation ruled with arrogance and insensitivity, excluding the Roman Catholics from a significant part in the nation's life by partial and unjust penal laws, however ineffectively applied, they are reported to have been. Their attempt to suppress Roman Catholic beliefs and culture, and to reduce their social, economic and political significance in Ireland still rankles in the heart of Roman Catholics two centuries later, which is not surprising; indeed what is surprising is both the patience and generosity of those Roman Catholics who do not allow memories of such unjust and unchristian treatment to dominate their present understanding of the relation of Christians and Christian churches in Ireland. And this is the vast majority of the Roman Catholic people of Ireland. These eighteenth century measures have, of course, to be judged in the context of their time and in the state of religious conflict that disturbed Europe after the Reformation of the sixteenth century and the widespread religious wars of the seventeenth century. The Penal Laws applied against the Roman Catholic population of Ireland were a mirror of the Penal Laws applied against the Protestants of France a little earlier. But unjust measures in one country cannot be presented to justify their use in another country, particularly when both countries are Christian.

The series presented to his students an expansive survey of the Irish nation's political and church history, and it was an exercise he personally found fulfilling, if daunting:

> I particularly appreciate the opportunity which the General Theological Seminary is giving me to review at leisure the course of my life in the ministry of the Church of Ireland and to tease out a little further the history of the relationship between the churches in Ireland, and to help me to make sense of the situations in which I have spent most of my life and in which I have had in many ways to cope without always understanding the rationale and the aetiology involved; and to see these problems in a wider and longer historical context.[3]

In September 2002, Donald was delighted, along with the Rev. Raymond Davey (from the Presbyterian Church in Ireland and a former director of the Corrymeela reconciliation centre) and the Rev. Edmund Mawhinney (a former president of the Methodist Church in Ireland and leading ecumenist) to be honoured by the Pontifical University at St Patrick's College, Maynooth, with an honorary doctorate. Expressing thanks to Cardinal Desmond Connell, Chancellor of the University and its president, Msgr Dermot Farrell, for the honour conferred both on him and on his fellow recipients by this 'ancient and renowned pontifical University', Donald noted that the college was named in honour of St Patrick, a man of peace and reconciliation whose life and ministry 'has shone with a clarity undimmed by the centuries to our own day'. Modern ecumenism, tracing its origin to the end of the nineteenth century and throughout the twentieth century, was 'a strong and hardy growth surviving two world wars and many other threatening vicissitudes to emerge as a truly worldwide movement'. However, much remained to be done 'to fulfil those words in the seventeenth chapter of the Gospel according to St John "*ut unum sint* – that they may be one".'

Nancy was able in retirement to rediscover something of her American heritage. As well as accompanying Donald during his visiting professorship in New York in 1997, she went with Helen to San Francisco in 2002 to a conference organised by the *Colonial Dames*, an association of people whose ancestors had fought in the American Revolution: 'Mum was eager for us [daughters] to become members of this.' Donald and Nancy enjoyed robust good health in the first phase of their retirement, but were to experience a health scare in late 2003 when Nancy was diagnosed with non-Hodgkin's lymphoma, The treatment for this condition, including several rounds of chemotherapy, was successful, although it did leave her with some lasting balance problems.

The Cairds kept up their long-standing friendship with Cyril and Philippa Patton. These get-togethers naturally consisted of 'ordinary domestic chat' but in Cyril's recollection, also included 'talk about serious issues of the day: the political scene, the religious scene ... he was somewhat sceptical of Irish politicians ... but very objective in his views.'

In retirement, Donald and Nancy had more time to enjoy the company of their children and, in due course, their grandchildren. 'My father was always fantastic with children,' observed Ann in 2008. 'You could see when [the] kids came to the house, they would be eating out of his hand. Even now when he is older and the tolerance level is not as high ... he would sit and read to them ... and he would see little quirks in everyone's character.' John and his wife Julie would bring their children on visits to Dun Laoghaire, where, with Donald as 'Grandad', they had 'great fun, he'd get ping-pong balls and put them in his eyes or [wear] a funny hat ...' He also found painting pictures relaxing from time to time, a pastime he enjoyed pursuing during stays in Kerry.

Living in the diocese, Donald maintained a low public profile in deference to his successors as Archbishop of Dublin: Walton Empey (1996), followed by John Neill (2002) and Michael Jackson (2010). He and Nancy enjoyed their membership of the Friends of Christ Church Cathedral, attending the annual lunch coinciding with the feast of the Holy Trinity. In retirement, the Cairds had more contact with Frances Pakenham Walsh (Donald's contemporary at Trinity in the 1940s), Nancy joining her and another friend from Rathmichael days, Patricia Butler, on annual trips to Salzburg in Austria for the Mozart winter festival. Donald, who 'wasn't interested in music and was a little deaf' came along on one of these trips. Up to 2010, he attended events for retired clergy in the dioceses three or four times a year.

Irish language interests in retirement
Not long after his retirement, in June 1996, Donald participated in *Éigse Thomais Bháin*, a cultural festival on Inis Meáin, one of the Aran Islands. In his address opening the Éigse, entitled 'The Language and Reconciliation', he confessed to having known little about Tomás Bán previously, but

expressed appreciation for the opportunity the invitation afforded to find out more.

Tomás Bán Ó Concheanainn was an Aran islander who had emigrated to America, and gave great assistance to Douglas Hyde during his visit there. He had been referred to in a book written by Hyde on his return from the United States at the start of the twentieth century, *Mo Thuras go Meiriceá*. The Gaelic League had made enormous progress in attracting Protestants into the language movement both North and South. Donald referred to the League's strength at that time as the biggest such political movement since Daniel O'Connell's Catholic Association some sixty years previously.

In his address, Donald praised the work of the League, and the spiritual aspect of its efforts to bring people together. One of the key resources in the League's campaign was the *timire* (tutor-organiser) who would strive to implement the League's aims at grassroots level. On his return from America, Tomás Bán was appointed by Patrick Pearse as a *timire*. The work was hard and grinding and required wholehearted commitment which Tomás Bán readily supplied: the establishment of Irish classes, the organisation of cultural meetings; gaining subscribers for the movement and undertaking long journeys by bicycle – all done for little money.[4]

In Dublin, Donald continued to lend his patronage to the annual interchurch service in Irish held for the Week of Prayer for Christian Unity in Christ Church Cathedral, taking a leading role in the service along with his Catholic counterpart, and delivering a joint blessing at its conclusion. He derived great pleasure from meeting members of the Irish language community, mainly Catholic, who attended the service and the subsequent reception in the cathedral crypt. He was on the panel of ministers who could celebrate *An Chomaoineach Naofa,* the Eucharist in Irish, for Cumann Gaelach na hEaglaise from time to time, and also celebrated an occasional service in Irish at St James's Church, Dingle, during visits to Kerry in the summer. In 1999, he was interviewed in Irish on TG4 as a guest of the politicians Máire Geoghegan-Quinn and Alan Dukes. A major documentary on the contribution of the Irish Protestant tradition to the Irish language, *No Rootless Colonists: Protastúnaigh agus an Ghaeilge*,[5] was broadcast by TG4 in 2003, in which Donald featured.[6]

The well-known writer in Irish, Risteárd Ó Glaisne, who, as we have seen, was a Methodist lay minister and devoted member of Cumann Gaelach na hEaglaise, died in 2003, At his funeral, Donald paid warm tribute to him, noting that while Ó Glaisne had suffered from TB, and had a lean build, he never allowed such frailty to interfere with his life.

He was always ready to give an account of his faith. A preacher, he was never too busy to give advice to a friend who would call on him in an hour of need.

Donald had also supplied translations into English of a number of Irish language hymns in the Church Hymnal, the inclusion of such hymns being widely welcomed in the church community. In the fifth edition of the hymnal, published in 2003, the following translations appear, credited to Donald and the Rev. Gary Hastings: *A Aonmhic na hÓighe, A Rí an Domhnaigh, Síormholadh is glóir duit, a Athair shioraí, Don Oíche úd i mBeithil, Fáilte Romhat a Rí na nAingeal, Gurab tú mo Bheatha* and *Deus meus, adiuva me.*

The first time this author made the acquaintance of Donald was at the launch of the Irish language translation of the Book of Common Prayer, *Leabhar na hUrnaí Coitinne 2004*, at a special festival in Downpatrick Cathedral in September 2004. A simple greeting and remark about the weather in Irish was exchanged on the street near the cathedral the morning after the launch, Donald's good humour and courtesy standing out in the memory of that briefest of moments. In 2006, Donald lectured on Douglas Hyde at the Celtic revival summer school, a joint venture between Christ Church Cathedral in Dublin and Áras Éanna arts centre on Inis Oírr, Aran Islands. He and his wife Nancy lodged once again at the house of Cóilí Conneeley on the island, Cóilí having passed on many years since, but his daughter Úna recalled Donald's visit in the 1960s when she was a young girl.

In an interview with the author in 2008, Donald said that he wrote out in manuscript any speeches which he had delivered in Irish over the years, as he never had anybody available to him able to type in the language. Both Ann and John expressed regret in not having developed their interest in Irish as their father himself had: 'he would take an interest and help us out – if we showed an interest [in the language], fine, but [we] never did ... I think the way Irish was presented in school killed it off ... I do regret not [pursuing] it,' reflected John.

Reflecting more widely on Donald's contribution, Frances Pakenham Walsh offered this view:

Being an absolutely non-Irish speaker and having no opportunity or desire [to learn it], in latter years I thought how marvellous it was: here we were, the Church of Ireland, we weren't the Church of Ireland at all! We were the *Church of England in Ireland* – as far as I was concerned, it was Donald Caird who started this. I'm afraid he never had so much influence on me that I started to learn Irish in middle age, but nevertheless ... there were [others], but as far as I was concerned, Donald Caird was the one who brought the Church of Ireland back to Ireland ... he was a quiet innovator but got there by getting people to think the same way he did. I think it was talking to people and getting to know people and then things went both ways.[7]

Donald himself said that he tried to keep up his Irish language associations and connections as a constant in a life of 'changing directions'. His lifelong contribution was recognised by the awarding of *Gradam an Phiarsaigh* (the Patrick Pearse award) in April 2010. Previous recipients of the award (made by a foundation, *Fondúireacht an Phiarsaigh*) included the scholar, poet and playwright Professor Sean Ó Tuama; Helen Ó Murchú, the educationalist and linguist; and Adi Roche, the founder of the Chernobyl Children's Project. At a special dinner in the headquarters of *Comhaltas Ceoltóirí Éireann* in Monkstown, Co. Dublin, attended by members and representatives of Irish language organisations and friends and colleagues of Donald (including the rector of his parish in Dun Laoghaire, Victor Stacey), the award was presented by Minister for the Gaeltacht Patrick Carey TD to Nancy on her husband's behalf. Donald, whose health had declined around this time, was unable to be present, and his acceptance speech (the last public speech prepared by him prior to illness that year) was read out on his behalf.

This speech, in Irish, traced his early interest in the language and his involvement with Cumann Gaelach na hEaglaise over several decades. It concluded on a valedictory note:

> The Irish language was a subject of interest for me for much of my life, which permitted me to relax from time to time, and which gave me a sense of peace when I was under stress. I am very grateful to the people who I met through the Irish language movement, old and young, for their friendship and support. I wish them every success and hope that the welfare of the language can be promoted through their work and their goodwill. It is my view that a way is opening before us in the present time, despite difficulties which face us, and that a better life is before us than that which is behind. We must muster our confidence, and keep a strong hold on it.[8]

Addresses and writings in retirement
The first decade of his retirement saw Donald keep up a programme of addresses at public events for which he was in demand, and he also contributed articles and book reviews to various publications. In 1997, he wrote an article for the Church of Ireland's scholarly journal *Search*, in

anticipation of the 1998 Lambeth conference. Entitled 'Lambeth Conferences I Have Known', he outlined the structure of the conference and its working groups. There is an evocative description of the worldwide nature of the gathering of 'about six hundred bishops dressed all in convocation robes; red chimere, white surplice, purple cassock and black scarf':

> No assembly of churchmen impresses one with the same sense of the catholicity, the worldwide nature of the Anglican Church than does the Lambeth conference. Every shade of colour from English pink to Africa blue-black, every variation in height from lanky nilotic, to squat Japanese, every variety of hairstyle from American crewcut to the flowing locks and sweeping beard of barely visible Greeks, delight the eye, while the ear is entranced by such a variety of sounds that one might be tempted to think that the incident of Babel went a little too far in dividing rebellious man.

A 'London day' was a feature of both the 1978 and 1988 Lambeth conferences:

> A fleet of buses conveyed the whole conference to London, first to Westminster Abbey where a senior member of the conference preached at a sung Eucharist, followed by lunch in Lambeth Palace with a conducted tour of the palace grounds by the Archbishop of Canterbury and his wife. In 1988 Mrs Runcie, a distinguished concert pianist, played during lunch, and also accompanied solo singers and a choir. After lunch, again transported by bus, the whole conference proceeded to Buckingham Palace to be greeted by the Royal Family who were presented as a large family group to greet the bishops and their wives in a most gracious and welcoming style. Informally they moved amongst their guests greeting them and chatting quite unselfconsciously as though meeting on a rectory lawn, but surrounded by the magnificent grounds of the Palace while a military band played in the background, one of the pieces in 1978 being 'Consider yourself at home, Consider yourself one of the family'! The native costume worn by the bishops' wives from Africa and other eastern countries of the Pacific Islands gave an exotic and highly colourful character to the whole occasion. A tired but satisfied Conference returned to a late supper in Canterbury that evening.

Recalling the appointment of Archbishop of Armagh Robin Eames to chair a commission on the issue of ordination of women, charged with devising a solution to situations where provinces, and indeed dioceses, were divided on the matter, and whose 'eirenic system is at present in operation in a neighbouring province, the mother province of Canterbury', he noted that 'the Church of Ireland has made and is making significant contributions to the Lambeth conference.'[9]

Delivering the 'Bishop Stock Annual Address' at Killala in 1999, Donald noted how Joseph Stock had been one of the few Irish bishops appointed to the established church in the eighteenth century, most of the bishops having come from England. Stock (a former headmaster at Portora Royal School in Enniskillen) had deplored the foundation of the Orange Order in 1795 saying 'much it were to be wished … no such society had ever appeared among us to furnish to the Romanists too plausible a pretext for alarm and hostility against their Protestant brethren'. In the middle of the turmoil accompanying the French invasion in 1798, rebels and townspeople took over the Palace in Killala. Stock withdrew to his study, but 'would not fly under false colours'. The mutual, if grudging, respect he established with the French leader General Humbert (whom he would not mislead into believing he supported his cause, even though his two sons were being held hostage) was pointed to as a symbol of reconciliation for the new millennium – 'reconciliation has to be made by a large investment of courage, determination and indeed hard graft. It will not be achieved by fudge and hype, by weasel words and too loose definitions.'

Referring in his address to the Good Friday Agreement concluded the year before, Donald stated that isolation breeds exclusivity, a formula for needless fears, fears that destroy the real fulfilment and enjoyment of life. Stock was not overborne by the catchphrases of the French Revolution, *liberté, eaglité, fraternité*. They could stir the blood, but real improvement in the human condition would take a longer and quieter course. The Revolution could be turned into an empire with a despotic emperor in a matter of a few years. The various vicissitudes of Irish history did not drive Joseph Stock's family out of the country, and in the seventh generation his family was represented there that day by a judge of the Irish High Court – Catherine McGuinness, 'Stock's great great great great great granddaughter.'

In a typed address (undated) entitled 'Taking Our Christian Heritage into the Next Millennium', a picturesque analogy is drawn of a battered old famine suitcase taken by an emigrant to America and placed on a plinth by his great-grandson in his house, lit by a concealed light with a plaque saying 'our heritage'. It should, Donald said, perhaps more correctly have borne the legend 'our inheritance' because the heritage was much wider and deeper than the old black bag. We discover heritage throughout our lives – it is living, not something belonging to a fast fading past. Our heritage is powerful and influential in our lives even when, or perhaps particularly when, we are not concentrating directly on it. Tracing the Christian heritage of Ireland and the Celtic saints, the other traditions which had come to the island, the divisions of eastern and western Christianity, the penal laws and religious strife in Reformation Europe, up to the growth of the modern ecumenical movement, Donald concludes with the reflection that

> we may find that our Christian heritage will bring us into the third millennium rather than we who will bring it. The imminent approach of the third Christian millennium will surely be the time for Christians to recognise that they share a sufficient common heritage to allow them to discover a closer fellowship 'in truth and love' and present a common witness to a waiting world.

In an undated typescript for a sermon at Wesley College, Donald expressed appreciation for the strong sense of identity with which pupils there had been imbued, something which could often be appreciated only in retrospect. Expanding his observation to the wider Protestant community, he noted the radical social and political change in the country in the period between the First World War and Second World War, when many of the institutions which had helped to form the community's identity in the past had disappeared or were disappearing. Many found themselves 'to be a lost and exiled generation in their own country'. A substantial degree of Protestant emigration in the early years of the independent state 'should not and need not have happened if only that generation had listened to the voice of its wisest prophets'. These losses combined to lower the confidence of the community: 'for many people of the generation of my parents the acceptance of those radical changes was a slow and often painful process, and with some of them a sense of alienation remained for the rest of their lives.'

However, change was a natural condition of human life, and 'I believe that Wesley College was one of the institutions which enabled the Protestant community to maintain its identity while making the necessary adaptations to a new Ireland. The identity we learned here was essentially the Christian identity of service.' He recalled a question posed by the former Provost of Trinity College Dublin, Professor F. S. Lyons, at the end of a series of lectures given in London in 1979: 'can the Protestant community in the South of Ireland survive as a community?' Lyons replied to his own question. 'In all honesty I have to end this lecture by leaving the question open, though obviously it is the question on which all else depends.' He indicated that it was very important for Ireland, North and South, that this community should survive, because he said 'it stands for freedom of speech and thought, for liberty of conscience, for private judgement' and 'it is no longer a voice crying in the wilderness in Ireland today.'

Donald concluded that, if people were to accept their vocation as Christians, they would have little need to dwell too much on statistics or to turn in on their own community with undue concern,

> but we will have that assurance of identity which will enable us to step boldly out and to take our place without apology, but with charity and understanding in the life of our nation which over many years has shown clearly its appreciation of our commitment in service to the whole community.

A book of essays on the Protestant experience in the Republic of Ireland since independence, *Untold Stories*, published in 2002, featured an essay by Donald, reviewing the church's progress through the years of the development of the Irish state. He noted that in the immediate aftermath of the War of Independence and the establishment of the Free State, the Church of Ireland community had been very uncertain of its future. A delegation from the General Synod led by Archbishop John Gregg went to meet the leaders of the new government, and were assured by Justice Minister Kevin O'Higgins that they were regarded as 'part and parcel' of the nation and that their contribution would be welcomed. Gregg, said Donald, accepted this promise and tacitly encouraged members to stay and contribute to the life of the new state, giving 'courageous and unmistakable leadership' to his community by his commitment and by his constructive criticism of the policies of the government. In the wider Anglican world, 'in which his opinions held sway', his presentation and defence of the new state contributed to its broader international acceptance. Though there were incidences of terror and sudden death among members of the Protestant community during the War of Independence, they were not felt to constitute 'an organised vendetta' against a largely defenceless community.

In his article, Donald noted a strong physical resemblance and shared cautious scholarly approach between Taoiseach Éamon de Valera (who came to power in 1932) and Archbishop Gregg, despite tensions over introducing compulsory Irish in schools and changes to the procedure for the training of teachers in primary schools. While the years of the Second World War had seemed to deepen the isolation and separation of the two jurisdictions North and South, the General Synod continued throughout to meet in Dublin, holding together such diverse representation as 'members of the Orange Order alongside men and women who had taken part in the rebellion of 1916'. The opening up of the Irish state to the wider world in the 1960s under Taoiseach Sean Lemass along with the vision of senior civil servant Ken Whitaker had heralded a new era, also reflected in such ecumenical contacts as the visit of the Archbishop of Canterbury to Pope Paul VI. Those were days of euphoria; slower and more cautious states have followed.

In June 2003, the Byrne Perry summer school in Gorey, Co. Wexford invited Donald to give its Gordon Wilson Memorial Lecture.[10] Donald recalled that he and Wilson had first met in Wesley College in the early 1940s, Wilson being a year and a half his junior. Wilson came into Wesley with a good knowledge of spoken Irish, as his primary teacher in Manorhamilton had been both a good teacher and an Irish language enthusiast. However by the time he got to Leaving Certificate stage he had become weak in the subject. He described Wilson as a strongly focused person, recalling the particular 'set of his jaw in determination'. The school headmaster had said he had sufficient qualifications for medical school if he chose to follow that career, but Wilson was proud of his father's drapery business and decided to become apprenticed there. Donald recalled how, while chaplain at Portora in Enniskillen, he had met Wilson at various social occasions in the community.

The unforgettable words Wilson spoke when his daughter Marie was killed in the Enniskillen Remembrance Day bombing, and his statement that he would pray for the killers, made a deep impression. He had hesitated on grounds of presumption to speak of forgiving them (which was a matter for God, and there were families of others killed in that explosion to be borne in mind). Honours were bestowed on him in both Ireland and Britain, and he was appointed to the Senate in the Republic by Albert Reynolds. The family suffered further tragedy when Wilson's only son Peter was killed in a car crash in December 1994. When the IRA bombed Warrington in England in 1993, Gordon Wilson visited the parents of a young boy, Tim Parry, who had been killed as a result. Flowing from this meeting, the Parrys bore no disgust or hatred towards Ireland or the Republic. Wilson, who had taken the risk of meeting representatives of the IRA to plead for peace, lived to see the 1994 ceasefire, but did not survive to see the Good Friday agreement of 1998. He had, Donald concluded, spoken prophetically to his generation with integrity and courage, and Donald quoted the book of the prophet Ezekiel, chapter 2, verse 5: 'and whether they hear or refuse to hear … they will know that there has been a prophet amongst them.'

A book of essays, entitled *As by Law Established: the Church of Ireland since the Reformation* concerned with various aspects of the history of the Church of Ireland, was published in 1995, arising out of a conference held in University College Dublin. In a review prepared by Donald,[11] he notes the radical transformation in Irish historiography which had taken place over the previous sixty years, drawing an analogy with the fashion in which styles of portrait painting also changed through time:

> New studios, better lighting, new techniques, better material may render another portrait truer to the original, while not totally supplanting in the affections of those who knew the subject well, the older portrait which was life-size and commanding.

He made the observation that:

> If one can identify a central theme running through these fascinating studies it must be the search to discover why the Reformation was not more successful in Ireland than it actually has been, and to identify the elements which have impeded its progress. This search at first throws up the obvious answers – the land and the people. Ireland and the Irish were and are very different from England and the English, and to expect the same or nearly the same approach to the project of Reformation to show equal success in both countries was mistaken. The relative neglect of the Irish language as the vehicle of reformed Church doctrine, Church organisation and liturgy, when it was the language of such a large proportion of the nation was a basic error; and also the too close identification of the Church 'by Law established', with the institutions of the State, so that the Archbishops of the Church of Ireland were often the Lord Chancellors and Lord Treasurers of Ireland, militated against the wide acceptance of the Reformation. A reformation commencing with parliament and proceeding to the grassroots by law cannot be calculated to win the hearts and minds of the people. But even despite this approach, at least in the early days, the authors bring out clearly that the Church of Ireland has contributed to and greatly enriched many vital elements in the life of the nation.

A Roman Catholic priest, the Rev. Dr Niall Coll wrote a book (published in 2001) titled *Christ in eternity and time: modern Anglican perspectives*, in which he examined the treatment given to the question of the pre-existence of Christ in the writings of four renowned Anglican theologians of the twentieth century. Donald's review praises the book as being clearly written, but he defends with an economy of words in the concluding paragraph his own church's traditional method of decision-making:

> Dr Coll implies that the Anglican claim to 'comprehensiveness' in its theology far from being a virtue, is, if not a vice, then certainly a weakness due to having no central authority to direct the course of its theological speculation. He suggests that an institution like the Congregation for the

Doctrine of the Faith; The Holy Office would have guarded Anglican theologians against idle speculation in some theological matters; but more Anglican theologians would regard such direction as having other serious disadvantages.

Some Reflections

Musing on Protestant culture, and the maintenance of community identity in the era of the *Ne Temere* decree, Donald said that we tend to think of the Church of Ireland as a phenomenon in the cities, but many members of the Church live in small communities where their friendship, beyond the normal Sunday services, is usually maintained through organisations such as the Mothers' Union. However, he highlighted that many rural Protestants would also attend meetings of Macra na Feirme or the Irish Countrywoman's Association. A Rathmichael parishioner, Muriel Gahan (1897–1995) had been a pillar of the ICA for many years. He regarded the Mothers' Union as a great institution for the church:

> As a bishop, I would have said that if I wanted anything very well done and thoroughly done and openly done, I would ask the Mothers' Union to do it. I think the Mothers' Union is largely Church oriented – that was their key point of contact, but the Mothers' Union would always urge [its members] to support other women's groups.

Donald said that he had been raised in an area which was

> about seven per cent Church of Ireland when I was young, more in Dublin than [other places] you were all day long meeting people who didn't share your views on *some* matters. They often *did* share your views on political or scholastic or matters like that. You are always aware you had to be careful what you say, as that might be offensive ... I met a man in Clare who said I was the first Protestant he'd ever spoken to ... Protestants are cautious and weigh their words before giving expression.

Priests in the Church of Ireland are often as much leaders of their communities as figures of the church. Donald reflected on the differing role played by them. The Greek word *heiros* stood for the priest as intellectual leader of the people, 'the theologian, the person thinking ahead, analysing the function of priests, religion etc., and conveying back to the people'. The other role played by the priest was that of *sanctos*, the priest 'conducting the liturgy and things associated with it, baptism etc.' This was also mirrored to some extent in Jewish tradition, the *rabbi* or teacher, and the role of the *kohen*, concerned more with the ceremonial.

While these roles were more fused in the Christian tradition, the separate functions can be seen in the Roman Catholic Church, where the priest conducts the liturgy and offices, while frequently monks (who are not ordained) were the teachers. Donald mentioned that the present abbot of Glenstal Abbey in Limerick [Mark Patrick Hederman] had to be ordained when he was made abbot there. The differing roles of the priest as intellectual leader of the people, and as conductor of the liturgy, were also fused in the Anglican tradition.

Donald had known many Jewish pupils during his time at Wesley College in the war years, some of whom would have come to tea at his parents' house. Reflecting on the Penal Laws in Ireland in the seventeenth century, and the discriminations against Catholics, sometimes regarded by many Irish people as uniquely unjust and without parallel elsewhere, Donald recalled attending a lecture in Mary Immaculate teacher training college in Limerick, where a professor of history had outlined the commonality between the treatment of Huguenots in France some eighty to one hundred years prior to the Penal Laws in Ireland: 'I had never heard that, and the people in [Mary Immaculate College] took it very well.' This comparison was made by him in his lectures to the GTS, as we have seen.

The 'tremendous influence' of the Roman Catholic Church in Ireland was seen disseminated through the laity, and reflected in 'great institutions' like the [charitable] Society of St Vincent de Paul. 'I always remember as a child when de Valera was the President and Archbishop McQuaid ... I regarded them as the two rulers of Ireland ... I thought Ireland was run by three institutions, (1) Fianna Fáil and de Valera, (2) the GAA, (3) [Archbishop] McQuaid ...' This has lessened in more recent times, he felt. Donald said that his family had always been an open one, 'we were Anglican in that we attended the Church of Ireland, but most of our friends were Roman Catholic.' He characterised his family as 'middle-of-the-road Anglican', people who were not deeply emotionally attached to religion. His own interest in religion was fundamentally a spillover from his interest in philosophy: 'religion is a strange phenomenon and it always amazed me that people were particularly interested in religion.'

On Irish nationalism and politics, Donald said

I would describe myself probably as a cultural nationalist: Hyde is/was my hero. I never got very hot under the collar about nationalist issues. I don't think [my ancestors] the Broadbents or Dreapers ever got involved in politics. The Broadbents were supporters of Home Rule and Charles Stewart Parnell – they were liberals following Gladstone.

He recalls that his father, George, had developed a respect for de Valera, although he doesn't know if he ever voted for Fianna Fáil. George might well have been attracted to Labour – he would always 'try to help a man to keep his family [from dire straits]'. He himself had voted during his life for various political parties. His interest in the Irish language was distinct from any political outlook, and he offered the opinion that the Church of Ireland community, relative to its numbers, made a greater contribution to the revival of Irish than any other:

> I could never turn my back on the history of my own family – they were Dubliners though they did not originate there – the Strachans came from just north of Edinburgh. The Broadbents were border Scots I think. They came to Ireland because [their] trades were needed there ... [they had] sharp business instincts.

Cheerfully confessing to his lack of expertise in music, Donald said: 'I have a totally uncultured mind for music.' He liked music with a strong beat and tune he could follow, but could not follow it into the 'rarer atmosphere'. He would occasionally listen to Irish music

> but not the pipes – I like gently soothing music to the soul and mind. I think, hymnology, I like – [although] some lyrics are ridiculous or even blasphemous. I love old hymns I knew as a child. I like beautiful hymns like *Immortal Invisible* – one of the most beautiful hymns and it's metaphysically correct!

An incident which Donald found amusing in his episcopal ministry was connected with his duty to carry out an inspection of parishes. The bishop would arrive at the parish church, where he would meet various people such as the rector's churchwarden, the glebewarden and other parish officials. He would normally be accompanied by the Archdeacon of the diocese. The visit would involve an inspection of the church roof, the bells, books kept in the church, silverware and other embellishments, each item being ticked off in a large inventory book, which would contain details of items viewed at previous inspections. The party would then go out to look at the churchyard, inspecting the grasses, hedges, boundary walls and the graves. On one occasion, Donald, the Archdeacon and parish officials were walking through the graveyard, when they came upon a new grave plot, covered with white stone and green chips. This contrasted starkly with the older neighbouring graves which had grass growing on them and were not as clearly demarcated. The Archdeacon exclaimed: 'my God, look at this vulgarity here!' A voice then came in reply: 'I'm very sorry you don't like it, Archdeacon – I've just put this up to my mother!' It was the parish churchwarden.

Some assessments

In retirement, Nancy reflected that her role as Donald's wife was one of supporting him in the background, and always being cautious not to undermine his role in any public comments she might make. Although she held different views from her husband in relation to women's ordination, and despite the disappointment of some women in the church that she didn't take a role in promoting their cause, she was quite clear on where her contribution lay:

> I don't have a calling and no wish to be ordained. If I had more time, I would have been happy to help out at services, as a reader. I don't want to study theology. Hospitality is my thing – I am comfortable with it, I can do it, it brings people together and in its way, it is exceedingly useful. [When I married Donald] I had no expectation of what a rector's wife did. I did what work Donald couldn't do, be the housewife, the wife, the mother, the gardener and whatever organisation he wanted me to deal with. The modern trend of 'space', 'because I'm worth it', to me epitomises all that is ugly in a modern capitalistic society. I am a capitalist but not that self-centred ... [when] you live in a rectory you don't own, you use it to the benefit of the church, parish and community.

Donald's former fellow student at Trinity, and episcopal colleague for many years, Samuel Poyntz, in an interview with the author in 2010, reflected on Donald the man, and his contribution to the church:

> Donald Caird was a considerable wordsmith. Many of his sermons and addresses and writings were almost poetic. He had a remarkable turn of phrase that might be styled almost Churchillian! He was a man gifted with versification and no mean composer of limericks. Some are very good. The clergy and laity found in Donald Caird an attentive and attractive and lovable, firm and fair pastor and Father in God. While always loyal to the Anglican Communion and the Church of Ireland, he delighted in his encounters with other people. He could do well at times without the trappings of the episcopate. It was these contacts with people and situations which he found extremely fruitful in his years as Archbishop of Dublin and Metropolitan of the southern province [of the Church of Ireland]. I think he will be remembered for a way of life, the way he ordered his own church family life and his own kith and kin. He was greatly blessed in his choice of a wife, Nancy.

Poyntz characterised Donald's role as chairman of the Select Committee on the Revision of the Canons in the early 1970s as 'a major contribution by a new bishop'. It was 'no mean task trying to edit, revise and update a legal corpus as to what clergy and laity may do rather than what they are forbidden to do!' He also pointed out Donald's critical role in ensuring that the new Tallaght Hospital would remain a focus for the participation of the Protestant community in the Republic's health service, after its incorporation of the traditional Protestant teaching hospital, the Adelaide.

Highlighting Donald's philosophical mode of thought, he mentions two significant pieces of writing; his essay 'The Predicament of Natural Theology after the Criticism of Kant (published in 1970, where Donald revisits the thinking of a wide variety of philosophers over two centuries, ranging from David Hume to Whitehead and others), and his article 'From Atheism to Theology' (published in 2009 by Catalyst). In the latter, Donald outlines the path taken by Professor C.E.M. Joad (a man 'forgotten now, but fifty years ago, a known academic and brilliant broadcaster'), telling of his conversion from atheism through a belief in God and ultimately through a belief in the Christian understanding of God as presented in the formularies of the Church of England and the Anglican communion of churches. Joad was a 'profound philosopher of whom Donald thought highly' and he was, in Poyntz's view, trying to show Joad's continuing relevance to modern philosophical thought.

The paucity of writings from Donald is accounted for in Poyntz's mind by his having become so tied up with the work of a bishop, that it left little time:

> If you listen to the way Donald would speak and preach … you would see the places where [his philosophical training] would come through. He had a marvellous turn of phrase and some of his statements could be quite magisterial.[12]

Conclusion

In 2010, at the annual service for church unity in Irish at Christ Church Cathedral, Donald dedicated a new altar frontal in memory of the late Leslie Bryan. Bryan, as secretary, had assisted Dáithí Ó Maolchoille in steering the work of Cumann Gaelach na hEaglaise over a number of decades, maintaining regular services in Irish and the long Church of Ireland tradition of producing worship material in the language. A new committee under Ó Maolchoille's chairmanship secured funding in 2010 from *Foras na Gaeilge* to employ a full-time development officer, and in the period since Caroline Nolan's appointment to that position in 2011, there is evidence of a strong renewal of interest in Irish in Church of Ireland communities North and South, an increase in services and renewed engagement with schools and youth. Cumann Gaelach na hEaglaise could look to the centenary of its foundation in 2014 with optimism, and echo the words of hope and courage and spoken by Donald in his last public speech.

2010 was a momentous year, because in addition to receiving the *Gradam an Phiarsaigh* award already mentioned, Donald celebrated a series of key anniversaries: the sixtieth anniversary of his ordination in 1950; the fortieth anniversary of his consecration as bishop in Christ Church Cathedral; and the twenty-fifth anniversary of his translation to Dublin as Archbishop. The current Archbishop of Dublin, Michael Jackson, whom Donald had ordained as deacon in 1986 and priest in 1987, wrote to congratulate him, recalling the contribution which he had made 'in such a sustained and creative way to the life of the church intellectually, pastorally, liturgically and across so many diocese and communities'. A special service of evensong was held at Christ Church, and Donald, though frail, was in attendance. A reception was held in the cathedral crypt afterwards, where a large number of old friends and colleagues had gathered to congratulate him. Nancy joined her husband in cutting a cake specially baked for the occasion.

He was honoured the following year by Wilson's Hospital school in Co. Meath, at celebrations to celebrate the two hundred and fiftieth anniversary of the school's foundation. In recognition of his important contribution in establishing the board of governors, the school entrance hall was named *The Caird Hall* and a portrait of Donald unveiled there. It hangs opposite to that of Andrew Wilson, the founder, who in his will provided the funds for the construction of the first school building in 1761.

Bishop Paul Colton recalls being quite moved in very recent years when having confirmed Donald's granddaughter in Cork, Donald (who had by then become infirm) came up to him as he was leaving the church, 'his eyes watered up and he took my hand and kissed the ring ... as if ... he recognised a commonality ... I found that an intensely moving moment. Poignant. [It expressed] a way of ... being church.'[13]

Since 2011, Donald has resided at the Brabazon Home in Sandymount, Dublin. Surrounding him there, and like him in the autumn of their lives, are many familiar faces from the Church of Ireland community, known to him through his ministry over many years. Content in the care of the nursing staff, and of his chaplain (and former pupil at Portora), Canon Adrian Empey, he enjoys the frequent visits of his devoted wife, Nancy, and wider family. Less talkative now, this is perhaps a time for harvesting the abundant memories of a long life: both of ministry in the Church he served so faithfully, and of times spent in enjoyment of the company of the diverse peoples of his beloved Ireland.

Donald Caird's overall contribution to Irish life may be best summarised in words he himself used about his hero, Douglas Hyde:

D'fhan sé dílis dá thír is dá Eaglais. Bhain sé aoibhneas as áilleacht na tíre. Bhain sé aoibhneas as cuideachta a charad Gael. Bhain sé aoibhneas as ceol na teanga. Bhain sé aoibhneas as seana gacha dighe agus nua gacha bidh, agus thug sé adhradh do Dhia.[14]

(He remained loyal to his country and to his Church. He rejoiced in the beauty of the country. He rejoiced in the company of his Gaelic friends. He rejoiced in the music of the language. He rejoiced in the freshest of food and the oldest of wine and he gave glory to God.)

Notes

CHAPTER ONE

INTERVIEW SOURCES

Interviews with Donald Caird (DC)
Interview with Elizabeth Caird
Interview with Cyril Patton
Interview with Olive Waugh (accompanied by Basil Waugh)
Interview with Stella Bell (née Woods)
Interview with Bishop Samuel Poyntz
Interview with Vincent Denard
Interview with Frances Pakenham Walsh
Conversations with Ken Ryan

NOTES

[1] http://www.houseofnames.com/caird-family-crest.

[2] Emmeline's bound music sheets containing songs of the music hall variety are in the possession of Ms Elizabeth Caird.

[3] The King's House was once the Vice Regal lodge, reputedly stayed in by William of Orange after the Battle of the Boyne. Ken Ryan, a descendant of the Broadbents, mentions that the house had been rebuilt since King William's time. It was demolished in 1963 and is now the site of an industrial estate.

[4] DC believes the Broadbents had origins in the border region of Scotland/ northern England and came to Ireland following commercial opportunities. He believes they were involved in the fashioning of decorative iron e.g. for balconies of houses.

[5] Marriage notice for George Caird and Emily (née Dreaper).

[6] According to DC, both George Caird and his son Jim were Freemasons, the former interested in their charitable work, the latter finding membership of value in making introductions when visiting foreign sea ports – for many Russian seamen, membership was a way of associating discreetly outside the party system in the communist era.

[7] Interview with Olive and Basil Waugh, 25 November 2011.

[8] 'Appreciation: Commodore Jim Caird', *The Irish Times*, 30 June 1994.

[9] Interview with Stella Bell.

10 Ibid.
11 From lecture 'Gordon Wilson – A Reflection', delivered at Byrne Perry Summer School, 2003. The Professor of Psychiatry in Dublin University referred to was Prof. Tim McCracken.
12 Ibid.
13 From DC's lecture notes for Visiting Professorship at General Theological Seminary, New York, 1997.
14 'An Irishman's Diary', Pasty McGarry, *The Irish Times*, 2 December 1995.
15 'A View of the Revival of the Irish Language', DC in *Éire-Ireland* 25/2 (Summer 1990).
16 Address to *Éigse na nGlintí*, June 2000.
17 From *De Bhunadh Protastúnach*, Risteárd Ó Glaisne (author's translation).
18 DC recalls Lil Nic Dhonnchadh as a 'very powerful lady, slightly unapproachable' but very sharp, kind to him, and a speaker of a range of languages including Russian, German and French.
19 'A View of the Revival of the Irish Language', op. cit.
20 DC's address to *Éigse na nGlintí*, June 2000.
21 'A View of the Revival of the Irish Language', op. cit.
22 *The Clergy of the Church of Ireland*, T. G. Barnard & W. G. Neely, eds, 2006, p 258.
23 The School of Philosophy was established as such in 1964.
24 *A Dictionary of Irish Biography*, Henry Boylan.
25 See *De Bhunadh Protastúnach*, Risteárd Ó Glaisne, pp 410–11.
26 Daughter of (Robert) Erskine Childers, author of *The Riddle of the Sands* (1904) who famously sailed into Howth, North County Dublin in July 1914 in the yacht *Asgard* with arms from Germany for the Irish Volunteers.
27 Interview with Frances Pakenham Walsh, 25 November 2011.
28 Profile interview with Deaglán de Bréadun in *The Irish Times*, 'The Thinking Person's Bishop', 17 May 1984.
29 Minute Book of Cumann Gaelach na hEaglaise, RCB Library.
30 *Leabhar na hUrnaí Coitinne*, a new translation in Irish of the 1926 Book of Common Prayer, would eventually be published in 1965, using Gaelic type. A hymnal in Irish had been published three years earlier in 1962. See *An Ghaeilge in Eaglais na hÉireann*, Risteárd Giltrap, pp 114–28.
31 Reflection prepared by DC for broadcast in the Christmas season for RTÉ's *The Living Word* (undated manuscript, probably when Archbishop of Dublin).
32 'A View of the Revival of the Irish Language', DC, op. cit.
33 The Divinity Testimonium was an essential requirement for ordination in the Church of Ireland and for eligibility for the degree of Bachelor of Divinity (BD).
34 Profile interview with Deaglán de Bréadun, op. cit.
35 Profile interview with DC by Máirín de Búrca, *The Sunday Tribune*, 8 December 1985.

CHAPTER TWO

INTERVIEW SOURCES

Interviews with DC

Interview with John McDowell, former rector of St Mark's, Dundela; now Bishop of Clogher

Interview with Canon Adrian Empey and William (Bill) Vaughan

Interview with Dáithí Ó Maolchoille

NOTES

[1] The Lion on the Hill (*A History of St Mark's Church*, Dundela, Belfast, 1878–1998), J. C. Beckett.

[2] In a profile interview with Máirín de Búrca (*The Sunday Tribune*, 8 December 1985), DC comments: 'I am not by nature ... a political animal, and wherever I am, I just try to get on with the people around me. I liked Belfast, I was there three and a half years and I found the people friendly and decent.'

[3] This structure would function as the church hall when, in subsequent years, a larger church was built in the area by the first bishop's curate appointed to Knocknagoney, Jim Hartin.

[4] Bishop John McDowell refers to a statement of Lewis' that Christianity was 'the true myth' – all other myths were preparatory to that.

[5] Reflection prepared by DC for broadcast in the Christmas season for RTÉ's *The Living Word* (undated manuscript, probably when Archbishop of Dublin).

[6] DC's reflections on experiences in Belfast in manuscript notes for GTS lecture series, 1997.

[7] Risteárd Ó Glaisne in *De Bhunadh Protastúnach* (op. cit.) says that Donald taught Irish to some pupils from the South who hoped, like their fathers before them, to enter the legal profession, for which a knowledge of the language was a requirement.

[8] Máirín de Búrca, in her profile of DC, reports that he took a clear-eyed view of his teaching abilities: '"I like teaching and I can be successful with good pupils, I am not particularly good at inspiring the reluctant however," he says ruefully.'

[9] Profile interview with Máirín de Búrca, ibid.

[10] 'St David's College: Christmas Term 1957', article by James Sambrook in *The Link*, newsletter of the Lampeter Society/Cymdeithas Llambed, No LVI, March 2003.

CHAPTER THREE

INTERVIEW SOURCES

Interviews with DC
Interview with David Neligan
Interview with Nancy Caird
Interview with Dáithí Ó Maolchoille
Interview with Frances Pakenham Walsh
Interview with Valerie Jones

NOTES

1 Rathmichael was attached to St Patrick's as a prebendal parish by Archbishop Henry de Loundres (1213–28), the tithes for which supported one of the canons, and it still has a prebendal stall in the cathedral – see *Rathmichael: A Parish History*, Kathleen Turner (ed. G. O. Simms), p 16.

2 *A Gaelic Experiment: The Preparatory System and Coláiste Moibhí 1926–1961*, Valerie Jones, p 252.

3 Reflection prepared by DC for broadcast in the Christmas season for RTÉ's *The Living Word* (undated manuscript, probably when Archbishop of Dublin).

4 There are various tellings of the story. This quote is as recounted by David Neligan.

5 William Sharpe, Gwendolen's second husband, had trained under Harvey Cushing, the pioneer of neurosurgery at John Hopkins University. He lived in China at one stage around the year 1912, working at the first surgical unit in Peking. Many of the people he operated on there were people who would jump off trams, fall back and sustain head injuries. Sharpe tended to one extremely eminent patient: the son of the Emperor of China, who sustained a bad riding accident, fracturing his skull. William Sharpe was summoned and examined him in the Palace. He diagnosed a haematoma which needed to be drained, and advised that the patient go into hospital. However he was compelled to perform the operation in the Palace, without the benefit of anaesthetic. Fortuitously, the operation succeeded and he was paid a fee of $50,000 which was a great deal of money in those days. William Sharpe wrote his autobiography, detailing his experiences in the medical field. He was also noted for his social concern and commitments to the rights of the black population. He died in the late 1950s, a few years before Nancy married.

6 Gwendolen's brother Dudley Wolfe had been on the 1939 American expedition to the K2 mountain in Pakistan, and died in an accident on the way down. In 2002, Nancy's brother Dudley (the explorer's nephew) received a call from somebody to say they had identified (uncle) Dudley's gloves which had his name tag on them: Dudley Wolfe. Skeletal remains were also found.

7 As recounted in Irish in *De Bhunadh Protastúnach*, Risteárd Ó Glaisne, 2000.

8 *Rathmichael: A Parish History*, op. cit.

9 *Ossory Diocesan Magazine*, October 1969.

10   In an interview with the author, DC said that the Celtic Tiger era in Ireland (from the late 1990s) would have brought an increase in the numbers of Freemasons, as it brought people into contact with each other. 'Many would be entrepreneurial types who would need confidential support. I never found them threatening. I was never asked [to be a member]. Once or twice in Northern Ireland somebody – not in the church – suggested that I might get a parish if I was a member.' Masonic concepts of a Supreme Being or Architect were compared by Donald to approaches in modern theology. 'The only thing you won't find [in the Freemasons] is an atheist. But [it] can accommodate Judaism or Islam.'

11   DC's reflections in manuscript notes for GTS lecture series, 1997.

12   *Ossory Diocesan Magazine,* September 1970.

13   Ibid.

CHAPTER FOUR

INTERVIEW SOURCES

Interviews with DC
Interview with Nancy Caird
Interview with Ann Caird
Interview with John Caird
Interview with Helen Caird
Interview with Msgr Pádraig Ó Fiannachta
Interview with Walton Empey, formerly Bishop of Limerick, Bishop of Meath and Kildare and Archbishop of Dublin successively

NOTES

1   *The Church of Ireland Gazette,* 7 August 1970.

2   DC recalls that some proposals were made early in his episcopate to raise the status of St Mary's Church, Killarney to that of cathedral – however his feeling was that the dioceses did not need another cathedral.

3   *The Church of Ireland Gazette,* 9 October 1970.

4   *The Church of Ireland Gazette,* 23 October 1970.

5   *The Church of Ireland Gazette,* 23 October 1970.

6   Undated newspaper profile 'The week when the Bishop's wife from America got to know Limerick', by Mary Anderson.

7   Walton Empey recollects that, in his experience, the Church of Ireland people of Kerry, although few in number, were 'open and fun' and 'absolutely involved' with the wider community. He recollects an older Church of Ireland man showing him three All-Ireland (GAA) medals. Pictures of the current

[Gaelic] football team might be on display, 'but up in Killaloe [one might find] discreet plates of the Royal Family!'

8 David Neligan says that while DC would be entirely helpful in any matter raised by a clergyman that seriously concerned the operation of the dioceses or difficulties he might have, some of this clergy were a little wary of his tendency to flashes of impatience or exasperation on occasion, particularly if matters were being raised which he thought had already been dealt with – while conceding that such was probably an 'essential weapon' for someone trying to run a disparate organisation like a diocese.

9 Tale related by David Neligan – the hunting call 'Gone to Ground' is sounded to denote to the pack that the fox has gone to ground after which, as a rule, foxes are generally not pursued.

10 Programme for the annual dinner of the American Irish Historical Society, 11 October 1973.

11 DC's address to Limerick diocesan synod, 1975.

12 DC's address to Ardfert and Aghadoe diocesan synod, 1975.

13 Referred to in DC's address to Meath and Kildare diocesan synod, 12 October 1983.

14 DC's address to Limerick diocesan synod, 1975.

15 Nancy recalls DC 'leafing through the Encyclopaedia Britannica' for information on Bach, on whom he knew little, when preparing his speech for this event. It received an extremely positive reaction.

16 *The Limerick Leader*, 28 June 1975.

17 *The Limerick Leader*, 30 June 1975.

18 *The Limerick Leader*, 28 June 1975.

19 *The Limerick Leader*, 28 June 1975.

20 Casey's jurisdiction as a Catholic bishop was confined to Kerry.

21 *The Irish Press*, 13 July 1974.

22 In an appreciation of the late President carried on the front page of the *Kerryman* newspaper on Friday, 22 November 1974, the journalist Con Houlihan wrote that '… Erskine Childers was a Protestant – and something more. He believed in a state where minorities felt no sense of inferiority – and he lived to see his own church sadly diminished. The tragedy went deeper than formal religion – it was a defeat for freedom. His father had died for the dream of a Republic: the younger Childers was to see that dream perverted into the reality of a theocratic state.' Praising Childers' ideals, energy and conscientiousness as a Minister, the writer argued that, like his father, he had a lack of knowledge of real people – 'it was the dream of one whose life was spent in a world far above what Scott Fitzgerald called "the hot struggles of the poor".'

23 Letter from Rita Childers to DC, dated December 1974.

24 *History Show* – 'Erskine Childers' Presidency', Diarmaid Ferriter, RTÉ Radio 1 podcast, 23 October 2011.

25 Valedictory article in Irish titled 'Easpag Caird agus cultúr Luimní', by Séamus Ó Cinnéide, *The Limerick Leader*, 9 October 1976.

26 In relation to his attendance at many Irish language events with his wife, and Nancy's own lack of knowledge of the language, Donald comments: '*ní raibh sí buartha, [bhí sí] an-fhoighneach ... níor chuir sé stró uirthi bheith ag imeachtaí.*' (she wasn't worried, [she was] very patient ... attending [such] events did not bother her).

27 Undated press clipping, DC's papers, probably from *The Limerick Leader* newspaper.

28 Goodman was sometime Professor of Irish in Trinity College Dublin in 1879, combining this position with clerical duties in Skibbereen, alternating six months in each location. Among his students at Trinity College were Douglas Hyde and John Millington Synge. According to Pádraig Ó Fiannachta, Goodman's daughter lived in the Ventry area up to 1923, and was known as 'Miss Mary' to the Ó Fiannachtas.

29 DC's address to Ardfert and Aghadoe diocesan synod, 14 November 1973.

30 Interview with Mairéad Ní Chinneide for *The Irish Press*, quoted in *De Bhunadh Protastúnach*, Risteárd Ó Glaisne.

31 Undated press cutting in DC's papers, August or September 1971.

32 Interestingly, a submission from the Church of Ireland's Role of the Church committee to the All-Party (Oireachtas) Committee on Irish Relations in 1974 acknowledged that 'in the past, members of our church ... have not participated as fully as might have been in the political life of this state, either at local or central level', while noting that this may stem from the political tradition in which most members of the Church had been brought up, and from the 'sufferings, physical and psychological', to which many of them were subjected at the time. 'Nor should it be forgotten that the political tradition to which many members of the Church of Ireland belonged came to an end with independence, so that there was no opportunity for political organisation open to ex-Unionists in the way that the Nationalist party provided for the minority tradition in the North ... Unquestionably, the southern minority has never posed a political threat to the institutions of the State, but has always accepted the institutions born of the Treaty.'

33 Biographical information from University of Limerick Special Collections – The Dr Tiede Herrema Papers, Reference Code: IE 2135 P22 http://www2.ul. ie/pdf/249495877.pdf.

34 *The Irish Times*, 4 October 1975.

35 *The Irish Times*, 15 May 1974.

36 *The Irish Times*, 15 May 1974.

37 *The Church of Ireland Gazette* reports on General Synod, 18 May 1973.

38 *The Church of Ireland Gazette* reports on General Synod, 31 May 1974.

39 See *A History of the Church of Ireland 1691–2001*, Alan Acheson, p 141.

40 At the point of DC's move to Meath, their youngest daughter Helen had just begun senior infants' class at St Michael's, Pery Square. Ann, the eldest, had begun sixth class, while John was two years behind her.

41 Walton Empey, who later succeeded to this larger diocese, recalls walking from Kenmare in Co. Kerry to Clonfert in Co. Galway, a distance of some two

hundred and twenty kilometres, to raise money for the repair of the medieval doorway at Clonfert Cathedral, a vignette which illustrates the enormous responsibility imposed on the Church of Ireland to maintain its medieval buildings without state support at that time.

CHAPTER FIVE

INTERVIEW SOURCES

Interviews with DC
Interview with Nancy Caird
Interview with Ann Caird
Interview with John Caird
Interview with Helen Caird
Interview with Kenneth Milne
Interview with Dáithí Ó Maolchoille
Interview with Msgr Pádraig Ó Fiannachta

NOTES

1 Diocesan profile, *The Church of Ireland Gazette*, 1984.
2 DC's address to Meath diocesan synod, 24 November 1976.
3 'New Bishop of Meath makes civics plea to youth,' report in *The Irish Independent*, 19 November 1976.
4 Diocesan profile, *The Church of Ireland Gazette*, 1984.
5 Recounted by Kenneth Milne, who heard it from Walton Empey.
6 *Meath and Kildare Diocesan Magazine*, January 1978.
7 From author's interview with DC and from *Meath and Kildare Diocesan Magazine*, September 1977.
8 The *Meath and Kildare Diocesan Magazine* reported in July 1978 that John Paterson, a bachelor of thirty-nine years of age, was rector of St Bartholomew's and Leeson Park group of parishes in Dublin. Previously Assistant Dean of Residence in Trinity college, he had served two curacies in Northern Ireland before returning to Dublin. In Trinity, he had obtained a moderatorship in Oriental languages, and was also a distinguished musician, having been College organist during his years in Trinity. He was also honorary secretary of the Radio and TV committee for the Church of Ireland. In his first parish notes for the diocesan magazine, published in November 1978, Dean Paterson expressed his hope that the whole diocese would feel that St Brigid's in Kildare was their cathedral in which they would always be welcome. He soon announced, through the diocesan magazine, his intention to keep all the holy days of the Christian year by celebrating Holy Communion at the cathedral

and in the absence of a verger, sought volunteers so that the cathedral might be kept open to visitors on Saturday and Sunday afternoons in the summer months of 1979. The chaplaincy at the Irish army camp at the Curragh was part of the duties of the Dean of Kildare, and Dean Paterson's parish notes in December 1978 noted that 'all the officers have been going to great pains to see that their Church of Ireland chaplain feels as much as at home as the full-time Roman Catholic chaplains. It is much appreciated.'

9   Report in *The Irish Times*, 16 May 1978.
10   DC's address to diocesan synod, October 1984.
11   'Bishop's letter' in *Meath and Kildare Diocesan Magazine*, November 1979.
12   'The Thinking Person's Bishop,' profile by Deaglán de Bréadún, *The Irish Times*, 17 May 1984.
13   DC's address to diocesan synod, October 1979.
14   The Church of Ireland, Empey observed, was 'blessed' to be able to call upon a large number of business people who volunteer their time in its service – 'busy, busy people giving advice on financial committees etc.'
15   DC interview with Mainchin Seoighe, *The Irish Press*, November 1970.
16   DC's address to Ardfert and Aghadoe diocesan synod, 1974.
17   *The Irish Times* report on Ballymascanlon talks, 24 April 1975.
18   *Meath and Kildare Diocesan Magazine*, May 1978.
19   Report in *The Irish Times*, 14 March 1977.
20   The Rector of Ennis, the Rev. Hayden Foster, was reported in *The Irish Times* on 7 October 1979 as having suggested that the Church of Ireland should respond to the Pope's visit by declaring, perhaps in a preface, that the 39 Articles of Religion of the Church of Ireland should be seen in their historical perspective. The articles contained negative statements in relation to practices of the Roman Catholic religion and the Mass, statements which, according to Rev. Foster, played into the hands of people like the Rev. Ian Paisley. In fact, it would be twenty years before the Church of Ireland General Synod formally adopted a declaration referring to the Articles as 'historic formularies': '… historic documents often stem from periods of deep separation between Christian Churches. Whilst, in spite of a real degree of convergence, distinct differences remain, negative statements towards other Christians should not be seen as representing the spirit of this Church today.'
21   *A History of the Church of Ireland 1691–2001*, Alan Acheson, pp 251–2, and *George Otto Simms – A Biography*, Lesley Whiteside, p 148.
22   'Bishop's fears about effects of Pope's visit,' report in *The Irish Independent*.
23   'Two Irish Voices,' report in *The Tablet* newspaper, 22 March 1980.
24   Undated press cutting from 1977 entitled 'Lack of political interest regretted.'
25   Editorial, *The Irish Times*, 16 October 1980.
26   Two-part series entitled *The Protestant outlook* by Paul Murray, published in *The Irish Times* on 25 December and 29 December 1982.
27   'The Thinking Person's Bishop', profile by Deaglán de Bréadún, *The Irish Times*, 17 May 1984.
28   The Social Study conference, founded in 1952 by a group of individuals from

different parts of Ireland sharing an interest in social issues, is a voluntary organisation which aims to contribute to the formation of 'an enlightened public opinion based on Christian principles'. A residential summer school is held each year in which themes of current public interest are discussed. The papers presented at the 1984 conference were published in association with Co-operation North, edited by James McLoone.

[29] See 'Bishop attacks rivalry in churches' (report in *The Irish Press*, 8 August 1984) and 'Bishop wants new concept of national identity' (report in *The Irish Times*). At the same conference, the well-known teacher, writer and Methodist lay preacher, Risteard Ó Glaisne, said Protestants needed to relate at a deeper level to many aspects of Irish life. 'They have not received much leadership within their churches on this matter, where the mood has generally been one of caution.' Too many Protestants, like many middle-class Catholics, keep to people of their own social groupings. Happily, individual Protestants had taken the initiative in various useful and interesting social or cultural activities, but it was a pity that there was not more support for these from the Protestant people with whom they worshipped. From a Protestant point of view, a knowledge of Irish could be important, he said. Not only did it give direct insights into the country's tradition not available through any other source, it also enabled a Protestant to relate easily to Catholics.

[30] Diocesan profile, *The Church of Ireland Gazette*, 1984.

[31] Letters to the editor, *The Irish Times*, 19 January 1980.

[32] *Meath and Kildare Diocesan Magazine*, December 1979.

[33] Report in *The Irish Times*, 25 February 1980.

[34] Report in *The Irish Times*, 18 March 1978.

[35] 'Language could be "instrument of peace"', report in *The Irish Times*, 9 October 1978.

[36] DC's personal papers.

[37] Fishing trawler shipwrecked in the 1960s and washed onto the shore on Inis Oírr, where it still stands today.

[38] As recalled by Dáithí Ó Maolchoille. Author's translation.

[39] Diocesan profile, *The Church of Ireland Gazette*, 1984.

[40] 'A Visit to Uganda,' *The Church of Ireland Gazette*, 21 June 1985.

[41] Church of Ireland Notes, *The Irish Times* of 4 June 1985 and report of 11 June 1985.

CHAPTER SIX

INTERVIEW SOURCES

Interviews with DC
Interview with Nancy Caird
Interview with Cyril Patton

Interview with Ann Caird
Interview with John Caird
Interview with Helen Caird
Interview with Kenneth Milne
Interview with Dáithí Ó Maolchoille
Interview with Pádraig Ó Fiannachta
Interview with Valerie Jones
Interview with Muriel McCarthy
Interview with Canon Ginnie Kennerley
Interview with Rev. Gillian Wharton
Interview with the Ven Gordon Linney
Interview with Bishop Samuel Poyntz
Interview with former Archbishop of Armagh Robin Eames
Interview with former Archbishop of Dublin John Neill
Interview with Bishop Paul Colton
Interview with former Archbishop of Dublin Walton Empey

NOTES

1 'Archbishop faces sensitive task with hopeful enthusiasm', *The Irish Independent*, 12 June 1985.
2 Editorial, *The Irish Times*, 12 June 1985.
3 Christ Church Cathedral notes, *Church Review*, July 1985, presumably penned by Dean Salmon, who also noted that DC would have living near at hand Archbishops McAdoo and Simms, 'bishops still, and ready to support him in every way'.
4 The other big story in the newspapers on Monday, 30 September 1985 was news of the dramatic rescue of opposition Fianna Fáil leader Charles J. Haughey, his son Conor and three family friends early on the Sunday morning after their yacht, the Taurima, struck the Mizen rocks off Baltimore, Co. Cork, and sank within minutes. They had been attempting to sail the boat back from Dún Chaoin in Kerry (where the family had been holidaying on Haughey's private island, Inishvickillane) to Dublin. Haughey had in fact just launched a new book on the life of Seán a' Chóta, a brother of Kruger Kavanagh, on the Saturday evening prior to boarding the boat. He was represented at DC's enthronement by deputy party leader Brian Lenihan.
5 Editorial, *The Irish Press*, 30 September 1985.
6 Editorial, *The Irish Times*, 30 September 1985.
7 The 'Cold Ash report' (1983) of the Anglican–Lutheran joint working group, and the 'Niagara report' of the Anglican–Lutheran consultation on 'Episcope' (1987).
8 Resolution on Anglican–Lutheran relations, Lambeth conference report, 1988. See http://www.lambethconference.org/resolutions/1988/1988-4.cfm.
9 DC's address to diocesan synod, October 1988.
10 See section 'October' in http://www.vatican.va/holy_father/john_paul_ii/speeches/1989 as displayed on 4 June 2014.
11 Report of diocesan address, *Church Review*, November 1989.

12 A description of the origins of the Spanish Reformed Episcopal Church's Mozarabic liturgy as 'a curious jumble of fragments from the Roman, American, Irish and Portuguese liturgies, and some wonderful effusions' was quoted in 'An Irishman's Diary' by Patrick Comerford, *The Irish Times*, 3 January 1995.

13 'Bishop's letter', *Church Review*, December 1994.

14 John Neill recalls a conversation with Ó Fiaich around the time that Desmond Connell was appointed Archbishop of Dublin, and the Cardinal's response when asked if he knew him 'no, the only Archbishop I know in Dublin is Donald Caird!' Empey recalled Ó Fiaich speaking of DC in very warm terms.

15 Connell's area of speciality was the French philosopher Malebranche, who had inspired George Berkeley, philosopher and sometime Church of Ireland Bishop of Cloyne. DC says that Berkeley went to see Malebranche shortly before the latter's death.

16 *Church Review*, January 1990.

17 Church of Ireland Notes, *The Irish Times*, 18 October 1988 – quote from Archbishop.

18 DC's address to diocesan synod, October 1987.

19 *Church Review*, editions of October 1990 and May 1992.

20 'Bishop's letter', *Church Review*, December 1993.

21 DC's addresses to diocesan synod in 1986 and 1990.

22 'Bishop's letter', *Church Review*, May 1992.

23 The ecclesiastical province on the southern side of an imaginary line running roughly from Co. Louth in the east to Galway in the diocese of Tuam. The northern side of this line in fact incorporated northerly parts of the Republic (as far as Donegal) but these, ecclesiastically, were within the province of Armagh. Correspondingly, in this rough division of labours, the Archbishop of Armagh would be the prime spokesperson on matters internal to Northern Ireland.

24 The General Synod in 1991 in fact only 'noted and received' a motion which sought to make clear that conscientious objectors to women's ordination should suffer no impediment to their ministry nor should such views constitute any impediment to the exercise of ministry [generally] in the Church of Ireland. The motion was not 'affirmed', and there would therefore be no special provision for alternative episcopal oversight (flying bishops) for traditionalists or 'two integrities', as happened in England. See *Embracing Women*, Ginnie Kennerley, pp 109–12.

25 Paul Colton credits this dissenting stance of Donald's with teaching him that, if one were to be true to the church and one's calling as bishop, 'sometimes you had to take the line no-one else was taking. The first time I saw that was there. [it was] altogether different from what the other bishops were saying – more nuanced.'

26 One of Donald's successors as Archbishop of Dublin, John Neill, in an interview with the author, opined that one of the difficulties with regard to women in the diaconate (as the limit of progression possible) is that 'no one really knows what they want of a deacon'. He says that no one has ever really

discovered a role for them other than as the 'transitional deacons' in the Catholic and Anglican churches. He noted that in some Lutheran churches in northern Europe, 'they do secular jobs, some of them have very little liturgical function, although there are exceptions. In the Catholic Church, it is really a way of getting married clergy by the back door.'

27 Wharton recounts a number of amusing anecdotes reflecting the cultural shock which the advent of women priests caused in Ireland. 'People would stop me in the street and ... the best one was "excuse me, Father, are you really a woman?" – it just all comes out backwards! Three months after I was made deacon, we were standing outside Burdock's fish and chip shop [near Christ Church Cathedral] chatting before we went to our cars. I had a black blazer on, a black clerical shirt and a red skirt that was very full and had three slits in it. These two men walked past, skulled out of their heads! One says "a bleedin' woman priest, that is." The other said "ah, you're bleedin' drunk, you are." "No, look!" We were kind of conscious of this happening, and he came back and said "excuse me, love, is it Sister?" I said "not really, no," and he said "are you a priest?" I couldn't really explain the whole deacon/priest thing and said "yes I am." He said "ah, Jaysus, I knew you couldn't be a nun with slits in your skirt like that!" Then he spat on his hand and said "leave it there!" I shook hands!'

28 DC's regard for Paterson was warmly reciprocated: Kenneth Milne recalls Paterson making the observation that he owed all of his preferments to DC, who was 'somebody you could trust your life with'.

29 'Bishop's letter', *Church Review*, February 1989.

30 Address to diocesan synod, October 1995.

31 Gordon Linney feels it is a mistake to simply characterise the Church of Ireland as low church. He refers to two traditions which emerged from the nineteenth century Oxford Movement, a ritualist tradition, and a tradition related to the doctrine of the church itself. In the Church of Ireland, there is a high doctrine of the church, and in particular a great respect for the office of bishop, although (historically) a low-level of ritual.

32 Linney recalled an address given by DC as guest speaker at the Dublin clergy conference in the mid-1970s: 'Donald came and articulated an intelligent representation of how we interpret the Christian faith in the modern world. Some clergy at that time were quite conservative or evangelical, and would have liked a more biblical [approach] ... It was so stimulating and uplifting ... He was saying that we've got to be thinking theologically and intelligently in the modern world.'

33 This sense of caution born of bitter experience also seems to be echoed in his wariness of the media, which may stem from the LPYMA episode, referred to earlier, when Bishop of Limerick.

34 When Maurice Carey, Dean of Cork, expressed an interest in returning to Dublin, his appointment as chaplain to St John's (a trustee church) was settled by a committee chaired by Dean Paterson, who knew Carey as an excellent scholar. Carey was also held in high regard by DC.

[35] Author's interview with DC. For a detailed account of Dublin's Anglican nuns, see 'The Nuns' Story: The Community of St John the Evangelist', by the late Jennifer Moreton in *Search*, A Church of Ireland Journal, Spring 2003.

[36] 'Bishop's letter', *Church Review*, March 1986.

[37] Empey recalls that, at this remark, he threw his hands up in the air in exasperation, earning dagger looks from Thatcher.

[38] 'Bishop's letter', *Church Review*, September 1988.

[39] DC's address to diocesan synod, October 1988.

[40] *Episcopal Life* magazine, May 1991.

[41] *The Irish Times*, 11 January 1992.

[42] John Neill remarked that both himself and Diarmuid Martin (Roman Catholic Archbishop of Dublin at the time of writing) had commented on how the Irish state loved to look to Armagh, whereas the church spokesperson for Republic of Ireland matters is the Archbishop of Dublin. This focus on Armagh, he seems to think, strengthened during Robin Eames's time. There has, however, been some rebalancing in the period since. Neill noted that all Anglican archbishops of Dublin in recent years would have been nationalist in personal opinion, and therefore found it slightly difficult to relate to the church in the North – even Donald, who had served there in his early ministry.

[43] Private correspondence, DC's personal papers.

[44] A special peace service was held in Dublin's St Patrick's Cathedral on 5 December 1993, attended by President Robinson, and at which Gordon Wilson read one of the lessons.

[45] Faxed statement dated 16 December 1993, DC's papers.

[46] 'Bishop's letter', *Church Review*, January 1994.

[47] *Church Review*, January 1995.

[48] *Irish Independent* reports, 18 October 1995; *Irish Times* reports, 18 October 1995.

[49] *The Irish Times*, 16 February 1996.

[50] An important part of the developing peace process was the public articulation of a need for reconciliation and healing in respect of wrongs done by various protagonists in the past. This legacy of history was felt to be particularly acute in 1995, which was the one hundred and fiftieth anniversary of the outbreak of the potato blight which led to the Great Famine in Ireland. The Church of Ireland's role in the popular imagination had for a long time been a murky one, with instances of offering of relief being conditional on conversion to the Protestant faith: the legacy of 'souperism' continued to foster resentment in popular consciousness. The Church of Ireland Cathedral of St Mary in Tuam in the heart of the west of Ireland was the venue for a National Famine Commemoration Service in the summer of 1995, attended by the Taoiseach John Bruton, and other government representatives (and in which Donald took part). Archbishop Eames delivered a keynote sermon in which he expressed regret for the 'denominational imperative' which had been sometimes attached to famine relief, on the part of agents of the established church. This made a huge emotional impact 'to someone of my background', said Eames. 'I took my courage in both hands, and to me it was an opportunity

to say sorry for what happened and I never regretted doing that. It seems unlikely [Donald and myself] wouldn't have discussed that ... the northern province [of the church, Eames's jurisdiction] included Tuam [in the Republic], but I would never have done anything in Tuam without the knowledge of the "Irish" (southern) Primate.'

51 *Church Review*, January 1996.

52 'Protestants in the Republic should stop apologising for what they are – Dr Caird', report, *The Irish Times*, 19 August 1993.

53 1991 marked the seventy-fifth anniversary of the 1916 Easter Rising, and the first significant state commemoration held at the GPO since the outbreak of the Northern Troubles. In his letter in *Church Review* in March 1991, Donald acknowledged the rebellion 'which nearly did not take place ... but which with a strangely heroic lack of regard for their own lives a handful of men carried out against all odds. Its significance changes with the years and may change further. But the event remains and we remember it'.

54 DC's address to diocesan synod, October 1988.

55 A hanging fall (banner) for use in the civic pew in Christ Church Cathedral on Presidential visits was inaugurated by the late Dean John Paterson in President Mary McAleese's time in office. It featured a gold harp on a background of Presidential (or St Patrick's) blue.

56 DC's address to diocesan synod, October 1991.

57 'Bishop's letter', *Church Review*, February 1988.

58 Ibid.

59 *The Irish Times*, 12 May 1994.

60 'Douglas Hyde – observed from a distance', address delivered by DC at French Park, Roscommon, June 1988. A correspondent, Hector Legge, in a letter to Donald around this time, referred to Hyde's remarks about a growth in Gaelic spirit among Protestants in Belfast in the early years of the century asking 'where is the organisation that can really unite the Irish people on the points of culture and peace? What is the Gaelic League doing these days?'

61 *An Ghaeilge in Eaglais na hÉireann*, Risteárd Giltrap, p 147.

62 Ó Fiannachta had also stayed with the Guithín brothers. He recalled going into the island on a *naomhóg* (small rowing boat) around the year 1945 as a student priest in the company of an older priest, to celebrate Mass on the island on 15 August, the feast of the Assumption. A certain rock close to the island shore was known to the islanders as *An Seanduine* (the Old Man) and when one reached this point, often a single wave would carry one onto the shore. On this occasion however, the *naomhóg* came perilously close to the rock, and an elderly islander remonstrated with them: '*chuaigh sibh ró-chóngarach don Seanduine, ni théann tú ... ar an Seanduine nuair a bhíonn se á bhearradh féin agus sobal air!*' (you went too close to the old man, you don't ... approach the old man when he is shaving himself and foam on him!).

63 *The Irish Times*, 2 February 1996.

64 DC's sermon at a thanksgiving service for Coláiste Moibhí, 23 June 1995, as recounted in *Coláiste Moibhí*, Risteárd Ó Glaisne.

[65] Dáil debates, col. 1236–37, as quoted in *Coláiste Moibhí*, Risteárd Ó Glaisne.

[66] Report, *Church Review*, November 1994.

[67] McAdoo's input was guessed at as amounting to no more than a '*nihil obstat*' (rather than an *imprimatur*) by Walton Empey in an interview with the author.

[68] The Lambeth conference of Anglican bishops in 1958 received a committee report in which it was stated: 'In the strongest terms, Christians reject the practice of induced abortion, or infanticide, which involves the killing of a life already conceived (as well as a violation of the personality of the mother) save at the dictate of strict and undeniable medical necessity.' This is regarded as the classic statement of the Anglican view of abortion.

[69] 'New wording protects existing ban, says C of I', *The Irish Times*, 29 March 1983.

[70] *The Irish Times*, 4 April 1983.

[71] *The Irish Times*, 4 April 1983.

[72] *The Irish Times*, 24 August 1983.

[73] Editorial, *The Irish Independent*, 24 August 1983.

[74] DC's address to diocesan synod, October 1983.

[75] 'The Thinking Person's Bishop', profile by Deaglán de Bréadún, *The Irish Times*, 17 May 1984.

[76] Letters to the editor, *The Irish Times*, 13 March 1992.

[77] 'Archbishop attacks nullity law plans', report in *The Irish Times*, 1 December 1976.

[78] *The Irish Press*, 18 October 1979.

[79] *The Irish Times*, 12 June 1985.

[80] 'Speeches emphasise divergent views on divorce', *The Irish Times*, 30 September 1985.

[81] Author's renumbering.

[82] In a curious editorial greeting the election of Walton Empey as Donald's successor in 1996, *The Irish Times* said that the Republic needed leaders from the Protestant tradition to do three things: 'courageously criticise the still existing excesses of a once overweening Catholic ethos; take a lead in pushing forward the vital work of ecumenism, still in its infancy in Ireland; and proclaim to Northern Protestants that the Republic is not the Catholic dominated theocracy they still appear to fear, but a youthful, effervescent and rapidly changing society which cherishes the values of personal freedom and responsibility so dear to Protestants.' The leader writer, while noting that Archbishop Empey's predecessor was loved and respected for his wisdom, scholarship, gentleness and humour, expressed some criticism. If Donald had one shortcoming, it was that he shared the 'traditional southern Protestant reluctance to speak out strongly on moral-political issues which are the subject of national controversy. Thus, for example, the Protestant voice was largely missing from the debate on divorce last autumn,' *The Irish Times*, 15 June 1996. Empey in a subsequent statement however made clear how he himself interpreted the role of Archbishop: it was to preach the gospel.

[83] *The Irish Press*, 16 October 1991.

[84] *The Irish Times*, 19 May 1990.

[85] Profile piece, 'A philosopher steering clear of politics', *The Irish Times*, 5 October 1990.

[86] Editorial, *The Irish Times*, 27 May 1993.

[87] 'Hospital would allow abortions if law permits', *The Irish Times*, 27 May 1993.

[88] 'Bishop's letter', *Church Review*, April 1991.

[89] Ann recalled that as DC worked from a home office, the situation was 'good for us' as the children could go in and out and get help with homework, not generally disturbing him if he was having a meeting, 'but if we did, he would introduce us'. She recalls there were always 'comfortable armchairs', to which DC would repair, cover himself in a rug for twenty to thirty minutes and emerge 'totally refreshed'.

[90] Feature article by Lavinia Greacen, 'Independent Weekender', *The Irish Independent*, 29 July 1989.

[91] Profile piece by Máirín de Búrca, *The Sunday Tribune*, 8 December 1995.

[92] DC's son, John, described Patricia Hastings-Hardy as 'a lovely lady of a different era' – Victorian in manner. She drove a little blue mini, spoke 'very clipped BBC English, everything was done on little [index] cards ... she must have been in her late sixties or early seventies'. He described her as a 'blue-rinsed' lady 'with horn-rimmed spectacles'. DC recounted that Hastings Hardy's grandfather had received four citations for the Victoria Cross in the First World War. He had been headmaster of an English public school, but when he saw the boys going out to fight, he himself retired and entered the Army as chaplain. He wrote his autobiography *It's Only Me*, a story of eighteen months' service in the War. Every night he climbed out of the trenches and crawled on his back over 'no man's land' to find wounded soldiers. He would climb in under them and carry them on his back to safety. King George V was so impressed, he came out to the trenches and conferred the Victoria Cross on him. He was killed just a week later.

[93] 'Hosts and hostesses – the art of Irish hospitality', interview with Nancy Caird, 1996, Consuelo O'Connor.

[94] Author's interview with Cyril Patton.

[95] *The Church of Ireland Gazette*, 3 May 1996.

[96] 'Parting prayer at Easter is for permanent peace in Ireland', profile by Nicola Tallant, 1996.

CHAPTER SEVEN

INTERVIEW SOURCES

Interviews with DC
Interview with Nancy Caird
Interview with Ann Caird
Interview with John Caird
Interview with Helen Caird

Interview with Cyril Patton
Interview with Frances Pakenham Walsh
Interview with Bishop Samuel Poyntz
Interview with Bishop Paul Colton

Notes

1. Kenneth Milne emphasises the 'huge dislocations' which moves or promotions frequently entail for clergy: there are a variety of circumstances to manage. These frequently encompass upheavals for the friendships, interests and involvements of the cleric him or herself, his or her spouse and their children, adjustments to new neighbourhoods, new schools, etc.

2. Having been made a scholar of the house in Trinity in 1948, DC attended a scholar's reunion dinner in the eighth year of each decade. In 2008, by coincidence, his son in law Dick Greene was celebrating the twentieth anniversary of his own election as a scholar. In a poignant remark to the author prior to the 2008 dinner, DC said 'The Archbishop of Dublin has a purple dress – all the others wear black tie. I think I'm going to wear … purple dress this year for my last appearance.'

3. Typescript of lectures to the General Theological Seminary, DC's papers. Author's punctuation inserted.

4. Author's translation of excerpts from address given by DC: *Éigse Thomais Bháin: Teanga an Athmhuintearais*, Inis Meáin, 28 June 1996.

5. Directed by Louis Marcus.

6. DC also participated as an interviewee in the TG4 documentary: *Dr Kathleen Lynn: Dochtúir Réabhlóideach*, made by Loopline Films and directed by Sé Merry Doyle. It was broadcast in 2011.

7. Interview with the author, November 2011.

8. Author's translation.

9. *Search*, Church of Ireland Journal, Winter 1997. Author's punctuation inserted.

10. The Gordon Wilson Memorial Lecture was inaugurated in 1996, previous speakers having included Albert Reynolds (Taoiseach 1992–94), Bertie Ahern (Taoiseach 1997–2007) and Supreme Court Justice Susan Denham.

11. Typescript of review, DC's papers, of *As by Law Established: the Church of Ireland since the Reformation,* A. Ford, J. Maguire and K. Milne (eds), Lilliput Press.

12. Poyntz feels that the intellectual brilliance of Canon William Nesbitt Harvey, the rector of Sandford parish in DC's youth, would have stretched DC, although 'he never said it to me himself!'

13. Interview with the author, June 2013.

14. Author's translation, with thanks to Eoin MacCárthaigh of Roinn na Gaeilge in Trinity College and Clíona Ní Shúilleabháin of Trinity College Library for directing me towards the phrase's source.

Index